THE
LATIN WORKS
OF
DANTE

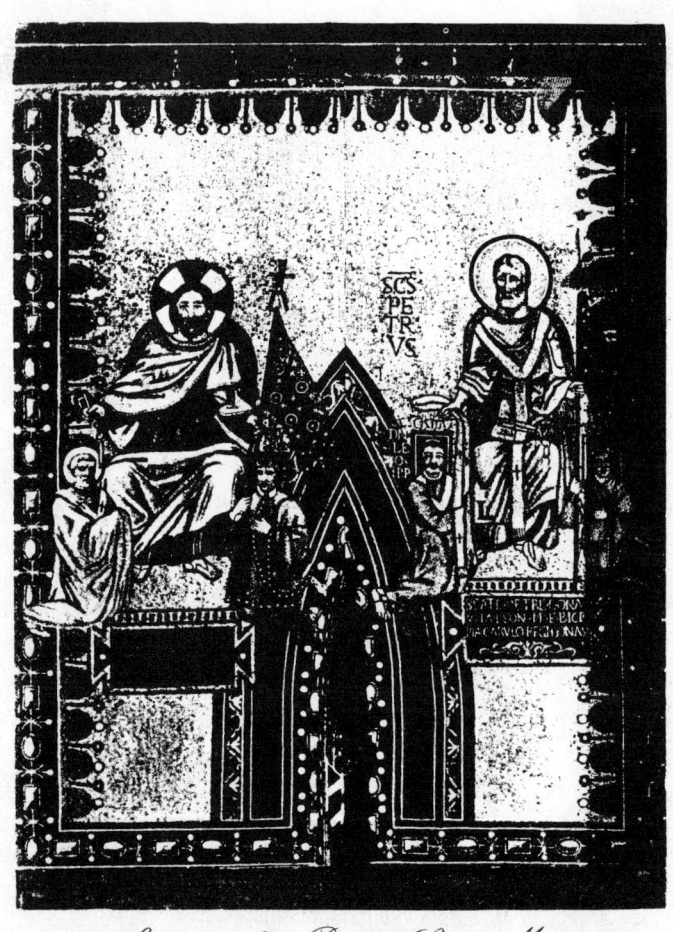

Side groups from Raphael's Lateran Mosaic,
Showing on one side Peter & Constantine deriving their authority direct from Christ
& on the other side Leo & Charlemagne deriving theirs from Peter.

A TRANSLATION OF THE LATIN WORKS OF DANTE ALIGHIERI

GREENWOOD PRESS, PUBLISHERS
NEW YORK

Originally published in 1904
by J. M. Dent and Co.

First Greenwood Reprinting 1969

Library of Congress Catalogue Card Number 69-13874

SBN 8371-1799-2

PRINTED IN UNITED STATES OF AMERICA

THE
DE VULGARI ELOQUENTIA,
DE MONARCHIA,
EPISTLES, AND ECLOGUES,
AND THE
QUAESTIO DE AQUA ET TERRA

CONTENTS

THE DE VULGARI ELOQUENTIA

	PAGE
THE FIRST BOOK	3
THE SECOND BOOK	65
APPENDIX I. (Date, etc.)	116
APPENDIX II. (Illustrations)	121

THE DE MONARCHIA

THE FIRST BOOK	127
THE SECOND BOOK	173
THE THIRD BOOK	225
APPENDIX	281

EPISTOLAE

LETTER I. (to Nicholas of Ostia)	295
LETTER II. (to Alexander da Romena)	298
LETTER III. (to Moruello Malaspina)	301
LETTER IV. (to the exile of Pistoja)	305
LETTER V. (to the Princes of Italy)	308
LETTER VI. (to the Florentines within)	316
LETTER VII. (to the Emperor Henry)	323
LETTER VIII. (to the Italian Cardinals)	331
LETTER IX. (to a Florentine friend)	340
LETTER X. (to Can Grande)	343

CONTENTS

ECLOGUES

	PAGE
INTRODUCTION	371
THE FIRST ECLOGUE	373
THE SECOND ECLOGUE	380

QUAESTIO DE AQUA ET TERRA

THE QUAESTIO, ETC.	387
NOTE TO THE QUAESTIO, ETC.	423
POSTSCRIPT TO THE QUAESTIO, ETC.	426
POSTSCRIPT TO THE DE VULGARI ELOQUENTIA	427
EDITORIAL NOTE	428
LIST OF TERMS EXPLAINED IN THE NOTES	viii

LIST OF PHILOSOPHICAL TERMS, Etc., EXPLAINED IN THE NOTES

	PAGE
STANDARDS	55 (text), 58 ff., 265, 266
LIFE	73
ESSENCE	134
FORM AND FIRST MATTER	155 ff., 409
AVERROES ON THE INTELLECT	136 f.
SEQUENCE, ANTECEDENT, AND CONSEQUENT	220, 224, 243, 366 f., 394 etc.
PARTICULAR FORMS	137
PREDICAMENTS (OR CATEGORIES), AND THE SIX PRINCIPLES	155, 265 ff., 390 f, 400
APPETITE	160
EXISTENCE, UNITY, GOODNESS	170, 179
LOCUS	220, 396
CONTRADICTORIES	220
DISTINCTIONS	240
MAJOR AND MINOR TERMS	242
INSTANTIA (*i.e.* OBJECTION OR REJOINDER)	243, 247, 408 f.
SUBSTANCE AND ACCIDENT	266

DATES OF HENRY'S EXPEDITION AND OF DANTE'S LETTERS . . . . . . 314 f.

THE
DE VULGARI ELOQUENTIA

BOOK I

CHAPTER I

[The author intends to treat of the vernacular or natural speech of mankind, which he distinguishes from the 'secondary' and 'artificial' speech of the learned, and declares to be the nobler. The treatise, as appears from the concluding passage of Book I. and the opening passage of Book II., was to embrace the vernacular of Italy in all its forms and ramifications, both literary and popular.]

Importance of the subject

SINCE we do not find that any one before us has treated of the science of the vernacular language, while in fact we see that this language is highly necessary for all, inasmuch as not only men, but even women and children, strive, in so far as nature allows them, to acquire it; and since it is our wish to enlighten to some little extent the discernment of those who walk through the streets [10] like blind men, generally fancying that those things which are [really] in front of them are behind them, we will endeavour, the Word aiding us from heaven, to be of service to the vernacular speech; not only drawing the water of our own wit for such a drink, but mixing with it the best of what we have taken or compiled from others, so that we may thence be able to give draughts of the sweetest hydromel.

The subject defined But because the business of every science is not to prove but to explain its subject, in order that men may know what that is [20] with which the science is concerned, we say (to come quickly to the point) that what we call the vernacular speech is that to which children are accustomed by those who are about them when they first begin to distinguish words; or to put it more shortly, we say that the vernacular speech is that which we acquire without any rule, by imitating our nurses. There further springs from this another secondary speech, which the Romans called grammar. And this [30] secondary speech the Greeks also have, as well as others, but not all. Few, however, acquire the use of this speech, because we can only be guided and instructed in it by the expenditure of much time, and by assiduous study. Of these two kinds of speech also, the vernacular is the nobler, as well because it was the first employed by the human race, as because the whole world makes use of it, though it has been divided into forms differing in pronunciation and vocabulary. It is also the nobler as being natural to us, whereas the other is [40] rather of an artificial kind; and it is of this our nobler speech that we intend to treat.

The original chapter headings, which are not by the hand of Dante and are inadequate and sometimes incorrect, have been replaced by summaries of the contents prefixed to each chapter. When in the notes appended to each chapter citations of passages from the *Divina Commedia* and the *Convivio* are followed by the letter *n.*, it is to be understood that the *notes* to those passages in the 'Temple Classics' edition are referred to.

I. THE FIRST BOOK

⁎ *The numbers inserted in the text in square brackets, used for reference in the notes and elsewhere, are those of the lines in Dr Moore's Oxford Dante. The original Latin text followed is that of Rajna's smaller edition (Florence, Successori Le Monnier, 1897). On the title, date, and history of this work, see Appendix I. p.* 116.

2. Compare *Paradiso,* II. 7; *De Monarchia,* I. 1 : 18, 19.

8. Compare *Convivio,* I. 11 : 18 ff. ; IV. 8 : 1-6.

10. Compare *Paradiso,* VIII. 94, 136.

11. The Word is here equivalent to the Wisdom of God, as in *Paradiso,* XIX. 44. Compare *Convivio,* II. 6 : 66.

12. Lit., 'To the speech of the vulgar peoples,' *i.e.* the different varieties of the vernacular in Italy. See below, I. 19.

17. *Sed quia unamquanque doctrinam oportet non probare sed suum aperire subiectum.* See *Convivio,* II. 14 : 14 ff. ; and compare *Paradiso,* XXIV. 70-78. The vernacular was not one of the recognised sciences (*Convivio,* II. 14 : 55 ff.), hence Dante here speaks of the learning relating thereto as *doctrina,* not *scientia.*

28. By grammar Dante here means a literary language of conventional origin, artificial construction, and permanent character ; with special reference to Latin. See below, I. 9 : 101*n.* In *Convivio,* I. 11 : 95 ff., he talks of 'the Grammar of the Greeks,' meaning their literary language, and alludes also to the literary language of Provence.

34. For Dante's own experience, see *Convivio,* II. 13 : 22 ff.

41. There is a contradiction, more apparent than real, between this passage and *Convivio,* I. 5 : 45-106, where Latin is proved superior to the vernacular (*a*) on the ground of nobility, because of its being unchangeable [as to this see below, *note* on I. 9 : 101] ; (*b*) because of its greater efficiency as a vehicle of thought, (*c*) because of the greater beauty due to its artificial character. To understand the relation between these two passages it must be borne in mind that in *Convivio,* I. 5 the comparison is between Latin as a literary language in the fixed and perfected state in which Dante supposed it to be, and the vernacular

in its state of continual change and lawlessness. From this point of view Latin was admittedly superior, nor is this superiority denied in the present treatise, since in II. 4 Dante proposes the Latin poets as models for imitation by the vernacular poets. But in the present passage the term 'vernacular' is not used in reference to literature at all, nor even confined to any nation in particular, but is merely taken in the sense of the natural speech of all mankind, 'which we acquire without any rule by imitating our nurses,' and as such is contrasted with 'grammar,' to which artificial language the natural speech of mankind was obviously superior as a mode of oral communication. Nor was its superiority in respect of origin less obvious. For the vernacular, originating in nature (the child of God), stood, to adopt Dante's quaint conceit (see *Inferno*, XI. 97 ff.), a degree nearer of kin to God than grammar, which was the creature of art, nature's humble disciple, and 'as it were the grandchild of God.'

CHAPTER II

[The author lays it down that man alone, as distinguished from the angels and the brutes, is endowed with speech. He shows that both for the angels and the brutes speech would have been unnecessary, and therefore repugnant to nature. He anticipates objections which might be founded on stories of animals talking, in the Bible and in Ovid, and on the fact that magpies and other birds can talk.]

Speech peculiar to man THIS [then] is our true first speech. I do not, however, say 'our' as implying that any other kind of speech exists beside man's; for to man alone of all existing beings was speech given, because for him alone was it necessary. Speech was not necessary for the angels or for the lower animals, but would have been given to them in vain, which nature, as we know, shrinks from doing. For if we [10] clearly consider what our intention is when we speak, we shall find that it is nothing else but to unfold to others the thoughts of our own mind. Since, then, the angels have, for the purpose of manifesting their glorious thoughts, a most ready and indeed ineffable sufficiency of intellect, by which one of them is known in all respects to another, either of himself, or at least by means of that most brilliant mirror in which all of them are represented [20] in the fulness of their beauty, and into which they all most eagerly gaze, they do not seem to have required the outward indications of speech. And if an objection be raised concerning the spirits who fell, it may be answered in two ways. First we may say that inasmuch as we are treating of those things which are necessary for well-being, we ought to pass over the fallen angels, because they perversely refused to wait for the divine care. Or secondly (and better), that the devils themselves only need [30], in order to disclose their perfidy to one another, to know, each of another, that he exists, and what is his power: which they certainly do know, for they had knowledge of one another before their fall.

The lower animals also, being guided by natural instinct alone, did not need to be provided with the power of speech, for all those of the same species have the same actions and passions; and so they are enabled by their own actions and passions to know those of others. But among those of different [40] species not only was speech unnecessary, but it would have been

Neither angels nor brutes speak

Of talking beasts in Scripture and in fable altogether harmful, since there would have been no friendly intercourse between them.

And if it be objected concerning the serpent speaking to the first woman, or concerning Balaam's ass, that they spoke, we reply that the angel in the latter, and the devil in the former, wrought in such a manner that the animals themselves set their organs in motion in such wise that the voice thence sounded clear like [50] genuine speech; not that the sound uttered was to the ass anything but braying, or to the serpent anything but hissing.

But if any one should argue in opposition, from what Ovid says in the fifth book of the *Metamorphoses* about magpies speaking, we reply that he says this figuratively, meaning something else. And if any one should rejoin that even up to the present time magpies and other birds speak, we say that it is false, because such action is not speaking, but a kind of imitation of the sound of [60] our voice, or in other words, we say that they try to imitate us in so far as we utter sounds, but not in so far as we speak. If accordingly any one were to say expressly 'Pica' [magpie], and 'Pica' were answered back, this would be but a copy or imitation of the sound made by him who had first said the word.

And so it is evident that speech has been given to man alone. But let us briefly endeavour to explain why this was necessary for him.

---

9. As in *De Monarchia*, 1. 3 : 21, and *Convivio*, III. 15 : 81, Dante adopts Aristotle's dictum that 'God and nature make nothing in vain' (*De Cœlo*, I. 4).

19. God is the mirror in which all things are reflected; and the angels and blessed spirits of Paradise,

ever gazing into this mirror, see, and therefore know, all things. This idea runs through the *Paradiso* (*e.g.*, XI. 19-21; XV. 61-63).

26. *i.e.* 'They anticipated the divine solicitude for their well-being.' The expression 'divine care' appears to be used in a pregnant sense as meaning 'The time appointed by God's providence.' See *Paradiso*, XIX. 48*n*.

31. St Thomas (*Summa Theol.*, part I., question 56, article 2) discusses the question whether one angel can know another, and decides it in the affirmative. He holds that the angels are distinguished from one another by the different degrees of their perfection, and that this difference is the cause of their being able to know one another. He holds also that this difference in the degrees of their perfection persisted in the angels who fell (see *Summa Theol.*, part I., question 109, article 1), and Dante's expression 'what is his power' (*quantus est*) refers to this.

34. St Thomas (*Summa Theol.*, part I., question 107, article 3) declares that 'as regards things pertaining to natural knowledge (*naturalis cognitio*) there is no need for the manifestation of the truth either in angels or devils; because . . . from the very beginning of their condition they know all things pertaining to natural knowledge.' It appears, however, that in relation to matters outside 'natural knowledge,' the angels, both good and bad, have a faculty of manifesting their thoughts to one another by 'internal speech' (*ibid.*, article 1), which of course does not conflict with what Dante says in this chapter, for he is here only referring to external speech by words. Compare also *Convivio*, II. 7 : 10 ff

37. '*Actions and passions.*' See below, I. 16 : 21 *n.* and II. 8 : 12 ff., where these terms are exemplified; also *Convivio*, II. 10 : 67*n*.

54. Lines 295-299.

58. Compare *Convivio*, III 7, where Dante raises and answers the same objection.

CHAPTER III

[Inasmuch as human beings are not, like the brutes, guided as to their knowledge of one another by instinct alone, nor are they able, like the angels, to know each other's thoughts by intuition, but differ from both by the possession of reason together with senses, they require a means of communication which shall be both rational and sensible, and such is speech.]

Why speech is necessary for man SINCE, then, man is not moved by natural instinct but by reason, and reason itself differs in individuals in respect of discernment, judgment, and choice, so that each one of us appears almost to rejoice in his own species, we are of opinion that no one has knowledge of another by means of his own actions or passions, as a brute beast; nor does it happen that one man can enter into another by spiritual insight [10], like an angel, since the human spirit is held back by the grossness and opacity of its mortal body. It was therefore necessary that the human race should have some sign, at once rational and sensible, for the inter-communication of its thoughts, because the sign, having to receive something from the reason of one and to convey it to the reason of another, had to be rational; and since nothing can be conveyed from one reason to another except [20] through a medium of sense, it had to be sensible; for, were it only rational, it could not pass [from the reason of one to that of another]; and were it only sensible it would neither have been able to take from the reason of one nor to deposit in that of another.

Now this sign is that noble subject itself of

which we are speaking; for in so far as it is sound, it is sensible, but in so far as it appears to carry some meaning according to the pleasure [of the speaker] it is rational.

1-6. So great are the differences between the reason of one individual human being and that of another that each one of us may practically be considered as forming a species by himself, like an angel, but without an angel's intuitive power. (See *note* to *De Monarchia*, I. 3 : 55-62 below in this vol.)

4. If discernment (the fairest branch that rises from the root of reason (*Convivio*, IV. 8 : 1)) be absent, the judgment (or decision) will be sensual, or according to appearance only (*Convivio*, III. 10 : 22 ff.), and consequently a wrong choice will be made. Cf. *De Monarchia*, I. 12 : 17-37.

15. *Sensible*, *i.e.* perceptible by sense.

CHAPTER IV

[The origin of speech. It is proved that Adam was the first speaker, and that the first word he said was the name of God, addressed to God.]

SPEECH was given to man alone, as is plain from what has been said above. And now I think we ought also to investigate to whom of mankind speech was first given, and what was the first thing he said, and to whom, where, and when he said it; and also in what language this first speech came forth. Now, according to what we read in the beginning of Genesis, where the most sacred [10] Scripture is treating of the origin of the world, we find that a woman spoke before all others, I mean that most presumptuous Eve, when in answer to the

Origin of human speech

Speech in Eden inquiry of the devil she said, 'We eat of the fruit of the trees which are in Paradise, but of the fruit of the tree which is in the midst of Paradise God has commanded us not to eat, nor to touch it, lest peradventure we die.' But though we find it written that the woman spoke first, it is, however, reasonable for us to suppose that [20] the man spoke first; and it is unseemly to think that so excellent an act of the human race proceeded even earlier from woman than from man. We therefore resonably believe that speech was given to Adam first by him who had just formed him.

Now I have no doubt that it is obvious to a man of sound mind that the first thing the voice of the first speaker uttered was the equivalent of God, namely *El*, whether in the [30] way of a question or in the way of an answer. It seems absurd and repugnant to reason that anything should have been named by man before God, since man had been made by him and for him. For as, since the transgression of the human race, every one begins his first attempt at speech with a cry of woe, it is reasonable that he who existed before that transgression should begin with joy; and since there is no joy without God, but [40] all joy is in God, and God himself is wholly joy, it follows that the first speaker said first and before anything else 'God.' Here also this question arises from our saying above that man spoke first by way of answer: If an answer, was it addressed to God? For if so it would seem that God had already spoken, which appears to make against what has been said above. To which [50] we reply **The speech of God** that he might well have made answer when God questioned him ; but it does not follow from this that God uttered what we call speech. For who doubts that whatsoever is can be bent according to the will of God ? For by him all things were made, by him they are preserved, and by him also they are governed. Therefore since the air is made to undergo such great disturbances by the ordinance of that lower nature which is the minister and workmanship of God, that it causes the thunder to peal, the [60] lightning to flash, the water to drop, and scatters the snow and hurls down the hail, shall it not be moved to utter certain words rendered distinct by him who has distinguished greater things ? Why not ? Wherefore we consider that these observations are a sufficient answer to this difficulty, and to some others.

19. *The woman spoke first.* Dante seems to have overlooked *Gen.* ii. 20-24.
29. *El* This opinion is retracted in *Paradiso*, XXVI. 133-136 (which see). See all also below, I. 6 : 61.
37. *Cry of woe* (lit., Alas!). See *Wisdom* vii. 3.
63. *Distinguished greater things.* The allusion is perhaps to Gen. i. 4, 6. See *Paradiso*, XIX. 42.

CHAPTER V

[The time and place of Adam's first utterance.]

THINKING then (not without reason drawn as well from the foregoing considerations as from those which follow) that the first man directed his speech first of all to the Lord himself, we

When, why, and where man first spoke may reasonably say that this first speaker at once, after having been inspired by the vivifying power, spoke without hesitation. For in man we believe it to be more characteristic of humanity to be heard than to hear, provided he be heard and hear [10] as a man. If, therefore, that workman and origin and lover of perfection by his breath made the first of us complete in all perfection, it appears to us reasonable that this most noble of animals did not begin to hear before he began to be heard. But if any one raises the objection that there was no need for him to speak, as he was, so far, the only human being, whilst God discerns all our secret thoughts without any words of ours, even before [20] we do ourselves, we say with that reverence which we ought to use in judging anything respecting the eternal will, that though God knew, nay, even fore-knew (which is the same thing in respect of God) the thought of the first man who spoke, without any words being said, still he wished that the man should also speak, in order that, in the unfolding of so great a gift, he himself who had freely bestowed it might glory. And therefore it is to be believed that it is by God's appointment that we rejoice in the well-ordered play of our emotions.

[30] Hence also we can fully determine the place where our first speech was uttered; for if man was inspired with life outside Paradise, he first spoke outside; but if within, we have proved that the place of his first speech was within.

8. *To be heard than to hear.* Speech, that is to say, is a more brilliant and characteristic use of that gift

VI.   THE FIRST BOOK

of reason which distinguishes man from the brutes than merely hearing what is uttered by another.
  10. That is, as a man guided by reason and not as a beast. See *Convivio*, II. 8 : 24 ff. ; IV. 5 : 73-75.
  13. See *Paradiso*, XIII. 37-45, 82, 83, and XXVI. 91.
  23. See *Paradiso*, XVII. 37-42.
  25 Cf. *Purgatorio*, XXXI. 37-42 ; *Paradiso*, XVII. 7-12, and XXIV. 40 ff.
  34. St Thomas decides that Adam was formed *outside* Paradise (*Summa Theol.*, part I., question 102, article 3).

CHAPTER VI

[Dante, purposing to investigate what was the language spoken by Adam, takes occasion to inveigh against the petty local conceit of those (especially Florentines) who believe the place where they were born to be the most delightful in the world, and their native tongue to be the best in the world, and consequently that which Adam spoke. After this digression he declares that the primitive language spoken by Adam and his descendants until the confusion of tongues was Hebrew.]

SINCE human affairs are carried on in very many different languages, so that many men are not understood by many with words any better than without words, it is meet for us to make investigation concerning that language which that man who had no mother, who was never suckled, who never saw either childhood or youth, is believed to have spoken. In this as in much else Pietramala [10] is a most populous city, and the native place of the majority of the children of Adam. For whoever is so offensively unreasonable as to suppose that the place

What was the language of Adam?

Dante's love for Florence of his birth is the most delightful under the sun, also rates his own vernacular (that is, his mother-tongue) above all others, and consequently believes that it actually was that of Adam. But we, to whom the world is our native country, just as the sea is to the fish, though we drank of Arno before our teeth appeared, and though we love [20] Florence so dearly that for the love we bore her we are wrongfully suffering exile—we rest the shoulders of our judgment on reason rather than on feeling. And although as regards our own pleasure or sensuous comfort there exists no more agreeable place in the world than Florence, still, when we turn over the volumes both of poets and other writers in which the world is generally and particularly described, and take account within ourselves of the [30] various situations of the places of the world and their arrangement with respect to the two poles and to the equator, our deliberate and firm opinion is that there are many countries and cities both nobler and more delightful than Tuscany and Florence of which we are a native and a citizen, and also that a great many nations and races use a speech both more agreeable and more serviceable than the Italians do. Returning therefore to our subject, we say that [40] a certain form of speech was created by God together with the first soul. And I say ' a form,' both in respect of words and their construction and of the utterance of this construction; and this form every tongue of speaking men would use, if it had not been dissipated by the fault of man's presumption, as shall be shown further on.

In this form of speech Adam spoke [50]; Hebrew in this form of speech all his descendants spoke the until the building of the Tower of Babel, which primitive is by interpretation the tower of confusion; and language this form of speech was inherited by the sons of Heber, who after him were called Hebrews. With them alone did it remain after the confusion, in order that our Redeemer (who was, as to his humanity, to spring from them) might use, not the language of confusion, but of grace. Therefore Hebrew was [60] the language which the lips of the first speaker formed.

7. See above, V. 13*n*.
10. Pietramala was a village in the Apennines, about twenty miles south of Bologna. Fraticelli quotes a similar ironical saying about another insignificant place: 'So and so has travelled a great deal; he has even seen Peretola.'
19. Compare below, I. 8 : 13; *Convivio*, IV. 14 : 116; *Æneid*, VII. 715.
22. Compare *Convivio*, II. 12 : 4, where Dante speaks of the 'face' of his discourse, and below, *Epistle* VI. 143.
45. By 'construction' Dante means the grammatical arrangement of words in sentences (see below, II. 6). By the 'utterance of the construction' he means the pronunciation.
61. The statement here made as to the permanency of the language spoken by Adam and repeated below, I. 7 : 61 ff.; 9 : 51, cannot be reconciled with *Paradiso*, XXVI 124-126, where we are told that the language of Adam had entirely disappeared long before the building of Babel; and we must accordingly take it that Dante's opinion had undergone a change by the time he was working at the *Paradiso*. Scartazzini and D'Ovidio go so far as to say that the passage in the *Paradiso* was inserted expressly to correct this one.

CHAPTER VII

[Description of the building of Babel and of the confusion of tongues. Those who retained the primitive language did not join in the wicked work; and their language was spoken by their descendants, the Israelites, until their dispersion.]

The ignominy of the human race
It is, alas! with feelings of shame that we now recall the ignominy of the human race. But since it is impossible for us to avoid passing through it, we will hasten through it, though the blush of shame rises to our cheeks and our mind recoils. O thou our human nature, ever prone to sin! O thou, full of iniquity from the first and ever afterwards without cessation! Did it suffice for thy correction that, deprived of light through thy first [10] transgression, thou wast banished from thy delightful native land? Did it suffice, did it suffice that through the universal lust and cruelty of thy family, one house alone excepted, whatsoever was subject to thee had perished in the Flood, and that the animals of earth and air had already been punished for what thou hadst committed? Certainly this should have been enough! But as men are wont to say in the proverb, 'Thou shalt not ride on horseback before the third time,' thou, wretched one, didst choose rather to come to a wretched steed.

[20] See, reader, how man, either forgetting or despising his former discipline, and turning aside his eyes from the marks of the stripes which had remained, for the third time provoked the lash by his stupid and presumptuous pride! For incorrigible man, persuaded by the giant,

presumed in his heart to surpass by his own skill **How** not only nature, but even the very power that **Babel** works in nature, who is God; and he began to **was built** build a tower in Sennear, which was afterwards [30] called Babel, that is, confusion, by which he hoped to ascend to heaven; purposing in his ignorance, not to equal, but to surpass his Maker. O boundless clemency of the heavenly power! Who among fathers would bear so many insults from a son? But he arose, and, with a scourge which was not hostile but paternal and had been wont at other times to smite, he chastised his rebellious son with correction at once merciful and memorable. For almost the whole human race had come together [40] to the work of wickedness. Some were giving orders, some were acting as architects, some were building the walls, some were adjusting the masonry with rules, some were laying on the mortar with trowels, some were quarrying stone, some were engaged in bringing it by sea, some by land; and different companies were engaged in different other occupations, when they were struck by such confusion from heaven, that all those who were attending to the work, using one and the same language, left off the work on being [50] estranged by many different languages and never again came together in the same intercourse. For the same language remained to those alone who were engaged together in the same kind of work; for instance, one language remained to all the architects, another to those rolling down blocks of stone, another to those preparing the stone; and so it happened to each group of workers. And the human

The confusion of tongues race was accordingly then divided into as many different languages as there were different branches of the work; and the [60] higher the branch of work the men were engaged in, the ruder and more barbarous was the language they afterwards spoke.

But those to whom the hallowed language remained were neither present, nor countenanced the work; but utterly hating it, they mocked the folly of those engaged in it. But these, a small minority, were of the seed of Shem (as I conjecture), who was the third son of Noah; and from them sprang the people of Israel, who made use of the most ancient language until [70] their dispersion.

5. *Our mind recoils* ('*animusque refugiat*'). A reminiscence of Virgil's '*animus refugit*' (*Æneid*, II. 12). Compare *Inferno*, I. 25.

18. 'Thou shalt not ride on horseback before the third time,' *i.e.* thou shalt be punished at the third fault. Giuliani (writing in 1878) says that the proverb was still current. *Dar un cavallo* (lit., to give a horse) = to punish. The expression originated, it seems, in the practice of putting naughty boys astride the back of some one, in order to receive a whipping. There may also be an allusion here to the instrument of torture known as the wooden horse. This explanation is, however, exposed to the obvious objection that the human race had already been punished twice, viz., by the expulsion from Eden and the flood, while the third punishment, the confusion of tongues, was less severe than the other two. According to another explanation, the words *non ante tertium equitabis* should be rendered 'Thou shalt not be a rider till the third time,' with an allusion to the saying that one will not become a horseman till he has been thrown three times.

26. *i.e.* Nimrod (compare *Inferno*, XXXI. 77, 78; *Purgatorio*, XII. 34-36), who is called a giant in

Gen. x. 8, as read by St Augustin (*De Civitate Dei*, XVI. 3). The same authority (*ibid.*, XVI. 4) identifies the narrative of *Gen.* xi. 1 ff. (building of Babel) with the building of Babylon, and states that Nimrod was its founder (compare *Gen.* x. 10). The tradition that Nimrod built the tower of Babel was well established in the Middle Ages.

28. See for Dante's idea of nature, *De Monarchia*, II. 2: 15 ff.; *Convivio*, IV. 9: 15 ff.

34. *Of the heavenly power* (*imperii*). Compare *Paradiso*, XXXII. 117.

37. *Pia correctione, i.e.* with the correction which a tender father would administer (see *Convivio*, II. 11: 30 ff.; *Paradiso*, XVIII. 129).

67. A conjecture founded, no doubt, on *Gen* x. 21. It is curious that Dante calls Shem the third son of Noah, for in the biblical narrative he is always mentioned in priority to Ham and Japheth. If, however, Dante's words here, '*tertius filius Noe*,' be taken in the sense of ' one of Noah's three sons,' the difficulty disappears.

CHAPTER VIII

[Dante here confines his attention to Europe. Its inhabitants, coming from the East, brought a threefold language with them which accordingly, in process of time, became divided into three principal varieties of speech: (1) That prevailing over the North of Europe, subdivided afterwards into various tongues, almost all of which betray their common origin by the use of the affirmative particle *iò*. (2) That prevailing over the East of Europe and extending into Asia, spoken by the Greeks. (3) That prevailing in the South, now subdivided into the tongues distinguished by the affirmative particles *oc*, *oïl*, and *sì*. The boundaries of these languages described].

Consequence of the confusion

ON account of the confusion of tongues related above we have no slight reason for thinking that men were at that time first scattered through all

Lan-
guages of
Europe
the climes of the world, and the habitable regions and corners of those climes. And as the original root of the human race was planted in the regions of the East, and our race also spread out from there on both sides by a manifold diffusion of shoots [10], and finally reached the boundaries of the West, it was then perhaps that rational throats first drank of the rivers of the whole of Europe, or at least of some of them. But whether these men then first arrived as strangers, or whether they came back to Europe as natives, they brought a threefold language with them, and of those who brought it some allotted to themselves the southern, others the northern part of Europe, while the third body, whom we [20] now call Greeks, seized partly on Europe and partly on Asia.

Afterwards, from one and the same idiom received at the avenging confusion, various vernaculars drew their origin, as we shall show farther on. For one idiom alone prevailed in all the country which from the mouths of the Danube, or marshes of Mæotis to the western boundary of England, is bounded by the frontiers of Italy and France and by the ocean; though afterwards through the [30] Sclavonians, Hungarians, Teutons, Saxons, English, and many other nations it was drawn off into various vernaculars, this alone remaining to almost all of them as a sign of their common origin, that nearly all the above-named answer in affirmation *iò*.

Starting from this idiom, that is to say eastward from the Hungarian frontier, another language prevailed over all the territory in that direction comprised in Europe, and even extended beyond. [40] But a third idiom pre-vailed in all that part of Europe which remains from the other two, though it now appears in a threefold form. For of those who speak it, some say in affirmation *oc*, others *oïl*, and others *sì*, namely the Spaniards, the French, and the Italians. Now the proof that the vernaculars of these nations proceed from one and the same idiom is obvious, because we see that they call many things by the same names, as *Deum, celum, amorem, mare, terram, vivit* [50], *moritur, amat,* and almost all other things. Now those of them who say *oc* inhabit the western part of the South of Europe, beginning from the frontier of the Genoese; while those who say *sì* inhabit the country east of the said frontier, namely that which extends as far as that promontory of Italy where the Gulf of the Adriatic Sea begins, and Sicily. But those who say *oïl* lie in some sort to the north of these last; for they have the Germans [60] on their east and north; on the west they are enclosed by the English sea, and bounded by the mountains of Aragon; they are also shut off on the south by the inhabitants of Provence, and the precipices of the Apennines.

Languages of Spaniards, French, and Italians

3. The climes (*climata*) were seven zones into which the ancient geographers divided that part of the earth which was known to them. Each clime, going northward, included such a space that the mean length of the longest day was half-an-hour longer than that of the longest day in the previous clime to the south (Moore, *Studies in Dante*, 3rd series, 131).

43 *Oc* = Latin *hoc* (this); *oïl* results from the combination of affirmative *hoc* with *ille* (he); as if to the question, 'Did he do it?' the answer were given, 'Yes, he did.' *Sì* = *sic* (so).

44. The speakers of the language of *oc* are not

inaptly called Spaniards, since a dialect of the language we now call Provençal prevailed over the whole of Aragon and Catalonia; while the Kings of Aragon were, after the downfall of the Counts of Toulouse (1249), the representative princes of the language of *oc*. In the same way the troubadour Albert of Sisteron (*c.* 1220) refers to the speakers of the language of *oc* as Catalans. Compare below, II. 12 : 20.

50. The specimen words here chosen represent the most important notions (God, heaven, love, sea, earth, being, living, dying, loving). Dante rightly argues that the fact that 'almost all' the words in the languages of *oc*, *oïl*, and *sì* are forms of the same Latin originals proves the common origin of these languages, though his theory of the conventional origin of Latin, the literary language (see below, I. 9 : 93 ff.) prevents him from drawing the inference that they are derived from Latin. In fact, on his hypothesis, the vulgar tongue must have preceded the literary language.

61, 62. The statement that the mountains of Aragon formed part of the west boundary of the language of *oïl* is puzzling. Orosius (*Hist.* I. 2), who was much relied on by Dante (see Moore, *Studies in Dante*, 3rd series, p. 110), says that Gallia Narbonensis (which comprised the territory of the mediæval countships of Provence and Toulouse) was bounded on the west by Spain; and in the map of Marino Sanuto (reproduced in Beazley's *Prince Henry the Navigator*), which is about contemporary with this treatise, the Iberian Peninsula is twisted round northward in such a way that the east coast of Spain is made to run parallel with the north coast of Africa! and consequently the line of the Pyrenees (which, however, are not marked) would actually form the west boundary of Southern France. But even assuming that the 'mountains of Aragon' = the Pyrenees, and that Dante shared an opinion prevalent in his time that the Pyrenees stretched from north to south instead of from east to west, it is further necessary to assume, in order to explain this passage as it stands, that Dante supposed the Pyrenees to extend so far north as to form part of the west boundary of northern France. Mr Wicksteed suggests that the words ' *et montibus Aragonie terminati* ' (' and bounded by the mountains of Aragon') (lines 61, 62) have become displaced, and ought to be inserted immediately after the clause (lines 52, 53) ' *a Ianuensium finibus incipientes* (' beginning from the frontier of the Genoese'). In that case the term ' Mountains of Aragon ' does not mean the Pyrenees, but the mountains south of that range which enclose Aragon on the west, south, and east. By adopting this suggestion the difficulty about the west boundary of *oïl* is removed, and the statement as to the limits of *oc* is made more precise ; for Genoa and the mountains of Aragon (in the sense just explained) give approximately the east and west limits of the territory of *oc*, including its Spanish portion. It may be mentioned that Rajna makes similar transpositions in the text in two other places. (See his larger edition, p. 168, *note* 2 ; p. 188, *note* 5.)

63. The term Apennines appears to be here equivalent to the Pennine Alps, which may fairly be taken as forming part of the south boundary of the *oïl* territory.

CHAPTER IX

[Dante further restricts his survey to the threefold language of the South, and proves by the fact that many words are common to all its forms that the language was at first uniform. This leads to a discussion of the cause of the variation in languages, and an explanation of the institution of a conventional invariable literary language (grammar) to obviate the inconveniences due to the mutability of natural speech.]

WE must now put whatever reason we possess to the proof, since it is our purpose to investigate matters in which we are supported by the authority of none, namely, the change which has passed over a language which was originally of

The language of Southern Europe

at first uniform one and the same form. [And] because it is safer as well as quicker to travel by known paths, let us proceed with that language alone which belongs to us, neglecting the others. For that which we find in one [10] appears by analogy to exist in the others also.

The language, then, which we are proceeding to treat of is threefold, as has been mentioned above; for some of those who speak it say *oc*, others *sì*, and others *oïl*. And that this language was uniform at the beginning of the confusion (which must first be proved) appears from the fact that we agree in many words, as eloquent writers show, which agreement is repugnant to that confusion which expiated the crime [committed] [20] in the building of Babel.

The writers of all three forms of the language agree, then, in many words, especially in the word *Amor*. Giraut de Borneil says:—

> '*Sim sentis fezelz amics
> per ver encusera Amor.*' [1]

The King of Navarre:—

> '*De fine amor si vient sen et bonté.*' [2]

Messer Guido Guinizelli:—

> '*Nè fa amor prima che gentil core*
> [30] *nè gentil cor prima che amor natura.*' [3]

---

[1] 'If a faithful friend heard me, I would make accusation against love.'

[2] 'From pure love proceeds wisdom and goodness.'

[3] 'Before the gentle heart, in nature's scheme Love was not, nor the gentle heart ere love.'
               (Rossetti's translation.)

Let us now inquire why it is that this language **Cause of** has varied into three chief forms, and why **variation** each of these variations varies in itself; why, **in lan-** for instance, the speech of the right side of **guage** Italy varies from that of the left (for the Paduans speak in one way and the Pisans in another) ; and also why those who live nearer together still vary in their speech, as the Milanese and Veronese, the Romans and the Florentines, and even those who [40] have the same national designation, as the Neapolitans and the people of Gaeta, those of Ravenna and those of Faenza, and what is stranger still, the inhabitants of the same city, like the Bolognese of the Borgo S. Felice and the Bolognese of the Strada Maggiore. One and the same reason will explain why all these differences and varieties of speech occur.

We say, therefore, that no effect as such goes beyond its cause, because nothing can [50] bring about that which itself is not. Since therefore every language of ours, except that created by God with the first man, has been restored at our pleasure after the confusion, which was nothing else but forgetfulness of the former language, and since man is a most unstable and changeable animal, no human language can be lasting and continuous, but must needs vary like other properties of ours, as for instance our manners and our dress, according to distance of time and place [60]. And so far am I from thinking that there is room for doubt as to the truth of our remark that speech varies 'according to difference of time,' that we are of opinion that this is rather

The ver- to be held as certain. For, if we consider our
nacular other actions, we seem to differ much more
con- from our fellow-countrymen in very distant
tinually
changing times than from our contemporaries very remote
in place. Wherefore we boldly affirm that if
the ancient Pavians were to rise from the dead
they would talk in a language varying or differ-
ing from that of the modern [70] Pavians.
Nor should what we are saying appear more
wonderful than to observe that a young man is
grown up whom we have not seen growing. For
the motion of those things which move gradually
is not considered by us at all ; and the longer
the time required for perceiving the variation of
a thing, the more stable we suppose that thing
to be. Let us not therefore be surprised if the
opinions of men who are but little removed from
the brutes suppose that the citizens of the same
[80] town have always carried on their inter-
course with an unchangeable speech, because the
change in the speech of the same town comes
about gradually, not without a very long suc-
cession of time, whilst the life of man is in its
nature extremely short.

If, therefore, the speech of the same people
varies (as has been said) successively in course of
time, and cannot in any wise stand still, the
speech of people living apart and removed from
one another must needs vary in different ways ;
just as [90] manners and dress vary in different
ways, since they are not rendered stable either
by nature or by intercourse, but arise according
to men's inclinations and local fitness. Hence
were set in motion the inventors of the art of
grammar, which is nothing else but a kind of

IX. THE FIRST BOOK

unchangeable identity of speech in different times and places. This having been settled by the common consent of many peoples [100], seems exposed to the arbitrary will of none in particular, and consequently cannot be variable. They therefore invented grammar in order that we might not, on account of the variation of speech fluctuating at the will of individuals, either fail altogether in attaining, or at least attain but a partial knowledge of the opinions and exploits of the ancients, or of those whom difference of place causes to differ from us.

Invention of 'Grammar'

17. *Eloquent writers (doctores)*, *i.e.* poets whose writings have given them the authority of teachers. So again below, line 21 of this chapter, and 10: 25, 12: 10, 15: 45, and II. 5 : 24, where the word is translated 'teachers.'

25. On Giraut de Borneil, see *Purgatorio*, XXVI. 115*n*. This and the other Provençal poems quoted in this work are printed *in extenso* in Chaytor's *Troubadours of Dante* (Clarendon Press, 1902).

27. This King of Navarre was Thibaut IV., Count of Champagne (1201-1253), who in 1234 succeeded his uncle, Sancho VII., as King of Navarre, under the title of Teobaldo I. He took part with Louis VIII. of France in the crusade against the Albigenses. He is celebrated for his passion for Blanche of Castile, mother of St Louis, and ranks among the first of the lyric poets of Northern France in the thirteenth century (Toynbee).

30. These are the third and fourth lines of the first stanza of the canzone whose first line is quoted below (II. 5 : 42). On Guido Guinizelli, see *Purgatorio*. XXVI. 16*n*

50. See *Convivio*, IV. 23 : 46.

70. See *Convivio*, I. 5 : 55 ff.

101. Compare above, I. 1 : 28*n*. In view of *Convivio*, II. 14 : 83 ff., where Dante points out that changes had taken place and would take place in 'Grammatica,' the 'unchangeable identity' here ascribed to it must

be taken relatively and not absolutely. This is made clear by *Convivio*, I. 5 : 47 ff., where Dante asserts that 'in the ancient writings of the Latin comedies and tragedies which cannot be changed we see the same speech that we have to-day.' The Latinity of the present work would have made Cicero's hair stand on end. Compare *Convivio*, I. 5 : 50-52*n*.

CHAPTER X

[Declining to decide the question which of the three languages of *oïl*, *oc*, and *sì* merits the preference, Dante, after stating the claims which each of them might urge, confines himself to the vernacular Italian and enumerates the principal dialects of Italy, classified with reference to their position west or east of the Apennines, and refers to the numerous subordinate variations of speech.]

The languages of *oc*, *oïl*, and *sì* Our language being now spoken under three forms (as has been said above), we feel, when comparing it with itself, according to the three forms that it has assumed, such great hesitation and timidity in placing [its different forms] in the balances, that we dare not, in our comparison, give the preference to any one of them, except in so far as we find that the founders of grammar have taken *sic* as the adverb of affirmation, which seems to confer [10] a kind of precedence on the Italians, who say *sì*. For each of the three divisions [of our language] defends its pretensions by copious evidence. That of *oïl*, then, alleges on its behalf that because of its being an easier and pleasanter vernacular language, whatever has been translated into or composed in vernacular prose belongs to it, namely, the compilations of the exploits of the Trojans and Romans, the exquisite legends of King Arthur, and very many [20] other works of history and learning. Another, namely that of *oc*, claims that eloquent speakers of the vernacular first employed it for poetry, as being a more finished and sweeter language, for instance Peter of Auvergne and other ancient writers. The third also, which is the language of the Italians, claims pre-eminence on the strength of two privileges: first, that the sweetest and most subtle poets who have written in the vernacular are its intimate friends and belong to its household [30], like Cino of Pistoia and his friend ; second, that it seems to lean more on grammar, which is common: and this appears a very weighty argument to those who examine the matter in a rational way.

Their rival pretensions

We, however, decline to give judgment in this case, and confining our treatise to the vernacular Italian, let us endeavour to enumerate the variations it has received into itself, and also to compare these with one another. In the first place, then, we say that Italy has a twofold division [40] into right and left. But, if any should ask what is the dividing line, we answer shortly that it is the ridge of the Apennines, which like the ridge of a tiled roof discharges its droppings in different directions on either side, and pours its waters down to either shore alternately through long gutter-tiles, as Lucan describes in his second book. Now the right side has the Tyrrhenian Sea as its basin, while the waters on the left fall into the Adriatic. The districts on the right [50]

The dialects of Italy are Apulia (but not the whole of it), the Duchy [of Spoleto], Tuscany, and the March of Genoa. Those on the left are part of Apulia, the March of Ancona, Romagna, Lombardy, and the March of Treviso with Venetia. Friuli and Istria cannot but belong to the left of Italy, and the islands of the Tyrrhenian Sea, namely Sicily and Sardinia, must belong to, or be associated with the right of Italy. Now in each of these two [60] sides, and those districts which follow them, the languages of the inhabitants vary, as for instance the language of the Sicilians as compared with that of the Apulians, of the Apulians with that of the Romans, of the Romans with that of the Spoletans, of these with that of the Tuscans, of the Tuscans with that of the Genoese, of the Genoese with that of the Sardinians; also of the Calabrians with that of the people of Ancona, of these with that of the people of Romagna, of the people of Romagna with that of the Lombards, of the Lombards with that of the Trevisans and Venetians, and of these last with that of the [70] Aquileians, and of them with that of the Istrians; and we do not think that any Italian will disagree with us in this statement. Whence it appears that Italy alone is diversified by fourteen dialects at least, all of which again vary in themselves: as for instance in Tuscany the Sienese differ in speech from the Aretines; in Lombardy the Ferrarese from the Placentines; in the same city also we observe some variation, as we remarked above in the last chapter [80]. Wherefore if we would calculate the primary, secondary, and subordinate variations of the vulgar tongue of Italy, we should find that in **A thousand idioms in Italy** this tiny corner of the world the varieties of speech not only come up to a thousand but even exceed that figure.

18. *Biblia cum Troyanorum Romanorumque gestibus* (sic) *compilata.* The wording of this is very peculiar. I am assured by Dr Paget Toynbee that *Biblia* has nothing to do with the Bible in this passage. The literal rendering would therefore be 'The books compiled with the exploits (or 'gests') of the Trojans and Romans.' So Fraticelli and Giuliani. In his Dante Dictionary (s. v. *Lingua Oïl*) Dr Toynbee says: 'The Troy Romance referred to is doubtless the abridged French prose version (cent. xiii.) of the celebrated verse Roman de Troie of Benoît de Sainte-More which was written *circ.* 1160; while that of Rome may be some version of the verse Roman d'Énéas, written (probably by the same author) somewhat earlier, which was widely popular in the Middle Ages.'

But *Biblia* primâ facie means the Bible, and the more natural translation of the words would be 'The Bible compiled (or combined) with the 'gests' of the Trojans and Romans.' The phrase would thus seem to refer to a universal history, the thread of which was formed by the biblical narrative, but into which profane history, especially of Troy and Rome, was interwoven.

This would constitute the main region of the *redactum* or translated French, whereas the Arthurian legend would be the chief example of the *inventum* or original French composition. But it can hardly be said that there is any known French work which corresponds with sufficient closeness to this description to give us any security that this is the meaning. The nearest approach to it is the *Historia Scholastica* of Petrus Comestor (*Paradiso*, XII. 134), which was translated into French in the thirteenth century. It is thus described (Gröber, *Grundriss der Romanischen Philologie*, 1902, II. i. p. 189): 'A sort of encyclopædia of biblical history which presents a complete picture of the history and religion of antiquity, in which the dates of ancient history, sacred and profane, and the allegorical and historical exposition of biblical passages, are united with the exposition of the doctrines of the ancient philosophers.'

19. The word translated 'legends' (*ambages*) means 'turnings' or 'windings,' and figuratively 'digressions,' and was a kind of technical expression for the romances of adventure.

24. Peter of Auvergne was a celebrated troubadour of the earlier period (fl. 1150-1180). Little is known of his life. He passed a considerable time at the court of Raymond V., Count of Toulouse (1148-1194); visited, in 1158, the court of Sancho III. of Castile, and in the following year that of Raymond Berenger IV., Count of Barcelona. There is reason to think that he ended his days in the cloister. He affected and gloried in the obscure or subtle style of poetry of which Arnaut Daniel (somewhat later) became the chief master. But his most celebrated piece is in quite another vein, being a satire on the habits and personal appearance of contemporary poets.

30. 'His friend' is Dante himself. Cino, or in full Guittoncino of Pistoja, of the family of the Sinibuldi or Sigisbuldi, was one of the chief jurists and poets of his time. The date of his birth is not known. In 1297 he was a student at Bologna. He adopted the legal profession; was banished from his native town in 1301 with others of the Neri faction; returned in 1306 or 1307, and was an assessor when the government of the city was reformed in the interests of the Neri. He was sent as ambassador to Florence in 1309. In 1314 he took his Doctor's degree at Bologna, and subsequently lectured on law at Treviso, Siena, Florence, Perugia, and Naples. He died in his native city at the end of 1336 or the beginning of 1337, and was buried in the cathedral. His love poems are said to have been inspired by Selvaggia, daughter of Filippo Vergiolesi, who married into the well-known family of the Cancellieri. He himself married Margherita degli Ughi. A canzone by him on the death of Beatrice is quoted below (II. 6 : 71), and another, on the death of Dante, is extant. His most

XI.   **THE FIRST BOOK**   35

important legal work was a commentary on the first nine books of Justinian's Code. Besides commemorating Cino in this work, Dante is believed to have addressed an extant Latin letter to him (*Epistola* IV., p. 305, in this volume), and also five sonnets, but does not refer to him in the Comedy. For some of the information given in this note I am indebted to the kindness of Mr E. G. Gardner.

32. *i.e.* common to the 'many peoples' by whose 'common consent' it was established (above, 9 : 98).

46. *Pharsalia* II. 391-438.

83. Cf. Giovanni del Virgilio's poetic Epistle to Dante (lines 15, 16), 'Clerks scorn the vernaculars, even though they varied not, whereas there are a thousand idioms.' There may be here an allusion to the present passage.

CHAPTER XI

[In view of the many discordant varieties of the Italian vernacular, Dante purposes to search for a language fitted to belong to the whole of Italy, and proceeds in this and the next four chapters to reject the claims of the principal dialects to occupy that position. He first rejects the dialects of Rome, the March of Ancona, Spoleto, Milan, Bergamo, etc., Aquileia and Istria, Casentino, Prato, and Sardinia.]

As the Italian vernacular has so very many discordant varieties, let us hunt after a more fitting and an illustrious Italian language ; and in order that we may be able to have a practicable path for our chase, let us first cast the tangled bushes and brambles out of the wood. Therefore, as the Romans think that they ought to have precedence over all the rest, let us in this process of uprooting or clearing away give them (not

The Roman dialect

Dialects of Central Italy, Milan, etc. undeservedly) precedence [10], declaring that we will have nothing to do with them in any scheme of a vernacular language. We say, then, that the vulgar tongue of the Romans, or rather their hideous jargon, is the ugliest of all the Italian dialects; nor is this surprising, since in the depravity of their manners and customs also they appear to stink worse than all the rest. For they say '*Mezzure, quinto dici?*'[1] After them, let us get rid of the inhabitants of the March of Ancona, who say, '*Chignamente scate sciate?*'[2] [20] with whom we reject the Spoletans also. Nor must we forget that a great many canzoni have been written in contempt of these three peoples, among which we have noticed one correctly and perfectly constructed, which a certain Florentine named Castra had composed. It began:—

> '*Una fermana scopai da Casciòli
> Cita cita sen gia'n grande aina.*'[3]

[30] And after these let us weed out the people of Milan and Bergamo with their neighbours, in reproach of whom we recollect that some one has sung:—

> '*Enti l'ora dei vesper,
> Ciò fu del mes d'ochiover.*'[4]

After them let us sift out the Aquileians and

---

[1] 'Sir, what sayest thou?'
[2] Meaning uncertain.
[3] 'I met a peasant-girl (?) from Cascioli: she was slinking off in a great hurry.'
[4] 'At the hour of evening, in the month of October.'

Istrians, who belch forth with cruelly harsh accents, '*Ces fastu?*'[1] And with these we cast out all the mountainous and rural dialects, as those of Casentino and Prato, which by the extravagance of their accent always seem discordant [40] to the citizens dwelling in the midst of the towns. Let us also cast out the Sardinians, who are not Italians, but are, it seems, to be associated with them; since they alone seem to be without any vulgar tongue of their own, imitating Latin as apes do men: for they say, '*Domus nova*'[2] and '*dominus meus*.'[3]

The Sardinian dialect

26. Nothing else is known of Castra. The poem in question, which is very obscure and difficult, is headed in the only MS. in which it is preserved by the name 'Messer Osmano.' It is suggested by Monaci (who prints the poem in his *Crestomazia italiana*, p. 493) that this name may be either a pseudonym, or else the name of the person to whom the poem was addressed.

42. It is curious to find the town of Prato (about ten miles from Florence) given as an instance of a mountainous and rural district. Possibly its dialect resembled that spoken among the neighbouring Apennines; or the insertion of Prato here may (as Rajna suggests) be due to a piece of local spite (*spirito di campanile*) on Dante's part. (Compare *Inferno*, XXVI. 8, 9).

47. There are at least two places called *Domus novas* in Sardinia, and Rajna thinks it likely that this proper name is the source of the first of these examples.

[1] 'What doest thou?'   [2] 'New house.'
[3] 'My lord.'

CHAPTER XII

[The examination of the Sicilian dialect is interrupted by a digression on the degeneracy of the present magnates of Italy as compared with the Emperor Frederick II. and his son Manfred, the patrons of the Sicilian school of poetry. After the digression, the local Sicilian dialect is summarily rejected, as is that of Apulia, the evidence of disqualification being the fact that the local poets did not compose in the local dialect, but in that language which belongs to the whole of Italy.]

Sicilian poets
HAVING sifted, so to speak, the Italian vernaculars, let us, comparing together those left in our sieve, briefly choose out the one most honourable and conferring most honour. And first let us examine the genius of the Sicilian, for the Sicilian vernacular appears to arrogate to itself a greater renown than the others, both because whatever poetry the Italians write is called Sicilian, and because we find that very many [10] natives of Sicily have written weighty poetry, as in the canzoni, '*Ancor che l'aigua per lo focho lassi*,'[1] and '*Amor che lungiamente m'ài menato.*'[2] But this fame of the land of Trinacria appears, if we rightly examine the mark to which it tends, only to have survived by way of a reproach to the princes of Italy, who, not in a heroic but in a plebeian manner, follow pride. [20] But those illustrious heroes Frederick Cæsar and his happy-born son Manfred, display-

---

[1] 'Even though through fire water forsakes [its great coldness].'
[2] 'O love, who long hast led me.'

ing the nobility and righteousness of their character, as long as fortune remained favourable, followed what is human, disdaining what is bestial; wherefore those who were of noble heart and endowed with graces strove to attach themselves to the majesty of such great princes; so that in their time, whatever the best Italians attempted first appeared [30] at the court of these mighty sovereigns. And from the fact that the royal throne was Sicily it came to pass that whatever our predecessors wrote in the vulgar tongue was called Sicilian; and this name we also retain, nor will our successors be able to change it. Racha, racha! what is the sound now uttered by the trumpet of the latest Frederick? What is that uttered by the bell of Charles II.? What is that uttered by the horns of the powerful Marquises John and Azzo? What is that uttered by the flutes of the other [40] magnates? What but 'Come, ye murderers; come, ye traitors; come, ye followers of avarice.'

Degeneracy of Italian princes

But it is better to return to our subject than to speak in vain: and we declare that if we take the Sicilian dialect, that namely spoken by the common people, out of whose mouths it appears our judgment should be drawn, it is in nowise worthy of preference, because it is not uttered without drawling, as for instance here [50]: '*Tragemi d'este focora, se t'este a boluntate.*'[1] If, however, we choose to take the language as it flows from the mouths of the highest Sicilians, as it may be examined in the canzoni quoted before, it differs in nothing from that language

---

[1] 'Draw me from these fires, if it is thy will.'

The Apulian dialect which is the most worthy of praise, as we show further on.

The Apulians also, because of their own harshness of speech, or else because of their nearness to their neighbours who are the Romans and the people of the March [of Ancona], make use of shameful barbarisms, for they say [60], '*Volzera che chiangesse lo quatraro.*'[1]

But though the natives of Apulia commonly speak in a hideous manner, some of them have been distinguished by their use of polished language, inserting more *curial* words into their canzoni, as clearly appears from an examination of their works, for instance, '*Madonna, dir vi voglio,*'[2] and '*Per fino amore vo sì letamente.*'[3]

[70] Wherefore it should become clear to those who mark what has been said above, that neither the Sicilian nor the Apulian dialect is that vulgar tongue which is the most beautiful in Italy, for we have shown that eloquent natives of those parts have diverged from their own dialect.

12-14. *Ancor che,* etc. *Amor che,* etc. The opening lines of two canzoni by Guido delle Colonne, a judge and notary of Messina (fl. 1257-1288). He accompanied Edward I. to England when that monarch was returning from crusade on the death of Henry III. (1272), and he was the author of a History of Troy (founded on a French romance), on the strength of which he is commemorated by Chaucer (Hous of Fame, III. 379). There is some reason to think he belonged to the great Roman house of Colonna. The expression 'weighty poetry' refers to the dignity of its subject matter (see below

[1] Meaning uncertain.
[2] 'Lady, I will tell you [how love has seized me].
[3] 'For pure love I go so joyfully.'

II. 4); on the Sicilian school of poetry see Gaspary's *Early Italian Literature* (Œlsner's translation, pp. 55 ff.).

16. The 'mark to which it tends' is the inciting of the other Italian princes to emulate Frederick II. and Manfred in their fostering of this literary vernacular.

21. Cæsar, here=emperor, as in *Paradiso*, I. 29. Frederick II., son of the Emperor Henry VI. by Constance, heiress of the Norman kingdom of Naples and Sicily, was born at Jesi, 1194; succeeded his father as king of Naples and Sicily, 1197; was crowned as emperor by Honorius III. in 1220; deposed by Innocent IV. at the council of Lyons (1245), and died in 1250. His reign was one long struggle with the papal power. As he is commemorated here for his munificent patronage of literature and learning, so in *Inferno*, X. 119 he is condemned as an epicurean on account of his irreligious life.

Benegenitus eius Manfredus. *Benegenitus* is an oddly chosen epithet, in view of Manfred's illegitimacy. It seems to be used in the same sense as *ben nato* in *Purgatorio*, V. 60, and *Paradiso*, V. 115; or the expression may allude to Manfred's personal beauty (*Purgatorio*, III. 107), just as the corresponding *mal nati* seems in *Convivio*, III. 4: 81 to mean ill-favoured; or perhaps Dante intends to assert that Manfred was the *spiritually* legitimate son of his father. On Manfred, see *Purgatorio*, III. 103-145*n*.

35. *Racha.* This expression of contempt is taken from Matt. v. 22.

37. *i.e.* Frederick II., king of Sicily from 1296 till 1337. He was the son of Peter III. of Aragon by Constance, daughter of Manfred. See *Convivio*, IV. 6: 182*n*; *Purgatorio*, VII. 115-120*n*; *Paradiso*, XIX. 130*n*; XX. 63.

38. On Charles II., king of Naples, see *Purgatorio*, VII. 124-129*n*. By the instrument here assigned to this monarch in the orchestra of princes, Dante seems to intimate that he thinks him fit for nothing but to ring a bell in church, which is quite in accordance with the contempt he expresses for king Charles in many other places.

38. John I., surnamed the Just, marquis of Montferrat, succeeded his father, William V. (or VII.), in 1292, married, in 1296, a daughter of Amadeus V., count of Savoy, and died in 1305. The reason why Dante blames this prince is uncertain. At the time of his accession to the marquisate, he was frequenting the court of Charles II. of Naples, which may perhaps in part account for it.

38. Azzo VIII., marquis of Este, succeeded his father Obizzo II. in 1293 and died in 1308. In 1305 he married Beatrice, daughter of Charles II. of Naples, as his second wife, a transaction denounced in *Purgatorio*, XX. 80. In *Purgatorio*, V. 77, 78, Dante charges him with murder, and in *Inferno*, XII. 112 with parricide (see also *Inferno*, XVIII. 55-57). In 1303 Azzo took part with the Neri of Florence in a futile attempt to drive the Bianchi refugees out of Bologna and to upset the government of that city. The horns, assigned as instruments to the marquises John and Azzo, may indicate their pride (see *Inferno*, XXXI. 71 in connection with *Purgatorio*, XII. 34-36).

43. Compare *De Monarchia*, II. 12 : 21-23.

50. *Tragemi*, etc. The third line of a poem in the form of a dialogue between a lover and his mistress. Its date is not earlier than 1231. The author appears to have been a minstrel in a humble way of life (Gaspary, *op. cit.* 71-74). His name, said to be Cielo dal Camo, or D'Alcamo, has long been a subject of inconclusive discussion.

54. *That language which is most worthy of praise*, i.e. the highest form of the language of Italy described below in chapters 16-18 of this book.

64. *Curial.* See below, I. 18 : 34.

67. *Madonna*, etc. The first line of a canzone by Jacopo da Lentino, a noted poet of the Sicilian school who flourished in the first half of the thirteenth century. He was known (it is said, on account of his skill in the legal profession) as the Notary, and by that name is associated in *Purgatorio*, XXIV. 55-57 (where see note) with Bonagiunta of Lucca and Guittone of Arezzo, as having been ' held back ' by the ' knot ' of conventionality from attaining to the excellence of the ' sweet new style.'

XIII.   **THE FIRST BOOK**   43

69. *Per fino*, etc. The first line (quoted again below, II. 5) of a canzone by Rinaldo d'Aquino, another poet of the Sicilian School and contemporary with the Notary. He seems to have been a person of some standing, is said to have engaged in a poetic correspondence with the emperor Frederick II., and probably acted as Manfred's viceroy in the province of Otranto and Bari in 1257.

CHAPTER XIII

[The Tuscan claim to the possession of the illustrious vernacular is indignantly denied, the speech of Florence, Pisa, Lucca, Siena, and Arezzo being rejected in detail. Guido Cavalcanti, Lapo Gianni, Cino of Pistoja, and 'another' (Dante himself) are commended for deviating from the Tuscan dialect. The claim of the Umbrian cities is dismissed in a parenthesis, and Genoa is disposed of in a few lines.]

NEXT let us come to the Tuscans, who, infatuated through their frenzy, seem to arrogate to themselves the title of the illustrious vernacular; and in this matter not only the minds of the common people are crazed, but we find that many distinguished men have embraced the delusion; for instance Guittone of Arezzo, who never aimed at the curial vernacular, Bonagiunta of Lucca, Gallo of Pisa [10], Mino Mocato of Siena, and Brunetto of Florence, whose works, if there be leisure to examine them, will be found to be not curial but merely municipal. And since the Tuscans exceed the rest in this frenzied intoxication, it seems right and profitable to deal with the dialects of the Tuscan towns one by one, and to

The Tuscan dialects

The take off somewhat of their vain glory. The
Tuscan Florentines open their mouths and say,
dialects '*Manichiamo introque* [20].—*Noi non facciano atro*';[1] the Pisans, '*Bene andonno li fanti De Fiorensa per Pisa*';[2] the people of Lucca, '*Fo voto a Dio che in gassarra eie lo comuno de Lucca*';[3] the Sienese, '*Onche renegata avesse io Siena!*'[4] '*Ch'ee chesto?*'[5] the Aretines, '*Vo tu venire ovelle?*'[6] (We do not intend to deal with Perugia, Orvieto [30], and Città Castellana at all, because of their close connection with the Romans and Spoletans.) But obtuse as almost all the Tuscans are in their degraded dialect, we notice that some have recognised wherein the excellence of the vernacular consists, namely, Guido, Lapo, and another, all Florentines, and Cino of Pistoja, whom we now undeservedly put last, having been not undeservedly driven to do so. Therefore if we examine the Tuscan [40] dialects, reflecting how the writers commended above have deviated from their own dialect, it does not remain doubtful that the vernacular we are in search of is different from that which the people of Tuscany attain to.

But if any one thinks that what we say of the Tuscans may not also be said of the Genoese, let him but bear this in mind, that if the Genoese

---

[1] 'Let us eat meantime—we do nothing else.'
[2] 'Truly the soldiers of Florence are going through Pisa.'
[3] 'Thank God the commonwealth of Lucca is in happy case' (Fraticelli).
[4] 'Would that I had never forsworn Siena!'
[5] 'What is this?'
[6] 'Wilt thou come somewhere?' (Rajna).

were through forgetfulness to lose the letter *z*, **The Genoese** they would have either to be dumb altogether, **dialect** or to discover some new [50] kind of speech, for *z* forms the greatest part of their dialect, and this letter is not uttered without great harshness.

7. Guittone di Viva, born near Arezzo in 1230, gained renown as a composer of love-poems; entered about 1266 that religious order instituted by Pope Urban IV., whose members, owing to their luxurious life, came to be known as Jovial Friars (*Frati Gaudenti;* see *Inferno,* XXIII. 103*n*.). Guittone, however, seems to have formed a creditable exception. His later poems were on religious, moral, and political subjects. In 1293 he helped to found the monastery of S. Maria degli Angeli at Florence, in which city he died in the following year. He is again unfavourably criticised below (II. 6 : 86). Compare *Purgatorio,* XXIV. 56; XXVI. 124.

8. Bonagiunta Orbiciani flourished in the latter part of the thirteenth century, and was a poet and notary of Lucca. Compare *Purgatorio,* XXIV. 19 ff.

9. Gallo of Pisa was a contemporary of Bonagiunta. Two canzoni by him are extant. Of Mocato nothing is known, but it has been suggested that he may be identical with one Meo di Mocata, one of whose poems is extant.

10. *i.e.* Brunetto Latini, on whom see *Inferno,* XV. 23*n*

20. The second Florentine phrase is probably an answer to the first, and the two together may be intended for a gibe at Dante's fellow-countrymen (Rajna).

35 *The excellence of the vernacular,* i.e. the illustrious language the author is now in search of.

36. On Guido Cavalcanti, see *Inferno,* X. 60*n*.

36. Lapo Gianni belonged to the Ricevuti family, and was a distinguished lyric poet and an intimate friend of Dante and Guido Cavalcanti. He was a notary, and was still living in May 1328.

39. Dante is compelled to put Pistoja last, because it deserves it; but doing so involves putting Cino

last, which he does not deserve. Dante's hatred of Pistoja (see *Inferno*, XXIV. 126; XXV. 10-12) was no doubt due to the fact of its having been the place where the feud of the Bianchi and Neri began, which was the source of the troubles that devastated Florence.

CHAPTER XIV

[Crossing the Apennines, the author notices the prevalence of two alternating types of dialect, one distinguished by its softness, the other by its harshness; the first prevails in Romagna; the second in Brescia, Verona, Vicenza, Padua, and Treviso; both are rejected, as is also the dialect of Venice.]

Two types of dialect in Italy (1) the smooth LET us now cross the leaf-clad shoulders of the Apennines, and hunt inquiringly, as we are wont, over the left side of Italy, beginning from the east.

Entering Romagna, then, we remark that we have found in Italy two alternating types of dialect with certain opposite characteristics in which they respectively agree. One of these, on account of the softness of its words and pronunciation, seems so feminine [10] that it causes a man, even when speaking like a man, to be believed to be a woman. This type of dialect prevails among all the people of Romagna, and especially those of Forlì, whose city, though the newest, seems to be the centre of all the province. These people say *deuscì* in affirmation, and use '*Oclo meo*'[1] and '*Corada mea*'[2] as terms of endearment. We have heard that some of them

---

[1] 'My eye.'   [2] 'My heart.'

have diverged in poetry from their own dialect, namely the Faentines Thomas and [20] Ugolino Bucciola.

There is also, as we have said, another type of dialect, so bristling and shaggy in its words and accents that, owing to its rough harshness, it not only distorts a woman's speech, but makes one doubt whether she is not a man. This type of dialect prevails among all those who say *magara*,[1] namely the Brescians, Veronese, and Vicentines, as well as the Paduans, with their ugly syncopations of all the participles in *tus* and denominatives in *tas*, as [30] *mercò* and *bontè*. With these we also class the Trevisans, who, like the Brescians and their neighbours, pronounce *f* for consonantal *u*, cutting off the final syllable of the word, as *nof* for *novem*, *vif* for *vivo*, which we disapprove as a gross barbarism.

(2) the rough

Nor do the Venetians also deem themselves worthy of possessing that vernacular language which we have been searching for; and if any of them, trusting in error, should cherish any delusion on this point, let him remember whether he has ever said [40] ' *Per le plage de Dio tu non veràs.*' [2]

Among all these we have noticed one man striving to depart from his mother-tongue, and to apply himself to the *curial* vernacular language, namely Ildebrandino of Padua.

Wherefore, on all the dialects mentioned in the present chapter coming up for judgment, our decision is that neither that of Romagna nor its opposite (as we have mentioned), nor that of

---

[1] ' Would it were so.'
[2] ' By God's wounds thou shalt not come.'

Venice is that illustrious vernacular which we are seeking.

14. *The newest (novissima).* A singular epithet for a city of the antiquity of Forlì (*Forum Livii*), said to have been founded B.C. 207 by M. Livius Salinator, after his defeat of Hasdrubal on the Metaurus. I am, however, informed by Dr Paget Toynbee that Prof. Rajna, in a letter written to him, suggests that *novissima* may here be taken in the sense of 'lowest in rank,' an expression of contempt possibly due to the ignominious failure of the attack on Florence made by the exiled Bianchi in March 1303 (known as the second war of Mugello), under the command of Scarpetta degli Ordelaffi, the head of the Ghibelline party at Forlì. 'It would be very like Dante,' says Dr Toynbee, 'to have a hit at Forlì on some such grounds.'

20. Ugolino Bucciola belonged to the important family of the Manfredi of Faenza, being a son of that Alberigo Manfredi whose treacherous murder of his kinsman is alluded to in *Inferno*, XXXIII. 118-120. Ugolino was born about 1245. He belonged to the Guelf party, and after a turbulent career was compelled to retire to Ravenna, where he died in 1301. Two sonnets by him, of little merit, are extant. Thomas, whom Dante here couples with Ugolino, belonged to the same family; he flourished about 1280 and was a judge. Several of his poems are extant.

30. The Italian forms are *mercato* (market) and *bontà* (goodness). In the first example the 'participle in *tus*' is *mercatus* (from *mercor*). In the second the 'denominative in *tas*' in *bonitas* (from *bonus*).

34. *Novem* is the Latin for 'nine' (Ital. *nove*).

43. Ildebrandino, otherwise Aldobrandino dei Mezzabati of Padua, held the office of 'Captain of the People' at Florence from May 1291 till May 1292. A sonnet of his in reply to one of Dante's (No. XLIV. in the Oxford Dante) is extant.

CHAPTER XV

[The dialect of Bologna, though the best of the local dialects, is not that courtly and illustrious language which the author is in search of.]

LET us now endeavour to clear the way by tracking out what remains of the Italian wood.

We say, then, that perhaps those are not far wrong who assert that the people of Bologna use a more beautiful speech [than the others], since they receive into their own dialect something borrowed from their neighbours of Imola, Ferrara, and Modena, just as we conjecture that all borrow from their neighbours, as Sordello showed with respect to his own Mantua, which is adjacent to [10] Cremona, Brescia, and Verona; and he who was so distinguished by his eloquence, not only in poetry but in every other form of utterance forsook his native vulgar tongue. Accordingly the above-mentioned citizens [of Bologna] get from those of Imola their smoothness and softness [of speech], and from those of Ferrara and Modena a spice of sharpness characteristic of the Lombards. This we believe has remained with the natives of that district as a relic of the admixture of the immigrant Longobards with them [20]: and this is the reason why we find that there has been no poet among the people of Ferrara, Modena, or Reggio; for from being accustomed to their own sharpness they cannot adopt the courtly vulgar tongue without a kind of roughness; and this we must consider to be much more the case with the people of Parma, who say *monto* instead of *multo*. If, therefore,

The Bologna dialect relatively the best

the people of Bologna borrow from both these kinds of dialect, as has been said, it seems reasonable that their speech should [30] by this mixture of opposites remain tempered to a praiseworthy sweetness; and this we without hesitation judge to be the case. Therefore if those who place the people of Bologna first in the matter of the vernacular merely have regard in their comparison to the municipal dialects of the Italians, we are disposed to agree with them; but if they consider that the dialect of Bologna is, taken absolutely, worthy of preference, we disagree with them altogether [40]; for this dialect is not that language which we term courtly and illustrious, since if it had been so, the greatest Guido Guinizelli, Guido Ghisilieri, Fabruzzo, and Onesto, and other poets of Bologna would never have departed from their own dialect; and these were illustrious writers, competent judges of dialects. The greatest Guido, wrote: '*Madonna lo fermo core*';[1] Fabruzzo [50], '*Lo meo lontano gire*';[2] Onesto, '*Più non attendo il tuo secorso, Amore*';[3] and these words are altogether different from the dialect of the citizens of Bologna.

And since we consider that no one feels any doubt as to the remaining towns at the extremities of Italy (and if any one does, we do not deem him worthy of any answer from us), little remains to be mentioned in our discussion. Wherefore [60] being eager to put down our sieve so that we may quickly see what is left in it, we say

(marginal note: but not good enough for illustrious writers)

---

[1] 'Lady, the steadfast heart.'
[2] 'My going afar.'
[3] 'No more do I await thy succour, Love.'

that the towns of Trent and Turin, as well as Alessandria, are situated so near the frontiers of Italy that they cannot possess pure languages, so that even if their vernaculars were as lovely as they are hideous, we should still say that they were not truly Italian, because of their foreign ingredients. Wherefore if we are hunting for an illustrious Italian language, what we are hunting for [70] cannot be found in them.

The frontier dialects

General note to lines 1-33.
The reasoning by which the relative superiority of the Bologna dialect is established is less clearly expressed than is usual with Dante. The following free paraphrase is submitted as a plausible explanation of this difficult passage. 'The peoples of every city borrow from their neighbours, and their dialects are better or worse (from the literary point of view) according to the character resulting from the mixture of the borrowed elements with the original speech. Hence the superiority of the Bologna dialect: for though the sharpness borrowed from Ferrara and Modena is bad in itself, it mixes well with the smoothness and softness borrowed from Imola. The same truth is illustrated as regards Mantua by the case of Sordello. The dialect of this place is bad, because of the badness of the elements borrowed from Cremona, Brescia, and Verona. Sordello, in fact, after some literary attempts in this dialect, found it so unsuitable that he forsook his native tongue entirely, wrote exclusively in Provençal, and became a Provençal to all intents and purposes.' It is no doubt true that so far no writings of Sordello have been discovered which are not in Provençal; but Dante's language certainly suggests the possibility of his having written in his native tongue, and Bertoni, who in 1901 printed two Provençal poems by Sordello previously unknown, printed with them another poem in a North Italian dialect, of which he thinks that Sordello may have been the author (*Giornale storico della letteratura italiana*, vol. xxxviii. pp. 269 ff.) It has been suggested, however, that the expression ' as Sordello

showed,' etc., may refer not to any poems in Italian, but to some definite utterance of Sordello in regard to the Mantuan dialect, in which, possibly, he justified himself for adopting Provençal, with other Italian poets, as his literary vehicle.

2. Compare above, II. 5, 6.

8. *All borrow from their neighbours, e.g.* the Apulians, Orvietans, etc. (above, 12 : 13).

9. There is much uncertainty about the earlier period of Sordello's life, and authentic dates are wanting. He was probably the son of a knight in needy circumstances, and was born at Goïto near Mantua about 1200. It is most likely (in spite of his own vigorous disclaimers) that he followed the calling of a professional minstrel. About the year 1225 (?) he carried off from Verona Cunizza (see *Paradiso*, IX. 33 *n.*), wife of Richard, Count of S. Bonifazio, daughter of Ezzelino II. of Romano, and sister of Ezzelino III., at the instigation of the latter, and perhaps also of his brother Alberic. There is very strong reason to believe that subsequently to this Sordello carried on an intrigue with Cunizza. While staying at a castle in the neighbourhood of Treviso belonging to three members of the Strasso family, he secretly married their near relative Otta. About 1230 (?) he left Italy, and after various wanderings settled down in Provence. Here he secured the friendship and patronage of Blacatz, one of the chief nobles of the country, a noted protector of troubadours, and something of a poet himself, whose death was commemorated by Sordello in the most famous of his pieces (see *Purgatorio*, VI. 58 *n.*). By the early part of 1233 Sordello had secured a footing at the court of Raymond Berenger IV., Count of Provence, and passed the rest of his life in the service of that prince, and of his son-in-law and successor, Charles of Anjou. Sordello, who at some time unknown received the honour of knighthood, followed Charles in his Italian expedition in 1265, and in September 1266 was lying in prison at Novara. It is uncertain whether he had been present at the battle of Benevento in the preceding February, when Manfred was defeated by Charles, who thereby secured the kingdom of Naples and Sicily. In 1269 Charles

XV. THE FIRST BOOK

bestowed on Sordello certain castles in the Abruzzi; and it seems that Charles (or perhaps his predecessor Raymond Berenger) had also provided Sordello with a second wife. The time, place, and manner of Sordello's death are unknown. His poems, so far as at present known, are forty-two in number, and with the exception of a long didactic work, are exclusively lyrical.

24. 'Courtly' (*aulicum*). This term is explained below, I. 18 : 42, 43. G. Ghisilieri (1244-1278) was a cousin of G. Guinizelli. Fabruzzo belonged to the great family of the Lambertazzi and is said to have been a nephew of the Fabbro mentioned in *Purgatorio*, XIV. 100. None of the works of these poets are known to exist. Onesto was a Doctor of Laws of Bologna and was living in 1301. His poetic reputation seems to have been higher than that of the other two here associated with him, for a certain number of his poems have survived and he is honourably mentioned, both by Cino of Pistoja and by Petrarch.

48. *Madonna*, etc. This canzone is attributed to G. Ghisilieri below, II. 12 : 40 ff., where the same quotation is given as an example of a canzone beginning with a line of seven syllables. *Donna* is there substituted for *Madonna*. Reading *Madonna*, the vowel of the article *lo* would not be sounded. Rajna conjectures that in the present passage a quotation from Guinizelli has dropped out, and that Ghisilieri's name has also dropped out before the words *Madonna*, etc.

50. *Lo meo*, etc. Quoted again below, II. 12 : 46.

CHAPTER XVI

[Having failed to discover in any of the local dialects a language fitted for the whole of Italy, Dante argues by analogy that there must be, as in all our other actions, some common measure or standard of comparison for the local dialects. This is what he is in search of, a language common to all parts without being peculiar to any; and this language he declares to be illustrious, cardinal, courtly, and curial; epithets explained in the next two chapters.]

A standard of comparison
AFTER having scoured the heights and pastures of Italy, without having found that panther which we are in pursuit of, in order that we may be able to find her, let us now track her out in a more rational manner, so that we may with skilful efforts completely enclose within our toils her who is fragrant everywhere but nowhere apparent.

Resuming, then, our hunting-spears, we say that in every kind of things there must be one thing by which [10] all the things of that kind may be compared and weighed, and which we may take as the measure of all the others; just as in numbers all are measured by unity and are said to be more or fewer according as they are distant from or near to unity; so also in colours all are measured by white, for they are said to be more or less visible according as they approach or recede from it. And what we say of the predicaments which indicate [20] quantity and quality, we think may also be said of any of the predicaments and even of substance; namely, that everything considered

XVI. THE FIRST BOOK

as belonging to a kind becomes measurable by that which is simplest in that kind. Wherefore in our actions, however many the species into which they are divided may be, we have to discover this standard by which they may be measured. Thus, in what concerns our actions as human beings simply, we have virtue [30], understanding it generally; for according to it we judge a man to be good or bad; in what concerns our actions as citizens, we have the law, according to which a citizen is said to be good or bad; in what concerns our actions as Italians, we have certain very simple standards of manners, customs, and language, by which our actions as Italians are weighed and measured. Now the supreme standards [40] of those activities which are generically Italian are not peculiar to any one town in Italy, but are common to all; and among these can now be discerned that vernacular language which we were hunting for above, whose fragrance is in every town, but whose lair is in none. It may, however, be more perceptible in one than in another, just as the simplest of substances, which is God, is more perceptible in a man than in [50] a brute, in an animal than in a plant, in a plant than in a mineral, in a mineral than in an element, in fire than in earth. And the simplest quantity, which is unity, is more perceptible in an odd than in an even number; and the simplest colour, which is white, is more perceptible in orange than in green.

Having therefore found what we were searching for, we declare the ¡illustrious, cardinal,

required for the local dialects

56 DE VULGARI ELOQUENTIA Ch.

The standard language of Italy courtly, and curial vernacular language in Italy to be that which belongs to all [60] the towns in Italy but does not appear to belong to any one of them, and by which all the municipal dialects of the Italians are measured, weighed, and compared.

2-5. 'The panther by its fragrant breath attracts other animals to itself, when it wishes to feed, and devours those it chooses' (Benvenuto da Imola).

10. Compare *De Monarchia*, III. 12 : 2 ff.

21. On the predicaments or categories, see note to *De Monarchia*, III. 12 : 1-3 in this volume. 'Substance' has two meanings. (*a*) As the first of the predicaments it means individual existence in the abstract. (*b*) It also means some individual thing existing on its own account.

37. '*Customs*,' or perhaps 'dress,' as the word (*habitus*) is translated above, 9 : 58, 90, and below, II. 1 : 37. The Italian equivalent, *abito*, is used in this sense in *Inferno*, XVI. 8, and *Purgatorio*, XXIX. 134.

60-63. It is now recognised that the illustrious language which Dante separates from all the local dialects in Italy, is in fact mainly based on the speech of Tuscany, which he so bitterly derides. As Gaspary very well puts it (*op. cit.*, 257): 'Nowadays we also say that no dialects correspond exactly to the literary language; but at the same time we recognise that the relation in which the latter stands to the single dialects is very various, that this literary language is based on one of these dialects, from which it arose by merely eliminating certain elements, whereas it is distinguished from the others by its phonetics and forms. As D'Ovidio noted, Dante was not yet able to draw this distinction, the distinction between language and style; he denominated both of them as *lingua*, and did not recognise that the literary language he employed was derived from the Tuscan, in spite of the divergencies detected by him.'

CHAPTER XVII

[Meaning of the epithet illustrious as applied to the language common to all Italy. This language is illustrious (1) by training, *i.e.* purification from unsuitable elements; (2) by its inherent power; (3) by the honour it confers on its followers.]

WE must now set forth why it is that we call this language we have found by the epithets illustrious, cardinal, courtly, and curial; and by doing this we disclose the nature of the language itself more clearly. First, then, let us lay bare what we mean by the epithet illustrious, and why we call the language illustrious. Now we understand by this term 'illustrious' something which shines forth illuminating and [10] illuminated. And in this way we call men illustrious either because, being illuminated by power, they illuminate others by justice and charity; or else because, having been excellently trained, they in turn give excellent training, like Seneca and Numa Pompilius. And the vernacular of which we are speaking has both been exalted by training and power, and also exalts its followers by honour and glory.

Now it appears to have been exalted by training, inasmuch as from amid so many rude Italian [20] words, involved constructions, faulty expressions, and rustic accents we see that it has been chosen out in such a degree of excellence, clearness, completeness, and polish as is displayed by Cino of Pistoja and his friend in their canzoni.

And that it has been exalted by power is

The standard language is illustrious

its plain; for what is of greater power than that power which can sway the hearts of men, so as to make an unwilling man willing [30], and a willing man unwilling, just as this language has done and is doing?

Now that it exalts by honour is evident. Do not they of its household surpass in renown kings, marquises, counts, and all other magnates? This has no need at all of proof.

But how glorious it makes its familiar friends we ourselves know, who for the sweetness of this glory cast [even] our exile behind our back. Wherefore we ought deservedly to proclaim this language illustrious.

24. The remarkable statement that the 'illustrious' language has been 'chosen out' implies that in Dante's view it owed its formation to a deliberate selection by himself and other poets of the most suitable materials from among the various local dialects. Some of the elements of the 'illustrious' speech were present in every place (above, 16 : 1-7, 45, 46); and it was the function of the 'illustrious' writers to gather them together and so bring to perfection that form of the language which belonged to the whole of Italy without being the exclusive possession of any part. These 'illustrious' writers, in fact, pursued consciously and of set purpose on an extended scale the same course of action which the inhabitants of the different Italian towns pursued as it were instinctively and on a restricted scale (see above, 15 : 1-10). In this treatise, however, while rejection (the negative part of the process) is dwelt on in detail, selection (the positive part) is explicitly mentioned here only. It is interesting to notice, in connection with Dante's theory of the 'illustrious' language, that one of the latest and most authoritative writers on phonetics, Otto Jespersen, in discussing the question of the test of the standard or correct language of any country, comes to the conclusion (as

I am informed) that that man speaks a language most correctly from whose speech it is least possible to tell from what part of the country he comes.

An interesting and singularly close analogy to Dante's attempt to erect a standard Italian above the dialects has been furnished in our own day by Norway. The literary and cultivated language of Norway is a modified form of Danish which attained this position in consequence of the political union for some centuries of Denmark and Norway. But the real language of Norway, spoken by the peasants in various dialects throughout the kingdom, is more closely allied to Swedish than to Danish. About the middle of the nineteenth century Ivar Aasen studied the Norsk language in its whole extent, and in his *Norsk Grammatik* (Cristiania, 1864) attempted to demonstrate its ideal unity, and the possibility of its becoming a recognised language of general currency by the elimination of purely local elements. Amid the great diversity of the dialects of Norway, Aasen found in the classical Icelandic literature a standard of comparison for the testing of the local dialects which Dante lacked. A systematic attempt has since been made to establish a literary Norsk on the lines laid down by Aasen. The New Testament has been translated into this ideal or typical peasant Norsk and has sometimes been read from the pulpit in that form; and a number of plays and stories, not all, nor exclusively, dealing with peasant life, have been written in it. It may be added that the analogies between this movement and Dante's attempt have not escaped the Norsk writers themselves, one of whom has made an express appeal to Dante's authority and example. It will be noted that the chief difference between the two cases lies in the fact that Aasen was able to formulate his principle of selection and to find an objective historical justification for it; whereas Dante, having only his literary sense to guide him, actually exalted his own Tuscan into the central or typical form (see as to this above, 16 : 60-63*n*). It is interesting to note further that Aasen wrote the *Norsk Grammatik* not in his ideal Norsk, but in the Dansk-Norsk, the recognised

60   DE VULGARI ELOQUENTIA   Ch.

medium of literature and scholarship, just as Dante wrote of his ideal Italian in Latin.

32-34. The Latin text, differently punctuated, may be translated thus: 'Do not they of its household, kings, marquises, etc., surpass all in renown?' Rajna adopts this punctuation, but it seems to yield a sense at variance with chapter 12 above, where Dante has indiscriminately condemned all the magnates of Italy. According to the punctuation adopted in the text Dante contrasts the renown enjoyed by himself and his brother poets, the familiar friends (compare *Convivio*, I. 12 and 13) of the illustrious language, with the infamy he has poured on the Italian princes.

CHAPTER XVIII

[Explanation of the epithets cardinal, courtly, and curial, applied to the illustrious language.]

The standard language is 'cardinal' Nor is it without reason that we adorn this illustrious vernacular language with a second epithet, that is, that we call it cardinal: for as the whole door follows its hinge, so that whither the hinge turns the door also may turn, whither it be moved inward or outward, in like manner also the whole herd of municipal dialects turns and returns, moves and pauses according [10] as this illustrious language does, which really seems to be the father of the family. Does it not daily root out the thorny bushes from the Italian wood? Does it not daily insert grafts or plant young trees? What else have its foresters to do but to take away and bring in, as has been said? Wherefore it surely deserves to be adorned with so great a name as this.

THE FIRST BOOK

Now the reason why we call it 'courtly' is that if we Italians had a court [20] it would be spoken at court. For if a court is a common home of all the realm and an august ruler of all parts of the realm, it is fitting that whatever is of such a character as to be common to all [parts] without being peculiar to any, should frequent this court and dwell there; nor is any other abode worthy of so great an inmate. Such in fact seems to be that vernacular language of which we are speaking; and hence it is that those who frequent all royal palaces [30] always speak the illustrious vernacular. Hence also it is that our illustrious language wanders about like a wayfarer, and is welcomed in humble shelters, seeing we have no court.

This language is also deservedly to be styled 'curial,' because 'curiality' is nothing else but the justly balanced rule of things which have to be done; and because the scales required for this kind of balancing are only wont to be found in the most excellent courts of justice, it follows that whatever in our actions [40] has been well balanced is called curial. Wherefore since this illustrious language has been weighed in the balances of the most excellent court of justice of the Italians, it deserves to be called curial. But it seems mere trifling to say that it has been weighed in the balances of the most excellent court of justice of the Italians, because we have no [Imperial] court of justice. To this the answer is easy. For though there is no court of justice of Italy in the sense of a single [supreme] court, like the court of the king of

'courtly' and 'curial'

Literary tribunal of Italy Germany, still the members of such a court are not wanting. And just as the members [50] of the German court are united under one prince, so the members of ours have been united by the gracious light of Reason. Wherefore, though we have no prince, it would be false to assert that the Italians have no [such] court of justice, because we have a court, though in the body it is scattered.

19. By 'court' (*aula*) Dante means the sovereign's residence. He implies that there ought to be an emperor keeping his court at Rome.

38. *Courts of justice* (*curiis*). Dante is no doubt referring to those assemblies held by sovereign princes (with special reference, of course, to the emperor) at the chief festivals, which were attended by the nobles and prelates of the realm, and in which national affairs of the greatest importance were transacted, and disputes between the magnates of the realm determined.

55. In the lamented absence of an imperial court of justice, the arbiters of literary excellence must be deemed to be the writers of the illustrious vulgar tongue 'scattered' in different parts of Italy, but 'united by the gracious light of Reason' and giving sentence by their writings and practice. It would therefore seem that Dante's ideal government would have included an imperial Academy of Letters.

CHAPTER XIX

[The illustrious, cardinal, courtly, and curial language belongs to the whole of Italy, and is the Italian vulgar tongue. The author announces his purpose to treat in the succeeding books of the use of this illustrious language, and afterwards to discuss the lower forms of the vernacular in detail.]

Now we declare that this vernacular language, which we have shown to be illustrious, cardinal, courtly, and curial, is that which is called the Italian vernacular. For just as a vernacular can be found peculiar to Cremona, so can one be found peculiar to Lombardy; and just as one can be found peculiar to Lombardy, [so] can one be found [10] peculiar to the whole of the left side of Italy. And just as all these can be found, so also can that which belongs to the whole of Italy. And just as the first is called Cremonese, the second Lombard, and the third Semi-Italian, so that which belongs to the whole of Italy is called the Italian vernacular language. For this has been used by the illustrious writers who have written poetry in the vernacular throughout Italy, as Sicilians, Apulians, Tuscans, natives of Romagna, and men of both the Marches. And because our intention is [20], as we promised in the beginning of this work, to give instruction concerning the vernacular speech, we will begin with this illustrious Italian as being the most excellent, and treat in the books immediately following of those whom we think worthy to use it; and for what, and how, and also

The standard language common to all Italy

Plan of the rest of the work where, when, and to whom, it ought to be used. And after making all this clear, we will make it our business to throw light on the lower vernaculars, gradually coming down to that which [30] belongs to a single family.

> 30. This curious passage is illustrated by a quotation from Trissino's dialogue *Il Castellano* see Appendix I. p. 117). Giovanni Rucellai, the 'Castellano' of the castle of St Angelo, says to Filippo Strozzi, 'Every man, and family, and district has some peculiarities of speech which others have not; my brother Palla, for instance, has some peculiarities in his language which I do not share; while your brother Lorenzo has some which you have not; and so likewise there are some points in which the speech of our family differs from that of yours.'

BOOK II

CHAPTER I

[Beginning to carry out the scheme set forth in I. 19, the author declares that the illustrious Italian language is equally fit for use in prose and in verse. But as poetry seems to be a model for prose writers, he will first treat of the use of the language in metre. He begins by inquiring whether all poets writing in the vernacular should use the illustrious language, and proves that only those that have knowledge and genius are at liberty to do so.]

URGING on once more the nimbleness of our wit, which is returning to the pen of useful work, we declare in the first place that the illustrious Italian vernacular is equally fit for use in prose and in verse. But because prose writers rather get this language from poets, and because poetry seems to remain a pattern to prose writers, and not the converse, which things [10] appear to confer a certain supremacy, let us first disentangle this language as to its use in metre, treating of it in the order we set forth at the end of the first book.

Let us then first inquire whether all those who write verse in the vernacular should use this illustrious language; and so far as a superficial consideration of the matter goes, it would seem that they should, because every one who

The language of poets a pattern for prose-writers

Ought all versifiers to use the illustrious language? writes verse ought to adorn his verse as far as he is able. Wherefore, since nothing affords so great an adornment [20] as the illustrious vernacular does, it would seem that every writer of verse ought to employ it. Besides, if that which is best in its kind be mixed with things inferior to itself, it not only appears not to detract anything from them but even to improve them. Wherefore if any writer of verse, even though his verse be rude in matter, mixes the illustrious vernacular with his rudeness of matter, he not only appears to do well, but to be actually obliged to take this course [30]. Those who can do little need help much more than those who can do much, and thus it appears that all writers of verse are at liberty to use this illustrious language. But this is quite false, because not even poets of the highest order ought always to assume it, as will appear from a consideration of what is discussed farther on. This illustrious language, then, just like our behaviour in other matters and our dress, demands men of like quality to its own; for munificence demands men of great resources, and the purple, men of noble character, and in the same way [40] this illustrious language seeks for men who excel in genius and knowledge, and despises others, as will appear from what is said below. For everything which is suited to us is so either in respect of the genus, or of the species, or of the individual, as sensation, laughter, war; but this illustrious language is not suited to us in respect of our genus, for then it would also be suited to the brutes; nor in respect of our species, for then it would be suited to all men; and as to this there is no question; for no one will say that this language is suited to dwellers in the mountains dealing with rustic concerns [53]: therefore it is suited in respect of the individual. But nothing is suited to an individual except on account of his particular worth, as for instance commerce, war, and government. Wherefore if things are suitable according to worth, that is the worthy (and some men may be worthy, others worthier and others worthiest) [60], it is plain that good things will be suited to the worthy, better things to the worthier, and the best things to the worthiest. And since language is as necessary an instrument of our thought as a horse is of a knight, and since the best horses are suited to the best knights, as has been said, the best language will be suited to the best thoughts. But the best thoughts cannot exist except where knowledge and genius are found; therefore the best [70] language is only suitable in those in whom knowledge and genius are found; and so the best language is not suited to all who write verse, since a great many write without knowledge and genius; and consequently neither is the best vernacular [suited to all who write verse]. Wherefore, if it is not suited to all, all ought not to use it, because no one ought to act in an unsuitable manner. And as to the statement that every one ought to adorn his verse as far as he can [80], we declare that it is true; but we should not describe an ox with trappings or a swine with a belt as adorned, nay rather we laugh at them as disfigured; for adornment is the addition of some suitable thing.

No; for the best language is suited only to the best thoughts

Of mixing superior with inferior things As to the statement that superior things mixed with inferior effect an improvement [in the latter], we say that it is true if the blending is complete, for instance when we mix gold and silver together; but if it is not, the inferior things appear worse [90], for instance when beautiful women are mixed with ugly ones. Wherefore, since the theme of those who write verse always persists as an ingredient distinct from the words, it will not, unless of the highest quality, appear better when associated with the best vernacular, but worse; like an ugly woman if dressed out in gold or silk.

6. *Prose writers.* 'Both among the Greeks and among the Latins, verse received attention long before prose; for all compositions were in early times in verse, while the study of prose flourished later' (St Isidore, *Etym.* i. 37).

18. *As far as he is able.* Compare *Convivio*, IV. 30 : 15 ff.

25. *Even though his verse be rude in matter* (*quanquam rude versificetur*). It is clear from what Dante says at the end of the chapter, where he is showing the fallacy of this reasoning, that the phrase *rude versificetur* refers to poverty of matter, rather than to rudeness of style.

38. *Munificence* (*magnificentia*). See *Paradiso*, XXXI. 88*n*.

39. Compare *Convivio*, IV. 29 : 16 ff.; *Paradiso*, XVIII. 91.

44. *Laughter.* Compare *Vita Nuova*, 25 : 17 ff.; Letter to Can Grande, § 26, line 504. Man's genus is 'animal'; his species, 'rational animal'; sensation is proper to him as 'animal,' laughter, as 'rational animal.' Waging war is proper to him if his individual circumstances justify it (compare *Paradiso*, VI. 106).

56. Compare *Paradiso*, VIII. 139-148.

64. Compare *Convivio*, I. 5 : 80 ff.

80. *Ox with trappings* (*bovem epiphyatum*). An example borrowed at second-hand from Horace, *Epist.* I. xiv. 43 (Toynbee).

90. See *Convivio*, IV. 29 : 89 ff.

CHAPTER II

[The illustrious language must only be used in treating of the worthiest subjects, *i.e.* Arms, Love, and Virtue.]

AFTER having proved that not all those who write verse, but only those of the highest excellence, ought to use the illustrious vernacular, we must in the next place establish whether every subject ought to be handled in it, or not; and if not, we must set out by themselves those subjects that are worthy of it. And in reference to this we must first find out what we understand by that which we call *worthy*. We say that a thing which has worthiness is worthy, just as we say that [10] a thing which has nobility is noble; and if when that which confers the habit is known, that on which the habit is conferred is [also] known, as such, then if we know what worthiness is, we shall know also what *worthy* is. Now worthiness is an effect or end of deserts; so that when any one has deserved well we say that he has arrived at worthiness of good; but when he has deserved ill, at worthiness of evil. Thus we say that a soldier who has fought well has arrived at worthiness of victory; one who has ruled well, at worthiness of a kingdom; also that a liar has arrived at [20] worthiness of shame, and a robber at worthiness of death.

Meaning of 'worthy'

Degrees of worthiness But inasmuch as [further] comparisons are made among those who deserve well, and also among those who deserve ill, so that some deserve well, some better, and some best; some badly, some worse, and some worst; while such comparisons are only made with respect to the end of deserts, which (as has been mentioned before) we call *worthiness*, it is plain that worthinesses [30] are compared together according as they are greater or less, so that some are great, some greater, and some greatest; and, consequently, it is obvious that one thing is worthy, another worthier, and another worthiest. And whereas there can be no such comparison of worthinesses with regard to the same object [of desert] but [only] with regard to different objects, so that we call *worthier* that which is worthy of greater objects, and *worthiest* that which is worthy of the greatest, because no thing can be more worthy [than another] in virtue of the same qualification, it is evident that the best things are worthy of the best [objects of desert], [40] according to the requirement of the things. Whence it follows that, since the language we call illustrious is the best of all the other forms of the vernacular, the best subjects alone are worthy of being handled in it, and these we call the *worthiest* of those subjects which can be handled; and now let us hunt out what they are. And, in order to make this clear, it must be observed that, as man has been endowed with a threefold life, namely, vegetable, animal, and rational, he journeys along a threefold road [50]; for in so far as he is vegetable he seeks for what is useful, wherein he is of like nature with plants; in so far as he is animal he seeks for that which is pleasurable, wherein he is of like nature with the brutes; in so far as he is rational he seeks for what is right —and in this he stands alone, or is a partaker of the nature of the angels. It is by these three kinds of life that we appear to carry out whatever we do; and because in each one of them some things are greater, some greatest, within the range of their kind, it follows that those which are greatest [60] appear the ones which ought to be treated of supremely, and consequently, in the greatest vernacular.

Subjects worthy of the illustrious language

But we must discuss what things are greatest; and first in respect of what is useful. Now in this matter, if we carefully consider the object of all those who are in search of what is useful, we shall find that it is nothing else but safety. Secondly, in respect of what is pleasurable; and here we say that that is most pleasurable which gives pleasure by the most exquisite object of appetite, and this [70] is love. Thirdly, in respect of what is right; and here no one doubts that virtue has the first place. Wherefore these three things, namely, safety, love, and virtue, appear to be those capital matters which ought to be treated of supremely, I mean the things which are most important in respect of them, as prowess in arms, the fire of love, and the direction of the will. And if we duly consider, we shall find that the illustrious writers have written poetry in the vulgar tongue on these subjects exclusively; namely, Bertran de Born [80] on Arms, Arnaut Daniel on Love, Giraut de Borneil on

Illus-
trations
Righteousness, Cino of Pistoja on Love, his friend on Righteousness. For Bertran says :—

> '*Non posc mudar c'un cantar non exparja.*'[1]

Arnaut: '*L'aura amara fals bruols brancuz clairir.*'[2]
Giraut: '*Per solaz reveillar
[90] que s'es trop endormitz.*'[3]
Cino: '*Digno sono eo de morte.*'[4]
His friend: '*Doglia mi reca nello core ardire.*'

I do not find, however, that any Italian has as yet written poetry on the subject of Arms.

Having then arrived at this point, we know what are the proper subjects to be sung in the highest vernacular language.

34-40. The meaning seems to be this: There are certain things (objects of desert) to be awarded according to the degree of the worthiness of certain other things (recipients of those objects). Some recipients have the qualification of being worthy, others that of being worthier, others that of being worthiest. The worthy are qualified to have the good things, the worthier, to have the better things, and the worthiest, the best things. We do not call one recipient worthier than another as being worthy of the *same* thing, but rather as being worthy of a *different*, and better thing. Throughout this passage, and in the practical applications of his principle, Dante ignores, though he does not deny, the fact that one recipient may be worthy, another worthier, and a third worthiest of the *same* thing. His procedure, in short, resembles that of an examiner who

---

[1] 'I cannot choose but utter a song.'
[2] 'The bitter blast strips bare the leafy woods.'
[3] 'For the awakening of gallantry which is too fast asleep [I thought to labour].'
[4] 'Worthy am I of death.'

issues a list of successful candidates divided into three classes, but puts the names in each class alphabetically, and not in order of merit. There is an order of merit in each class, but it is ignored; and the only information given is that so-and-so has passed in the first, second, or third class. Thus below in this chapter Dante, on this principle, awards the illustrious language to arms, love, and righteousness, giving them, as it were, a first class. But he is not concerned to put them in an order of merit. All alike having attained the qualification of worthiest, all alike receive the object of desert, the illustrious language. The 'requirement of the things' means the right (if one may say so) of the object of desert to insist on the attainment by the recipient of the proper qualification, and the correlative right of the recipient who has attained the qualification to receive the object of desert.

47. '*Man has been endowed with a threefold life*' (*tripliciter spirituatus est*). So in *Vita Nuova*, 2: 19 ff., the three kinds of life with which man is endowed are identified with 'natural,' 'vital,' and 'animate' spirits. It is, however, most important to observe that Dante was careful to maintain the unity of the individual vital principle or soul (by which terms the whole of the immaterial part of man is meant), endowed with the three kinds of life here mentioned, and rejected the doctrine of those who held that the vital principle consisted of so many distinct essences to *each* of which the name of soul might be applied. See *Purgatorio*, IV. 1-6; XXV. 37 ff.; *Convivio*, III. 2: 78 ff.; 3: 35 ff.; IV. 7: 110 ff.

55. '*Partaker of the nature of the angels.*' See *Purgatorio*, XI. 10; *Convivio*, III. 7: 74 ff.; *Letter to Can Grande*, 531 ff.; and compare *Convivio*, IV. 19: 52 ff.

75. Compare below, 4: 61.

85. *Non posc*, etc. This poem, an imitation as to its metrical structure of the one by A. Daniel, quoted below, 13: 12, was written in the early summer of 1188, on the outbreak of war between Richard Cœur-de-Lion and Philip Augustus. In it the poet expresses his regret at not being able himself to join in the fray. On Bertran de Born, see *Inferno*, XXVIII. 118-142*n*.

88. *L'aura*, etc. Arnaut Daniel (fl. 1180-1200) was certainly the greatest of the troubadours from the merely technical point of view; and it is his extraordinary metrical skill and originality that cause Dante to place him above G. de Borneil as 'a better craftsman of the mother-tongue,' in *Purgatorio*, XXVI. 115 ff. It should not be forgotten, however, that in the present passage Dante associates G. de Borneil with himself as a singer of righteousness, which A. Daniel certainly was not.

94. *Doglia*, etc. See *Convivio*, page 412, where the poem is translated. G. de Borneil's very fine poem, '*Si per mon Sobre-totz no fos*' (quoted for a different purpose below, 6 : 55), shows a considerable resemblance to this canzone of Dante's, both in subject (the baseness and folly of avarice) and in treatment, and would (one might think) be a better example of a poem on righteousness than '*Per solaz reveillar*,' which is a lament on the decay of gallantry (a commonplace with the troubadours from first to last) very much in the spirit of *Purgatorio*, XIV. 103 ff.

CHAPTER III

[The canzone is the noblest form of poetry, and therefore the subjects which have been proved worthy of the illustrious vulgar tongue ought to be treated of in canzoni.]

Different forms of poems But now let us endeavour carefully to examine how those matters which are worthy of so excellent a vernacular language are to be restricted. As we wish, then, to set forth the form by which these matters are worthy to be bound, we say that it must first be borne in mind that those who have written poetry in the vernacular have uttered their poems in many different forms, some in that of canzoni, some in that of ballate, some in that of sonnets, some [10] in other illegitimate and irregular forms, as will be shown farther on. Now we consider that of these forms that of canzoni is the most excellent; and therefore, if the most excellent things are worthy of the most excellent, as has been proved above, those subjects which are worthy of the most excellent vernacular are worthy of the most excellent form, and consequently ought to be handled in canzoni. Now we may discover by several reasons that the form of canzoni is such [20] as has been said. The first reason is that though whatever we write in verse is a canzone, the canzoni [technically so called] have alone acquired this name; and this has never happened apart from ancient provision.

The canzone the highest form

Moreover, whatever produces by itself the effect for which it was made, appears nobler than that which requires external assistance. But canzoni produce by themselves the whole effect they ought to produce; which ballate do not [30], for they require the assistance of the performers for whom they are written; it therefore follows that canzoni are to be deemed nobler than ballate, and therefore that their form is the noblest of any, for no one doubts that ballate excel sonnets in nobility of form.

Besides, those things appear to be nobler which bring more honour to their author; but canzoni bring more [honour] to their authors than ballate; therefore [40] they are nobler [than these], and consequently their form is the noblest of any.

Furthermore, the noblest things are the most fondly preserved; but among poems canzoni are

Canzoni the noblest poems the most fondly preserved, as is evident to those who look into books; therefore canzoni are the noblest [poems], and consequently their form is the noblest.

Also, in works of art, that is noblest which embraces the whole art. Since, therefore [50], poems are works of art, and the whole of the art is embraced in canzoni alone, canzoni are the noblest poems, and so their form is the noblest of any. Now, that the whole of the art of poetic song is embraced in canzoni is proved by the fact that whatever is found to belong to the art is found in them; but the converse is not true. But the proof of what we are saying is at once apparent; for all that has flowed from the [60] tops of the heads of illustrious poets down to their lips is found in canzoni alone. Wherefore, in reference to the subject before us, it is clear that the matters which are worthy of the highest vulgar tongue ought to be handled in canzoni.

22-24. See below, 8: 12, with *note*. Dante here seemingly gives us to understand that the adoption of the name was not casual but by the deliberate choice of those who invented the thing or by the early framers of technical language.

30. *Ballate* (from *ballare*, to dance) were intended to be sung by dancers.

43. *Poems*. Lit., 'those things which have been sung.' See the definition of poetry in the next chapter, line 20.

60. 'Philosophers say that the seat of the imagination is in the extremity of the concavity of the brain, which is in the forehead' (F. da Buti).

CHAPTER IV

[The author begins to treat of the form of the canzone. The regular (*i.e.* Latin) poets proposed as models for the vernacular poets' imitation. Choice of subject and its bearing on the style to be adopted, viz., tragic, comic, or elegiac. The illustrious language appropriated to the tragic style. Definition of the tragic style, in which alone the subjects worthy to be handled in canzoni are to be sung. Denunciation of those who attempt the tragic style without the proper equipment.]

HAVING then laboured by a process of disentangling [to show] what persons and things are worthy of the courtly vernacular, as well as the form of verse which we deem worthy of such honour that it alone is fitted for the highest vernacular, before going off to other topics, let us explain the form of the canzone, which many appear to adopt rather at haphazard than with art; and let us unlock the workshop of the art of that form which has hitherto been adopted in a casual way [10], omitting the form of ballate and sonnets, because we intend to explain this in the fourth book of this work, when we shall treat of the middle vernacular language. *The form of the canzone*

Reviewing, therefore, what has been said, we remember that we have frequently called those who write verse in the vernacular poets; and this we have doubtless ventured to say with good reason, because they are in fact poets, if we take a right view of poetry, which is nothing else but [20] a rhetorical composition set to music. But these poets differ from the great

Subject and style poets, that is, the regular ones, for the language of the great poets was regulated by art, whereas these, as has been said, write at haphazard. It therefore happens that the more closely we copy the great poets, the more correct is the poetry we write; whence it behoves us, by devoting some trouble to the work of teaching, to emulate their poetic teaching.

Before all things therefore we say that each one [30] ought to adjust the weight of the subject to his own shoulders, so that their strength may not be too heavily taxed, and he be forced to tumble into the mud. This is the advice our master Horace gives us when he says in the beginning of his 'Art of Poetry' ['Ye who write] take up a subject [suited to your strength'].

Next we ought to possess a discernment as to those things which suggest themselves to us as fit to be uttered, so as to decide whether they ought to be sung in the way of tragedy, comedy, or elegy. By tragedy we bring in (*sic*) the higher style [40], by comedy the lower style, by elegy we understand the style of the wretched. If our subject appears fit to be sung in the tragic style, we must then assume the illustrious vernacular language, and consequently we must bind up a canzone. If, however, it appears fit to be sung in the comic style, sometimes the middle and sometimes the lowly vernacular should be used; and the discernment to be exercised in this case we reserve for treatment in the fourth book. But if our subject appears fit to be sung in the elegiac style, we must adopt the lowly vernacular alone.

IV. THE SECOND BOOK

But let us omit the other styles and [50] now, as is fitting, let us treat of the tragic style. We appear then to make use of the tragic style when the stateliness of the lines as well as the loftiness of the construction and the excellence of the words agree with the weight of the subject. And because, if we remember rightly, it has already been proved that the highest things are worthy of the highest, and because the style which we call tragic appears to be the highest style, those things which we have distinguished as being worthy of the highest song [60] are to be sung in that style alone, namely, Safety, Love, and Virtue, and those other things, our conceptions of which arise from these; provided that they be not degraded by any accident.

The tragic style

Let every one therefore beware and discern what we say; and when he purposes to sing of these three subjects simply, or of those things which directly and simply follow after them, let him first drink of Helicon, and then, after adjusting the strings, boldly take up his *plectrum* and begin to ply it. But it is in the exercise of the needful caution and discernment [70] that the real difficulty lies; for this can never be attained to without strenuous efforts of genius, constant practice in the art, and the habit of the sciences. And it is those [so equipped] whom the poet in the sixth book of the *Æneid* describes as beloved of God, raised by glowing virtue to the sky, and sons of the Gods, though he is speaking figuratively. And therefore let those who, innocent of art and science, and trusting to genius alone, rush forward to sing of the highest subjects in the highest style, confess their folly

Presumptuous ignorance [80] and cease from such presumption; and if in their natural sluggishness they are but geese, let them abstain from imitating the eagle soaring to the stars.

20. Lit., 'a rhetorical fiction musically composed' (*fictio rethorica musice composita*). Compare *Convivio*, IV. 6 : 34-37.

28. '*To emulate their poetic teaching.*' There may perhaps be a specific reference here to Horace's *Ars Poetica*.

40. In Dante's time both tragedy and comedy had lost their dramatic character, and the distinction between them depended on the dignity of the subject, the character of the issue (Moore), and the style, as appears from the present passage. Cf. below, Letter to Can Grande, § 10.

62. An 'accident' is anything that can only exist as an attribute or experience of something else. See *Convivio*, I. 5 : 2, 3*n*.

67. Helicon was a mountain in Bœotia and a favourite resort of the Muses. Here, as in *Purgatorio*, XXIX. 40, the mountain stands for the springs of Aganippe, or Hippocrene, which flowed from it.

68. The plectrum was a small stick or quill for striking the strings of the lyre.

72. *Habit.* See *Convivio*, I. 1 : 15*n*.

73. *Æneid*, VI. 129-131.

CHAPTER V

[Of the different lines admissible in canzoni. The line of eleven syllables is the stateliest (see preceding chapter, line 53), and therefore the most eligible; next come the lines of seven, five, and three syllables. The line of nine syllables is obsolete, and lines with an even number of syllables are rarely used.]

Stateliness of lines We seem to have said enough, or at least as much as our work requires, about the weight of the subjects. Wherefore let us hasten on to **The** the stateliness of the lines, in respect of which **eleven-** it is to be observed that our predecessors made **syllabled** use of different lines in their canzoni, as the **line** moderns also do; but we do not find that any one has hitherto used a line of more than eleven [10] or less than three syllables. And though the Italian poets have used the lines of three and of eleven syllables and all the intermediate ones, those of five, seven, and eleven syllables are more frequently used [than the others], and next to them, that of three syllables in preference to the others. But of all these the line of eleven syllables seems the stateliest, as well by reason of the length of time it occupies as of its capacity in regard to subject, construction, and words [20]: and the beauty of all these things is more multiplied in this line [than in the others], as is plainly apparent; for wherever things that weigh are multiplied so also is weight. And all the teachers seem to have given heed to this, beginning their illustrious canzoni with a line of eleven syllables, as Giraut de Borneil:—

'*Ara auzirez encabalitz cantars.*' [1]

And though this line appears to be of ten syllables, it is in reality of eleven [30], for the last two consonants do not belong to the preceding syllable. And though they have no vowel belonging to them, still they do not lose the force of a syllable; and the proof of this is that the rhyme is in this instance completed by one vowel, which could not be the case except by

---

[1] 'Now you shall hear perfect songs.'

should virtue of another understood there. The king
pre- of Navarre writes:—
dominate
in the '*De fine Amor si vient sen et bonté,*'[1] where,
stanza if the accent and its cause be considered [40]
the line will be found to have eleven syllables.
Guido Guinizelli writes:—
'*Al cor gentil repara sempre Amore.*'[2]
The Judge [Guido] delle Colonne of Messina:—
'*Amor che lungiamente m' ài menato.*'[3]
Rinaldo d'Aquino:—
'*Per fino amore vo sì letamente.*'[4]
Cino of Pistoja:—
'*Non spero che già mai per mia salute.*'[5]
His friend:—
[50] '*Amor che movi tua vertù da cielo.*'
And though this line which has been mentioned appears, as is worthy, the most celebrated of all, yet, if it be associated in some slight degree with the line of seven syllables (provided only it retain its supremacy), it seems to rise still more clearly and loftily in its stateliness. But this must be left for further explanation.

We say also that the line of seven syllables follows next after that which is greatest in celebrity. After this we place the line of five, and [60] then that of three syllables. But the line of nine syllables, because it appeared to consist of the line of three taken three times, was either never held in honour or fell

---

[1] See above, p. 26.
[2] 'To the gentle heart love ever flies for shelter.'
[3] See above, p. 38.
[4] See above, p 40.
[5] 'I have no hope that e'er for my well-being.'

into disuse on account of its being disliked. **Odd and** As for the lines of an even number of syl- **even** lables, we use them but rarely, because of **numbers** their rudeness; for they retain the nature of their numbers, which are subject to the odd numbers as matter to form. And so, summing up what has been said, the line of eleven syllables appears to be the stateliest [70] line, and this is what we were in search of. But now it remains for us to investigate concerning exalted constructions and pre-eminent words; and at length, after having got ready our sticks and ropes, we will teach how we ought to bind together the promised faggot, that is the canzone.

19. *Construction.* This subject is dealt with in the next following chapter.
24. *Teachers.* See above, I. 9 : 17*n*.
36. *Understood there.* 'Dante's meaning is, The rhymes in a canzone must consist of two syllables, but the second vowel may occasionally disappear without, however, the consonants belonging to it losing the force of a syllable' (Böhmer). In giving a Provençal example, he implies that the rule was the same in that language. Here, however, he is wrong. In Provençal prosody the final unaccented syllable in a line was not counted. Thus, according to the Provençal reckoning, the line here quoted from G. de Borneil has ten syllables, and the line from Bertran de Born, quoted above, II. 2 : 85, '*Non posc mudar un cantar non exparja,*' has ten syllables also, though Dante would say that in both instances there were eleven. Moreover, as is pointed out by Mr Tozer in his essay on the metre of the *Divina Comœdia* (printed at the end of Moore's Textual Criticism of the D.C.), Dante's implied statement that the Provençal and Old French line of ten syllables is an abbreviated line of eleven syllables is historically impossible, since the monosyllabic rhyme and con-

sequently the ten-syllable line was the earlier. The eleven-syllable line became prevalent in Italy on account of the preponderance of dissyllabic endings in that language.

37-40. See above, I. 9 : 27*n*. The 'cause of the accent' is the presumed loss of a syllable. *Bonté* (derived from *bonitatem*) in Dante's view stands for *bonté-e*. 'Probably he found this observation confirmed by the melody of the poem. In another *chanson* by the same king, '*L'autrier par la matinée,*' in the original notation the note to which the first *e* of *matinée* is to be sung is repeated for the second *e*' (Böhmer).

42. *Amore.* See above, I. 9 : 30*n*.
44. See above, I. 12 : 12-14*n*.
46. See above, I. 12 : 69*n*.
47-49. See above, I. 10 : 30*n*.
50. See *Convivio*, p. 388.

63-68. Professor Saintsbury thinks that the statement that lines with an even number of syllables are 'rude' means that they do not suit the structure of Italian verse. This explanation no doubt gives the true cause of the rare use of such lines. But it is too simple for Dante. The true cause, according to him, is to be found in the 'rudeness' or inferiority of the even numbers, which attaches itself to lines made up of such numbers, and in an analogy between the even numbers and matter, and between the odd numbers and form. Now the relation of matter to form is such that when matter receives a form (*e.g.*, when marble receives the form of a statue), it is raised from potentiality, a state of inferiority (compare the *rudis indigestaque moles* of Ovid's chaos) to actuality, a state of superiority (see below in this volume, note on *De Monarchia*, I. 3 : 66-78). So when an even number receives the addition of an odd number it is raised from a state of inferiority to one of superiority. Therefore if, *e.g.*, a line of six syllables receives the addition of one syllable, a change will be effected analogous to that undergone by matter when it receives a form. Benvenuto of Imola remarks, commenting on the words, 'three and four times,' in *Purgatorio*, VII. 2 : 'Here note that the poet includes both numbers, *i.e.* the even and the odd, and he puts the odd first as the more perfect; whence among arithmeticians an odd number is called masculine, but an even number feminine, on account of its imperfection.' Compare above, I. 16 : 52-5.

CHAPTER VI

[Of construction, *i.e.* the arrangement of words in sentences. Different kinds of construction. The most excellent kind is alone suitable for the canzone.]

INASMUCH as our intention has reference to the illustrious vernacular, which is the noblest of all, and we have distinguished the things which are worthy of being sung in it, which are the three noblest subjects, as has been established above, and have chosen the form of canzoni for them, as being the highest form of any, and have also (in order that we may be able more perfectly to give thorough instruction in this form) already settled certain points, namely the style [10] and the line, let us now deal with the construction.

Now it must be observed that we call construction a regulated arrangement of words, as 'Aristotle philosophised in Alexander's time,' for here there are five words arranged by rule, and they form one construction. Now in reference to this we must first bear in mind that one construction is congruous, while another is incongruous; and inasmuch as, if [20] we recollect the beginning of our distinction, we are only pursuing the highest things, the incongruous con-

Of arrangements of words in sentences

Degrees of 'constructions' struction finds no place in our pursuit, because it has not even proved deserving of a lower degree of goodness. Let therefore illiterate persons be ashamed—I say, let them be ashamed of being henceforth so bold as to burst forth into canzoni, for we laugh at them as at a blind man making distinctions between colours.

It is, then, it seems, the congruous construction after which we are following. But here we come to a distinction of not less difficulty [30] before we can reach that construction which we are in search of, the construction, I mean, which is most full of refinement. For there are a great many degrees of constructions; namely, [first] the insipid, which is that of uncultivated people; as, 'Peter is very fond of Mistress Bertha.' [Then] there is that which has flavour but nothing else, which belongs to rigid scholars or masters; as, 'I, greater in pity than all, am sorry for all those who, languishing in exile, only revisit their native land in their dreams.' There is also [40] that which has flavour and grace, which belongs to some who have taken a shallow draught of rhetoric; as, 'The praiseworthy discernment of the Marquis of Este and his munificence prepared for all makes him beloved.' Then there is that which has flavour and grace and also elevation, which belongs to illustrious writers; as, 'Having cast the greatest part of the flowers out of thy bosom, O Florence, the second Totila went fruitlessly to Trinacria.' This degree of construction we call the most excellent [50], and this is the one we are seeking for, since, as has been said, we are in pursuit of the highest things. Of this alone are illustrious canzoni found to be made up as [that by] Giraut de Borneil,

'*Si per mon Sobre-totz no fos.*'[1]

[that by] Folquet of Marseilles,

'*Tan m'abellis l'amoros pensamens.*'[2]

[60] [that by] Arnaut Daniel,

'*Sols sui qui sai lo sobraffan quem sortz.*'[3]

[that by] Aimeric de Belenoi,

'*Nuls hom non pot complir addreciamen.*'[4]

[that by] Aimeric de Pegulhan,

'*Si com l'arbres que per sobrecarcar.*'[5]

[that by] the King of Navarre,

'*Ire d'amor qui en mon cor repaire.*'[6]

[that by] Guido Guinizelli,

'*Tegno de folle 'mpresa a lo ver dire.*'[7]

[that by] Guido Cavalcanti,

'*Poi che di doglia cor conven ch'io porti.*'[8]

[70] [that by] Cino of Pistoja,

'*Avegna che io aggia più per tempo.*'[9]

[that by] his friend,

'*Amor che nella mente mi ragiona.*'

Nor, reader, must you be surprised at our calling to memory so many poets; for we cannot point out that construction which we call the

Illustrative quotations

---

[1] 'Were it not for my All-excelling one.'
[2] 'So pleasing is to me the amorous thought.'
[3] 'I alone am he who knows the excessive grief which rises [in my heart].'
[4] 'No man can properly fulfil [what he has in his heart].'
[5] 'Even as the tree which through being overladen.'
[6] 'Sorrow of love which in my heart abides.'
[7] 'To say the truth, I hold his conduct foolish [who yields himself to one too powerful].'
[8] 'Since I must needs bear a heart of woe.'
[9] 'Albeit my prayers have not so long delayed' (Rossetti's trans.).

Classical models highest except by examples of this kind. And it would possibly be very useful in order to the full acquirement of this construction if we had surveyed the regular poets, I mean [80] Virgil, Ovid in his *Metamorphoses*, Statius, and Lucan, as well as other writers who have employed the most lofty prose, as Titus Livius, Pliny, Frontinus, Paulus Orosius, and many others whom friendly solitude invites us to consult. Let, then, those followers of ignorance hold their peace who praise up Guittone of Arezzo and some others who have never got out of the habit of being plebeian in words and in construction.

16. By 'a regulated arrangement of words,' and 'words arranged by rule,' Dante means a sentence free from barbarisms, *i.e.* errors in single words (Böhmer.)

17 ff. By a 'congruous construction Dante means a sentence free from solecisms, *i.e.* errors in syntax (Böhmer).

20. '*Beginning of our distinction.*' The reference is to II. 2, above.

42-44. *Laudabilis discretio marchionis Estensis et sua magnificentia preparata cunctis illum facit esse dilectum.* With a comma after *cunctis* the meaning is as in the text. With a comma after *preparata* the meaning is, 'The praiseworthy discernment of the Marquis of Este and his calculated munificence makes him universally beloved.'

32-50. The four typical sentences here given by Dante are, as to style, classified by Professor Saintsbury as follows : (1) Sheer prose ; (2) Efforts at style ; (3) Ornate prose without much distinction ; (4) Style achieved. The last three of the sentences are significant. The first of them contains a pathetic allusion to the author's exile. The second, taken in connection with the first and third, probably alludes to the welcome given by Azzo VIII., Marquis of Este, to Charles of Valois in

1301, when the latter, 'unarmed, save with the lance wherewith Judas tilted' (*Purgatorio*, XX. 73), was journeying to Tuscany. Azzo entertained him and his suite in the most princely style, and with 'praiseworthy discernment' made him a loan of 10,000 gold florins—which was never repaid (Prompt, *Traité de l'Eloquence vulgaire*, p. 26). In view of the opinion of Azzo expressed above (I. 12: 38), this second sentence must be ironical, as is apparently intimated by the curious words '*of some who have taken a shallow draught of rhetoric*,' which precede it. In the third sentence the allusion to Charles of Valois' infamous overthrow of the government of the Bianchi at Florence and his ignominious expedition to Sicily (Trinacria) is too plain to be mistaken. In Dante's time Totila was believed to have destroyed Florence, and the virtual destruction of the city (see *Convivio*, II. 14: 177), which in the poet's opinion Charles of Valois wrought in 1301 earns him the title of Totila II.

55. *Sobre-totz* (lit., above all) is a nickname, such as the troubadours frequently used, under which Giraut de Borneil addresses Bernart de Rovigna (fl. 1197), a Gascon nobleman and an intimate friend of the poet.

59. On Folquet, see *Paradiso*, IX. 94*n*.

63. A. de Belenoi (fl. 1250), a Gascon, nephew of the troubadour Peire de Corbiac. At first a cleric, he afterwards became a professional minstrel. He passed some time at the court of Raymond Berenger IV., count of Provence, and ended his days in Catalonia.

65. A. de Pegulhan was son of a merchant of Toulouse, and became one of the most celebrated among the later troubadours. His poetic career covered the central part of the thirteenth century. Among his patrons were Raymond VI., count of Toulouse, Peter II. of Aragon, Alfonso VIII. of Castile, the emperor Frederick II., and Azzo VI. and Azzo VII., marquises of Este. About fifty of his poems are extant.

57. *Ire d'amor*, etc. (It will be noticed that this citation, which in the Oxford Dante follows that from Giraut de Borneil, in Rajna's text follows that

from A. de Pegulhan.) The poem is not by the King of Navarre (see above, I. 9: 27*n*.), but by a friend of his, Gaces Brulez, who was a native of Champagne, of noble birth, and a renowned lyric poet.

69. *Poi che*, etc. One stanza only of this poem exists.

71. See above, I. 10: 30*n*.

73. This canzone is expounded in the third treatise of the *Convivio*. Compare *Purgatorio*, II. 112.

74. 'So many poets' (*autoribus*). See *Convivio*, IV. 6: 32-35.

80-85. The list of authors here given is interesting. As will be seen from Moore's *Studies in Dante* (1st series), Virgil's *Æneid*, Ovid's *Metamorphoses*, Statius' *Thebaïd* and Lucan's *Pharsalia* are among those Latin classics that have left the most numerous traces in Dante's writings. As to Livy, Dante's acquaintance with him was slight, and the same may be said of Pliny, whom he nowhere else mentions or refers to. Nor does the name of Frontinus (Governor of Britain, A.D. 75-78; Superintendent of the Aqueducts, 97; died, 106) occur elsewhere in Dante; though the poet's military experience (see *Inferno* XXI. 94 ff.; XXII. 1-9, and Lionardo Bruni's *Life*) may possibly have drawn his attention to Frontinus' *Strategematica*, or manual of the art of war. Paulus Orosius (fl. A.D. 415) was a historian much relied on by Dante, and personal sympathy no doubt accounts for his inclusion in the list.

86. On Guittone, see above, I. 13: 7*n*.

CHAPTER VII

[Classification of the words admissible into canzoni.]

Of different kinds of words

THE next division of our progress now demands that an explanation be given as to those words which are of such grandeur as to be worthy of being admitted into that style to which we have awarded the first place. We declare therefore

VII. THE SECOND BOOK

to begin with that the exercise of discernment **Of the** as to words involves by no means the smallest **choice of** labour of our reason, since we see that a great **words** many sorts of them can be found. For some words are *childish*, some *feminine*, and some [10] *manly* ; and of these last some are *sylvan*, others *urban* ; and of those we call urban we feel that some are *combed-out* and *glossy*, some *shaggy* and *rumpled*. Now among these urban words the combed-out and the shaggy are those which we call *grand* ; whilst we call the glossy and the rumpled those whose sound tends to superfluity, just as among great works some are works of magnanimity, others of smoke ; and as to these last, although when superficially looked at [20] there may be thought to be a kind of ascent, to sound reason no ascent, but rather a headlong fall down giddy precipices will be manifest, because the marked-out path of virtue is departed from. Therefore look carefully, Reader, consider how much it behoves thee to use the sieve in selecting noble words ; for if thou hast regard to the illustrious vulgar tongue which (as has been said above) poets ought to use when writing in the tragic style in the vernacular (and these are the persons whom we intend to fashion), thou wilt take care that the noblest words alone are left in thy sieve [30]. And among the number of these thou wilt not be able in any wise to place childish words, because of their simplicity, as *mamma* and *babbo*, *mate* and *pate* ; nor feminine words, because of their softness, as *dolciada* and *placevole* ; nor sylvan words, because of their roughness, as *greggia* and *cetra* ; nor the glossy nor the rumpled urban words, as

Of the choice of words *femina* and *corpo*. Therefore thou wilt see that only the combed-out and the shaggy urban words will be left to thee, which are the noblest, and members of the illustrious vulgar tongue [40]. Now we call those words *combed-out* which have three, or as nearly as possible three syllables; which are without aspirate, without acute or circumflex accent, without the double letters *z* or *x*, without double liquids, or a liquid placed immediately after a mute, and which, having been planed (so to say), leave the speaker with a certain sweetness, like *amore, donna, disio, vertute, donare, letitia, salute, securitate, defesa.*

We call *shaggy* all words besides these which appear either necessary [50] or ornamental to the illustrious vulgar tongue. We call *necessary* those which we cannot avoid, as certain monosyllables like *sì, no, me, te, se, a, e, i, o, u,* the interjections, and many more. We describe as *ornamental* all polysyllables which when mixed with combed-out words produce a fair harmony of structure, though they may have the roughness of aspirate, accent, double letters, liquids, and length [60]; as *terra, honore, speranza, gravitate, alleviato, impossibilità, impossibilitate, benaventuratissimo, inanimatissimamente, disaventuratissimamente, sovramagnificentissimamente,* which last has eleven syllables. A word might yet be found with more syllables still; but as it would exceed the capacity of all our lines it does not appear to fall into the present discussion; such is that word *honorificabilitudinitate*, which runs [70] in the vernacular to twelve syllables, and in grammar to thirteen, in two oblique cases.

In what way shaggy words of this kind are to

VII. THE SECOND BOOK

be harmonised in the lines with combed-out words, we leave to be taught farther on. And what has been said [here] on the pre-eminent nature of the words to be used may suffice for every one of inborn discernment.

Of the choice of words

8-17. See Prof. Saintsbury's interesting remarks on this classification of words (*History of Criticism*, II. 439-441).

19. Compare *Inferno*, XXIV. 47-51; *Psalms* XXXVII. 20; LXVIII. 2.

36. *Corpo* occurs in line 15 of the canzone '*Amor tu vedi ben*,' which Dante quotes with so much complacency below, 13: 90 ff.

41-47. We must assume that in Dante's time the initial aspirate, which is now never sounded in Italian, was in many cases heard. In excluding words with acute accent Dante excludes words ending in a short accented vowel (*oxytona*), like *vertù, securità*. In excluding words with circumflex accent he excludes words ending in a consonant whose last syllable contains a long vowel (*perispomena*) like *donar*. The alternative forms *vertute, securitate, donare*, are given among the succeeding examples as fulfilling the required conditions (Böhmer). It must be remembered that by the Latins (whom Dante would follow) *l* and *r* were alone regarded as liquids, as appears from the *Etymologies* of St Isidore (I. 4, 9), where he states that the Greeks counted *m* and *n* also as liquids.

45. *Planed* (*dolata*, where the Oxford Dante reads *locatam*). So A. Daniel in one of his poems (X. 2, Ed. Canello) speaks of planing his words, in allusion to his care in composition.

53. *a* is a preposition, *e* a conjunction; and they might also be the 3rd. sing. pres. ind. of *avere* and *essere* respectively; *i* would be a shortened form of the pronoun *io*; *o* the adverb meaning '*or*'; *u* is a parallel form of *ove* (where): *i* and *u* do not seem to be strictly 'inevitable' like the other vowels.

70. *Grammar*, i.e. Latin. See above, I. 1: 28*n*.; I. 9: 10*1n*. *Honorificabilitudinitatibus*, the thirteen-syllabled word here referred to, is introduced by Shakespeare into *Love's Labour's Lost*, Act V., sc. i.

CHAPTER VIII

[Meanings of the term canzone. Definition of the canzone in the technical sense in which Dante uses it.]

Meanings of 'canzone'. HAVING prepared the sticks and cords for our faggot, the time is now come to bind it up. But inasmuch as knowledge of every work should precede performance, just as there must be a mark to aim at, before we let fly an arrow or javelin, let us first and principally see what that faggot is which we intend to bind up. That faggot, then (if we bear well in mind all that has been said before), is the canzone [10]. Wherefore let us see what a canzone is, and what we mean when we speak of a canzone. Now canzone, according to the true meaning of the name, is the action or passion itself of singing, just as *lectio* is the passion or action of reading. But let us examine what has been said, I mean whether a canzone is so called as being an action or as being a passion. In reference to this we must bear in mind that a canzone may be taken in two ways. In the first way [20], as its author's composition, and thus it is an action; and it is in this way that Virgil says in the first book of the *Æneid*, 'I sing of arms and the man.' In another way, when, after having been composed it is uttered either by the author or by some one else, whether with or without modulation of sound; and thus it is a passion. For in the first case it is acted, but in the second it appears to act on some one else; and so in the first case **Mean-** it appears to be the action of some one, and in the **ings of** second it [30] also appears to be the passion of **'canzone'** some one. And because it is acted on before it acts, it appears rather, nay, altogether, to get its name from its being acted and being the act of some one than from its acting on others. Now the proof of this is, that we never say 'This is Peter's canzone,' meaning that he utters it, but meaning that he has composed it.

Moreover, we must discuss the question whether we call a canzone the composition of the words which are set to music, or [40] the music itself; and, with regard to this, we say that no music [alone] is ever called a canzone, but a sound, or tone, or note, or melody. For no trumpeter, or organist, or lute-player calls his melody a canzone, except in so far as it has been wedded to some canzone; but those who write the words for music call their words canzoni. And such words, even when written down on paper without any one to utter them, we call canzoni; and therefore [50] a canzone appears to be nothing else but the completed action of one writing words to be set to music. Wherefore we shall call canzoni not only the canzoni of which we are now treating, but also ballate and sonnets, and all words of whatever kind written for music, both in the vulgar tongue and in Latin. But, inasmuch as we are only discussing works in the vulgar tongue, setting aside those in Latin, we say that of poems in the vulgar tongue there is one supreme which [60] we call canzone by super-excellence. Now the supremacy of the canzone has been

'canzone' in the strict sense proved in the third chapter of this book. And since the term which has been defined appears to be common to many things, let us take up again the common term which has been defined, and distinguish by means of certain differences that thing which alone we are in search of. We declare therefore that the canzone as so called by super-excellence which we are in search of is a joining together in the tragic style of equal [70] stanzas without a *ripresa*, referring to one subject, as we have shown in our composition '*Donne che avete intellecto d'amore*'[1] [80]. Now the reason why we call it 'a joining together in the tragic style' is because when such a composition is made in the comic style we call it diminutively *cantilena*, of which we intend to treat in the fourth book of this work [74]. And thus it appears what a canzone is, both as it is taken generally, and as we call it in a super-excellent sense. It also appears sufficiently plain what we mean when we speak of a canzone, and consequently what that faggot is which we are endeavouring to bind up.

12. *Canzone* (*cantio*). Here, of course, and until the meaning is restricted in the latter part of this chapter to canzone in its technical sense, the word is equivalent to song in its most general acceptation; but as the word *song* cannot be used as an equivalent of canzone in its technical sense, I have thought it better to retain the Italian term throughout.

14. I retain the Latin *lectio*, since there is no word in English which expresses at once the 'action' and 'passion' of reading.

---

[1] 'Ladies that have understanding of love.'

15-30. I understand this passage as follows: The term canzone expresses (*a*) action, in reference to the author, and (*b*) passion, in reference to the audience. In the former case the author acts by composing the canzone; in the latter, the canzone, which has been 'acted,' *i.e.* composed by the author, may be said in its turn to act (*videtur agere*) on the audience, who undergo the 'passion.'

26. *Modulation of souna, i.e.* a musical setting.

70. The words '*without ripresa*' (*sine responsorio*) are added in order to distinguish the canzone from the ballata. The *ripresa* was the opening portion of the ballata, and was repeated at its close. Antonio da Tempo, in his treatise on vernacular rhymes (*Delle Rime Volgari*), written in 1332, says that ballate were commonly known as canzoni. Hence the necessity for the distinction.

72. *Donne*, etc. The first line of the first canzone in the *Vita Nuova*. It is quoted again below, 12 : 19. See *Purgatorio*, XXIV. 49-51. It will be noticed that the next sentence in the Oxford Dante text is in the translation transposed, in accordance with Rajna's text, to the end of the chapter.

CHAPTER IX

[Having in the preceding chapter defined the canzone as a joining together of stanzas, the author proceeds to define the stanza.]

INASMUCH as the canzone is a joining together of stanzas, as has been said, we must necessarily be ignorant of the canzone if we do not know what a stanza is, for knowledge of the thing defined results from knowledge of the things defining; and it therefore follows that we must treat of the stanza, in order, that is, that we may discover what it is, and what we mean to understand by it. And in reference to this matter we must observe that this word [10] has been in-

Of the stanza

The art of the canzone vented solely with respect to the art [of the canzone]; namely, in order that that in which the whole art of the canzone is contained should be called stanza, that is a *room* able to hold, or a receptacle for the whole art. For just as the canzone embosoms the whole theme, so the stanza embosoms the whole art; nor is it lawful for the subsequent stanzas to call in any additional scrap of the art, but only to clothe themselves with the art of the first stanza; from which it is plain that the stanza of which we are speaking will be the delimitation or [20] putting together of all those things which the canzone takes from the art; and if we explain them, the description we are in search of will become clear. The whole art, therefore, of the canzone appears to depend on three things: first, on the division of the musical setting; second, on the arrangement of the parts; third, on the number of the lines and syllables. But we make no mention of rhyme, because it does not concern the peculiar art of the canzone, for it is allowable in any stanza to introduce [30] new rhymes and to repeat the same at pleasure, but this would by no means be allowed if rhyme belonged to the peculiar art of the canzone, as has been said. Anything, however, relating to rhyme which the art, as such, is concerned to observe will be comprised under the heading 'Arrangement of the Parts.'

Wherefore we may thus collect the defining terms from what has been said, and declare that a stanza is a structure of lines and syllables limited by reference to a certain musical setting, and to the arrangement [of its parts].

24. The practice of setting canzoni to music fell into disuse not long after Dante's time (Carducci, *Studi letterari*, 301, 302).

29-32. Dante's argument is this: The subsequent stanzas must conform to the first stanza in those things which belong to the peculiar art of the canzone; but they need not so conform in the matter of identity of the rhymes; therefore rhyme does not belong to the peculiar art of the canzone.

35. '*Arrangement of the parts.*' Below, c. 13.

CHAPTER X

[The author enters on the discussion of the stanza, and in this chapter examines its structure in relation to the musical setting. The different kinds of stanza made use of in the canzone depended upon the musical setting for which they were designed.
I. The musical setting might consist of one continuous melody without any repetitions or division.
II. The musical setting might be divided into two different *Melodic Sections*, which Dante calls *Odes*, the repetition of *one* of which was compulsory, and might be made either—
  (*a*) Before the transition to the second ode (which transition Dante calls diesis). Here the *first* part of the stanza was divided into parts called feet (two in number, or, very rarely, three), each of course sung to the same ode. If the ode used in the *second* part of the stanza was not to be repeated, the second part of the stanza was called the sirma or coda.
  (*b*) After the diesis, or transition. Here the *first* ode was not to be repeated, and the *first* part of the stanza, which was consequently undivided, was called the *fronte* (*i.e.* brow), while the divisions of the *second* part of the stanza (each sung to the second ode) were called verses.

(*c*) Lastly, both odes might be repeated, and in this case both parts of the stanza were divided; the divisions of the *first* part being called feet, and those of the *second* verses.]

Of the musical setting of the stanza If we know that man is a rational animal, and that an animal consists of a sensible soul and a body, but are ignorant concerning what this soul is or concerning the body itself, we cannot have perfect knowledge of man, because the perfect knowledge of every single thing extends to its ultimate elements, as the master of the wise testifies in the beginning of the *Physics*. Therefore in order to [10] have that knowledge of the canzone which we are panting for, let us now compendiously examine the things which define its defining term; and first let us inquire concerning the musical setting, next concerning the arrangement [of the parts], and afterwards concerning the lines and syllables.

We say, therefore, that every stanza is set for the reception of a certain ode; but they appear to differ in the modes [in which this is done]; for some proceed throughout to one continuous ode [20], that is, without the repetition of any musical phrase, and without any diesis: and we understand by diesis a transition from one ode to another. (This when speaking to the common people we call *volta*.) And this kind of stanza was used by Arnaut Daniel in almost all his canzoni, and we have followed him in ours beginning—

'*Al poco giorno e al gran cerchio d'ombra.*'

But there are some stanzas which admit of a diesis [30]: and there can be no diesis in our sense of the word unless a repetition of **Of the** one ode be made either before the diesis, or **divided** after, or both. If the repetition be made before **stanza** [the diesis] we say that the stanza has feet; and it ought to have two, though sometimes there are three; very rarely, however. If the repetition be made after the diesis, then we say that the stanza has verses. If no repetition be made before [the diesis] we say that the stanza has a *Fronte* [40]; if none be made after, we say that it has a *Sirma* or Coda. See, therefore, Reader, how much licence has been given to poets who write canzoni, and consider on what account custom has claimed so wide a choice; and if Reason shall have guided thee by a straight path, thou wilt see that this licence of which we are speaking has been granted by worthiness of authority alone.

Hence it may become sufficiently plain how the art of the canzone depends on the division of the musical setting; and therefore let us go on to the [50] arrangement [of the parts].

The rules given in this chapter must be carefully borne in mind, or the further rules in the following chapters will be quite unintelligible.

2. See above, II. 2 : 47*n*. The soul is called sensible in so far as it is put into connection with external things by means of the senses.

8. The master of the wise is Aristotle. Compare *Convivio*, IV. 6 : 71 ff.

11. 'Its defining term' is the stanza. See the beginning of the preceding chapter.

21, 22. St Isidore (*Etym*. III. 19) explains the word diesis in this sense. In Greek music the word meant a quarter-tone.

25-27. In nine out of seventeen extant canzoni by A. Daniel for certain, and probably in more (since

Dante expresses himself thus), the undivided stanza is used (Canello, *Arnaldo Daniello*, p. 23). The purpose of setting the stanza to an undivided melody was to avoid the wearisome repetition of short melodic sections involved in the use of the divided stanza. This disadvantage would, however, be more apparent in the Provençal than in the Italian canzoni, since the stanzas of the former were as a rule both shorter and more numerous than those of the latter, and therefore the repetitions would be more frequent and recur at shorter intervals.

38. In *Convivio*, II. 2; III. 1, and elsewhere '*verso*' is used in the sense of stanza.

41. *Sirma* is the Greek σύρμα. It means anything trailed after one.

46. *By worthiness of authority*, *i.e.* by the virtue of the deservedly pre-eminent authority of the canzone.

CHAPTER XI

[The author, beginning to treat of the arrangement of the parts of the stanza, discusses the relation between its several parts in regard to the number of lines and syllables they contain.]

Of the relation between the several It appears to us that what we call the arrangement [of the parts of the stanza] is the most important section of what belongs to the art [of the canzone], for this depends on the division of the musical setting, the putting together of the lines, and the relation of the rhymes; wherefore it seems to require to be most diligently treated of.

We therefore begin by saying that the *fronte* with the verses, and the feet with the coda or sirma, and also the feet with the verses [10], may be differently arranged in the stanza. For sometimes the *fronte* exceeds or may exceed the verses in syllables and in lines; and we say parts of the stanza in regard to 'may exceed' because we have never yet met with this arrangement. Sometimes [the *fronte*] may exceed [the verses] in lines, and be exceeded by them in syllables; as, if the *fronte* had five lines, and each verse had two lines, while the lines of the *fronte* were of seven syllables and those of the verses of eleven syllables. Sometimes the verses [20] exceed the *fronte* in syllables and in lines, as in our canzone

'*Traggemi de la mente Amor la stiva.*'[1]

Here the *fronte* was composed of four lines, three of eleven syllables and one of seven syllables; for it could not be divided into feet, since an equality of lines and syllables is required in the feet with respect to one another, and also in the verses with respect to one another. And what we say of the *fronte* we might also say of the verses; for the verses might exceed the *fronte* in lines and be exceeded by it in syllables; for instance, if each verse had three lines of seven syllables [33] and the *fronte* were made up of five lines, two of eleven syllables and three of seven syllables.

And sometimes the feet exceed the coda in lines and syllables as in our canzone,

'*Amor che movi tua vertù da cielo.*'

Sometimes the feet are exceeded by the sirma [40] both in lines and syllables, as in our canzone,

'*Donna pietosa e di novella etate.*'[2]

[1] 'Love drags the plough-pole of my mind.'
[2] 'A very pitiful lady, very young.'
(Rossetti's trans.)

number of And just as we have said that the *fronte*,
lines and [though] exceeded [by the verses] in syllables
syllables may exceed them in lines, and conversely, so we
say of the sirma [in relation to the feet].

The feet likewise may exceed the verses in number, and be exceeded by them; for there may be in a stanza three feet and two verses, or three verses and two feet; nor are we limited by that number so as not to be able to combine more [50] feet as well as verses in like manner.

And just as we have spoken of the victory of lines and syllables in comparing the other parts of the stanza together, we now also say the same as regards the feet and verses [compared together]: for these can be conquered and conquer in the same way.

Nor must we omit to mention that we take feet in a sense contrary to that of the regular poets, because they said that a line consisted of feet, but we say that a foot consists of lines, as appears plainly enough.

Nor must we [60] also omit to state again that the feet necessarily receive from one another an equality of lines and syllables, and their arrangement, for otherwise the repetition of the melodic section could not take place. And we declare that the same rule is to be observed in the verses.

22-24. *Traggemi*, etc. This canzone is lost. Dante's practice in this chapter is not to give details as to the parts of the stanza when he cites a particular canzone. He doubtless expected the reader to hunt out the reference for himself. In this case, however, there seems to have been a possibility of misconceiving the structure of the first part of the stanza. Perhaps some peculiarity in the musical setting, or else (as Rajna suggests) the mere fact that the first part was composed of four lines was calculated to raise a suspicion that it might be divided into two feet, which is guarded against by the explicit statement in the text. As the verses (presumably) offered no such scope for misconception, details are not given about them.

38. This canzone is translated in *Convivio*, p. 388.
41. *Donna pietosa*, etc. The second canzone of the *Vita Nuova*.
50-54. In this case, of course, *both* parts of the stanza would be divided.
56. *Regular* (lit., regulated) *poets; i.e.* the Latin poets. Compare above, II. 4 : 21 ff.
60-64. The meaning simply is that the feet must exactly correspond in the number of their lines and syllables. Thus if the first foot has five lines, the second must also have five, and if the first line of the first foot has eleven syllables, the first line of the second must also have eleven, and so on.

CHAPTER XII

[Arrangement of the parts of the stanza in relation to the different kinds of lines employed.]

Combinations of lines in the stanza

There is also, as has been said above, a certain arrangement which we ought to consider in putting the lines together; and therefore let us deal with this, repeating what we have said above respecting the lines.

In our practice three lines especially appear to have the prerogative of frequent use, namely, the line of eleven syllables, that of seven syllables, and that of five syllables, and [10] we have shown that the line of three syllables follows them, in preference to the others. Of these, when we are attempting poetry in the tragic

Combinations of lines in the stanza style, the line of eleven syllables deserves, on account of a certain excellence, the privilege of predominance in the structure [of the stanza]. For there is a certain stanza which rejoices in being made up of lines of eleven syllables alone, as this one of Guido of Florence:—

'*Donna me prega, perch' io voglio dire.*' [1]

And we also say :—

'*Donne ch' avete intellecto d'amore.*' [2]

[20] The Spaniards have also used this line, and I mean by Spaniards those who have written poetry in the vernacular of *oc*. Aimeric de Belenoi [has written]—

'*Nuls hom non pot complir adrechamen.*' [3]

There is a stanza where a single line of seven syllables is woven in, and this cannot be except where there is a *fronte* or a coda, since (as has been said) in the feet and verses an equality of lines and syllables is observed. Wherefore also neither can there be [30] an odd number of lines where there is no *fronte* or no coda, but where these occur, or one of them alone, we may freely use an even or an odd number of lines. And just as there is a certain stanza formed containing a single line of seven syllables, so it appears that a stanza may be woven together with two, three, four, or five such lines, provided only that in the tragic style the lines of eleven syllables predominate in number, and one such line begin. We do indeed

---

[1] ' A lady prays me, therefore I will speak.'
[2] See above, p. 96.   [3] See above, p. 87.

XII. THE SECOND BOOK

find that some writers have begun with a line of seven syllables in the tragic style [40], namely, Guido dei Ghisilieri and Fabruzzo, both of Bologna, as thus:— **Combinations of lines in the stanza**

and, *'Di fermo sofferire,'* [1]
and, *'Donna, lo fermo core,'* [2]
and, *'Lo meo lontano gire,'* [3]

and some others also. But if we go carefully into the sense of these writers, their tragedy will not appear to have proceeded without a certain faint shadow of elegy.

[50] With regard to the line of five syllables also, we are not so liberal in our concessions; in a great poem it is sufficient for a single line of five syllables to be inserted in the whole stanza, or two at most in the feet: and I say 'in the feet,' because of the requirements of the musical setting in the feet and verses.

But it by no means appears that the line of three syllables existing on its own account should be adopted in the tragic style; and I say, 'existing on its own account,' because it often appears to have been adopted by way of a certain [60] echoing of rhymes, as may be discovered in that canzone of Guido of Florence, *'Donna me prega,'* and in the following of ours:—

'Poscia ch' Amor del tutto m' ha lasciato.'

And there the line of three syllables does not appear at all on its own account, but only as a part of a line of eleven syllables [68], answering like an echo to the rhyme of the line before.

[1] 'Of steadfast endurance.'
[2] See above, p. 50.   [3] See above, p. 50.

Special rules for feet and verses

[72] This further point also must be specially attended to with regard to the arrangement of the lines, [namely] that if a line of seven syllables be inserted in the first foot, it must take up the same position in the second that it receives in the first. For instance, if a foot of three lines has the first and last of eleven syllables, and the middle one—that is the second—of seven syllables [80], so the second foot must have the second line of seven syllables and the first and last of eleven syllables, otherwise the repetition of the melodic section, with reference to which the feet are constructed, as has been said, could not take place; and consequently there could be no feet.

And what we have said of the feet we say of the verses also; for we see that the feet and the verses differ in nothing but position, the former term being used before the diesis of the stanza, and the latter after it.

And we declare also that what has been said of the foot of three lines [90] is to be observed in all other feet. And what we have said of one line of seven syllables we also say of more than one, and of the line of five syllables, and of every other line.

[69] Hence, Reader, you are sufficiently able to choose how your stanza is to be arranged as regards the arrangement which it appears should be considered with reference to the lines.

4. *Repeating*, etc. See above, II. 5.
17. *Donna*, etc. The opening line of Guido Cavalcante's celebrated canzone on the nature of love.
19. Compare above, II. 8: 72*n*.
20-23. See above, I. 8: 44*n*.; II. 6: 63*n*.

XIII. THE SECOND BOOK 109

24-29. The canzone *Amor che nella mente*, etc., quoted above, II. 6 : 73, exemplifies the stanza here spoken of. See its first stanza in Appendix II.
40-46. See above, I. 15 : 42, 43, 48, 50, with notes.
49. See above, II. 4 : 36 ff.
52. *A great poem*, *i.e.* a canzone.
65. *Poscia*, etc. Translated, *Convivio*, page 404. See first stanza in Appendix II. below.
72. The sentence included in lines 69-72 (Oxford Dante) is transferred to the end of the chapter, as in Rajna's text.

CHAPTER XIII

[Rhyme in relation to the arrangement of the parts of the stanza.]

LET us apply ourselves to the relation of the **Of the** rhymes, not [however] in any way treating of **unrhymed** rhyme in itself; for we put off the special **stanza** treatment of them (*sic*) till afterwards, when we shall deal with poems in the middle vulgar tongue.

At the beginning of this chapter it seems advisable to exclude certain things : one is the unrhymed stanza, in which no attention is given to arrangement of rhymes [10] ; and Arnaut Daniel very often made use of this kind of stanza, as here :—

'*Sim fos Amors de joi donar ;* ' [1]
and we say : '*Al poco giorno.*'

Another is the stanza all of whose lines give the same rhyme ; and here it is plainly unnecessary to seek for any arrangement [of rhymes].

[1] 'If love were as bountiful in bestowing joy upon me [as I am towards her in purity and sincerity of affection].'

Of the rhymed stanza

And so it remains for us only to dwell upon the mixed rhymes. And first it must be remarked [20] that in this matter almost all writers take the fullest licence; and this is what is chiefly relied on for the sweetness of the whole harmony. There are, then, some poets who sometimes do not make all the endings of the lines rhyme in the same stanza, but repeat the same endings, or make rhymes to them, in the other stanzas: as Gotto of Mantua, who recited to us many good canzoni of his own. He always wove into his stanza one line unaccompanied by a rhyme [30], which he called the key. And as one such line is allowable, so also are two and perhaps more.

There are also some other poets, and almost all the authors of canzoni, who never leave any line unaccompanied in the stanza without answering it by the consonance of one or more rhymes.

Some poets also make the rhymes of the lines following the diesis different from the rhymes of the lines preceding it [40]; while some do not do this, but bring back the endings of the former [part of the] stanza, and weave them into the lines of the latter part. But this occurs oftenest in the ending of the first line of the latter part of the stanza, which very many poets make to rhyme with the ending of the last line of the former part; and this appears to be nothing else but a kind of beautiful linking together of the whole stanza.

Also with regard to the arrangement of the rhymes, according as they are in the *fronte* or coda, every wished-for licence should, it seems, be conceded [50]; but still the endings of the

XIII. THE SECOND BOOK

last lines are most beautifully disposed if they fall with a rhyme into silence.

Special rules as to the feet

But in the feet we must be careful; and [here] we find that a particular arrangement has been observed; and, making a distinction, we say that a foot is completed with either an even or odd number of lines, and in both cases there may be rhymed and unrhymed endings. In [the foot of] an even number of lines, no one feels any doubt [as to this]; but in the other, if any one is doubtful [60], let him remember what was said in the next preceding chapter about the line of three syllables, when, as forming part of a line of eleven syllables, it answers like an echo. And if there happens to be an unrhymed ending in one of the feet, it must by all means be answered by a rhyme in the other. But if all the endings in one of the feet are rhymed, it is allowable in the other either to repeat the endings, or to put new ones, either wholly, or in part, at pleasure, provided, however, that the order of the preceding endings [70] be observed in its entirety; for instance, if in a first foot of three lines, the extreme endings, that is, the first and last, rhyme together, so the extreme endings of the second foot must rhyme together; and according as the middle line in the first foot sees itself accompanied or unaccompanied by a rhyme, so let it rise up again in the second; and the same rule is to be observed with regard to the other kinds of feet. In the verses also we almost always obey this law; and we say 'almost,' because on account of [80] the above-mentioned linking together [of the two parts of the stanza], and combination of the final endings, it some-

Things to be avoided

times happens that the order now stated is upset.

Moreover, it seems suitable for us to add to this chapter what things are to be avoided with regard to the rhymes, because we do not intend to deal any further in this book with the learning relating to rhyme. There are, then, three things, which with regard to the placing of rhymes it is unbecoming for a courtly poet to use, namely, [first], excessive repetition of the same [90] rhyme, unless perchance something new and before unattempted in the art claim this for itself; just like the day of incipient knighthood, which disdains to let the period of initiation pass without any special distinction. And this we have striven to accomplish in the canzone '*Amor, tu vedi ben che questa donna.*'

The second of the things to be avoided is that useless equivocation which always seems to detract somewhat from the theme; and the third is roughness of rhymes [100], unless it be mingled with smoothness; for from a mixture of smooth and rough rhymes the tragedy itself gains in brilliancy.

And let this suffice concerning the art [of the canzone] so far as it relates to the arrangement [of the parts of the stanza].

2. See above, II. 9 : 27 ff.

12-14. *Sim fos*, etc. There is an important metrical difference between the poems here coupled together. In A. Daniel's, each stanza is unrhymed *in itself*, but every line rhymes with the corresponding line of every other stanza. In Dante's (which is a sestina, imitated from A. Daniel's sestina) there is no rhyme at all, but the end-words of each of the six lines of the first stanza recur in a different

XIII. THE SECOND BOOK

order (in each case) as the end-words of each of the succeeding five stanzas (see *Convivio*, p. 396, *note* 4).

21. *And this*, *i.e.* the free choice as to the arrangement of the rhymes.

26. Nothing further is known of Gotto of Mantua.

30. This device of putting one or more isolated rhymes in a stanza was common enough in the Provençal canzoni, and was carried to an extreme length by A. Daniel, who in no less than eight out of seventeen extant canzoni uses a stanza in which *all* the rhymes are isolated (compare *note* on lines 12-14 in this chapter).

40-47. This is exemplified in '*Donna pietosa*' (quoted above, II. 11 : 41). See its first stanza in Appendix II.

50-52. *i.e.* the concluding lines of the whole stanza should form a couplet.

53. The reason for 'care' in the feet (and verses) is of course the necessity of preserving uniformity between them. The *fronte* and coda (it will be remembered) are single members of the stanza.

55-63. '*Answers like an echo.*' It will be remembered that in the passage to which Dante here refers (above, II. 12 : 56-63) he had said that the line of three syllables was only admissible in the tragic style, as forming part of a line of eleven syllables, and rhyming with the ending of the line before. In the present passage his meaning is that, in the case of a foot with an odd number of lines (three, for instance), there might be room for doubt as to the possibility of avoiding (if so desired) an unrhymed line; and he suggests as a way of escape the expedient of making a line of eleven syllables follow the unrhymed line, which line of eleven syllables should incorporate a line of three syllables answering 'like an echo' the ending of the line otherwise unrhymed. The following rhyme-formula for the feet of a stanza will make this explanation quite clear: *AaBB : BbAA :* where the small letters *a*, *b*, indicate the three-syllabled lines incorporated respectively in the eleven-syllabled lines indicated by the capital letters *B*, *A* which follow them.

81. By the combination of the final endings is

meant the last lines of the stanza forming a couplet (above, lines 50-52 in this chapter).

82. *It sometimes happens*, etc. Thus, for instance, as Böhmer points out, in a stanza consisting of feet and verses, where the lines of the feet rhymed according to the formula *ABA : CBC*, if the lines of the verses rhymed according to the formula *DDE : FFE*, the rule would be observed; but if the verses rhymed according to the formula *CFE : FFE*, the rule would not be observed, on account of the first line of the first verse being made to rhyme with the last line of the second foot; similarly, in a stanza when the lines of the verses rhymed according to the formula *CDED : CDED*, the rule would be observed; but if they rhymed according to the formula *CDED : CDEE*, the rule would be broken, in order that the last two lines of the second verse might form a couplet.

96. *Amor tu vedi ben*, etc. An unrhymed poem with five words used as line-endings disposed in each stanza according to a scheme developed from that of the Sestina (see *Convivio*, p. 398. Metrical version by Plumptre, reproducing the peculiarities of the original, *Canzoniere*, p. 112).

97. By *equivocation* is meant the use of equivocal rhymes, *i.e.* words rhyming together which are written and pronounced alike but have different meanings. A. Daniel made large use of this device, especially in the canzone quoted above, II. 6 : 61.

CHAPTER XIV

[The author begins to treat of the number of lines and syllables in the stanza.]

HAVING sufficiently treated of two things belonging to the art in the canzone, it now appears that we ought to treat of the third, namely, the number of the lines and syllables. And in the first place we must make some observations with regard to the stanza as a whole; then we will make some observations as to its parts.

Of the length of the stanza in relation to the subject

It concerns us therefore first to make a distinction between those subjects which fall to be sung of [10], because some stanzas seem to desire prolixity, and others do not. For whereas we sing of all the subjects we are speaking of either with reference to something favourable or else to something unfavourable, so that it happens that we sing sometimes persuasively, sometimes dissuasively, sometimes in congratulation, sometimes in irony, sometimes in praise, sometimes in contempt, let those words whose tendency is unfavourable always hasten to the end, and the others gradually [20] advance to the end with a becoming prolixity. . . .

1-4. See above, II. 9 : 22-26.

APPENDIX I

On the History, Date, and Title of the *De Vulgari Eloquentia*

For about 200 years after Dante's death this book seems to have attracted little attention. It is mentioned by Boccaccio (*Vita di Dante*, ed. Milanesi, p. 67) and G. Villani (ix. 136). Filippo Villani makes no allusion to it in his Life of Dante. Lionardo Bruni, in his Life of Dante (1436), after mentioning the *De Monarchia*, which he describes as entirely without elegance of style, baldly states that 'he (Dante) wrote yet another book entitled *De Vulgari Eloquentia*'; which looks as if Lionardo had been acquainted with the former treatise, but not with the latter. Manetti, who died in 1459, and wrote his Life of Dante after Lionardo Bruni's had appeared, does not mention the book, while Giovanni Maria Filelfo (d. 1480) states indeed that the poet wrote a work *De Vulgari Eloquentia*, but follows this up in characteristic fashion by a fictitious quotation of its first sentence.

It was reserved for Gian Giorgio Trissino (1478-1550) to bring Dante's fragmentary work into prominent notice. Trissino made a considerable figure in the literary world of the early sixteenth century. He was keenly interested in the language and literature of his native country, and possessed a MS. of the *De Vulgari Eloquentia*, the ideas of which he readily embraced. He became an ardent champion of the doctrine that the language of the great writers of Italy—Dante, Petrarch, and Boccaccio—should be called Italian and not Tuscan; and with a view to the improvement of the written tongue proposed, after many years' consideration, as he tells us himself, that five new letters should be added, in order to remove certain ambiguities of pronunciation. This scheme (which he afterwards modified) Trissino recommended in a letter to the reigning Pope (Clement VII.). In January 1529, or according to Rajna a little later, Trissino published a dialogue called *Il Castellano*, in which the issue 'Tuscan *versus* Italian,' raised by implication in the letter to the Pope, is thrashed out. Trissino's views met with vehement opposition, and, as Rajna observes, the dialogue no doubt represents discussions actually held at Rome between Trissino and his opponents. In the dialogue he supports his contention that the highest form of the language should be called Italian and not Tuscan by quotations from the *De Vulgari Eloquentia*, his MS. of which he had very likely brought with him. In the same year, 1529, there appeared an anonymous Italian version of the *De Vulgari Eloquentia*, preceded by a dedicatory letter addressed by Giambattista Doria to Cardinal [Ippolito] dei Medici, in which the author of the version is merely referred to as 'somebody.' The circumstances of the publication were, however, such as to raise a strong presumption that the 'somebody' was

Trissino himself, for the version was issued at Vicenza by the same publisher (Tolomeo Janiculo of Brescia), who also published at about the same time the *Castellano*, the Letter to Clement VII., and two other acknowledged works by Trissino. These works were all printed in the same size, on the same kind of paper, and with the new letters of Trissino's invention; and in addition to this, the passages of the *De Vulgari Eloquentia* cited in the *Castellano* are quoted from the anonymous version. No one in fact now doubts that this version came from Trissino's pen. He probably thought that if he had put his name to it, his opponents would suspect him of having not translated, but fabricated the book. As a matter of fact the version was at first believed to be a fabrication; and for about half a century more the original was still unpublished and generally unknown. Not till 1577 was the Latin text first published at Paris by Jacopo Corbinelli, a Florentine refugee who, after many wanderings, had obtained an appointment at the court of Henry III. of France. Trissino's version was reprinted at Ferrara in 1583, and again at Venice in 1643 and 1696. Early in the seventeenth century another Italian version was made by Celso Cittadini. The MS. of it is now at Vienna, and some specimens of it are printed by Rajna in his larger edition of the Latin text. It is curious to notice that Trissino's version was the cause of the first reprint of the original, for it was in a reprint of Trissino's works at Verona in 1729 that the Latin text was next given to the world, in parallel columns with the Italian version.

Three MSS. only of the original are known to be in existence. The oldest, known as T, dating from the end of the fourteenth century, is in the Trivulzian Library at Milan. Another, known as G, dating from the early fifteenth century, is in the town library of Grenoble; and the third, which was written in the early part of the sixteenth century by order of Cardinal Bembo, is in the Vatican Library. Full information as to these MSS. will be found in Rajna's larger edition. We may, however, note here the curious coincidence by which, early in the nineteenth century T, the MS. from which Trissino's version was made, came into the possession of the Marquis Gian Giacomo Trivulzio, a member of whose illustrious family, Cesare Trivulzio, was an intimate friend of Trissino, who inscribed the *Castellano* to him. It is indeed far from impossible, says Rajna, that Trissino obtained that very MS. from Cesare Trivulzio.

The date of the work may, from internal evidence, be assigned with some confidence to the year 1304 (see discussion of the question in the Temple Classics *Convivio*, pp. 422-425). In addition to the internal evidence there is another circumstance tending to prove conclusively that the *De Vulgari Eloquentia* must be assigned to the earlier years of Dante's exile, and to negative the statement of Boccaccio (*ubi supra*) that the treatise was composed 'when Dante was already near his death'—the only external evidence against the early date of the work. It is impossible to state definitely when the Comedy began to be written, still less when the scheme of the poem began to be matured. But it is quite clear that by this time, whenever it was, Dante's views of the poetic art had undergone a radical change since the days when he had written the present treatise. The Comedy is in fact a repudiation of the doctrines of the *De Vulgari Eloquentia*. We find in the second book of the treatise (c. 2-4) that the highest subjects, arms, love, and righteousness are to be handled in the illustrious vulgar tongue, in canzoni, and in the tragic style; and intricate rules follow which are to be observed by the writers of canzoni. But in the Comedy we find that Dante has completely shifted his position. Arms, love and righteousness are there treated of, but not in canzoni, not in the tragic style, and not in the illustrious vernacular, as defined in the earlier treatise. If, when this treatise was being written, the Comedy was already in contemplation, we are landed in the absurd position that the greatest achievement of the poet's genius was classed by him among the 'other illegitimate and irregular forms of poetry' which in II. 3 : 10 he promises to discuss 'further on.' It is, indeed, not unreasonable to conjecture that the *De Vulgari Eloquentia* was interrupted by some temporary cause, and that its subsequent completion was abandoned by reason of the revolution in Dante's ideas as to the scope of poetry in the vulgar tongue wrought by his conception of the Divine Comedy.

With reference to the title, the designation *De Vulgari Eloquentia* is to be preferred to that of *De Vulgari Eloquio*, which has been sometimes used (though no difference in meaning is involved) for the following reasons: (1) Because

APPENDIX

in the treatise itself (I. 1 : 2 ; 19 : 21, 22) Dante refers to the subject-matter as *doctrina vulgaris eloquentie, doctrina de vulgari eloquentia;* (2) Because, in *Convivio,* I. 5 : 68, Dante expresses his purpose to write a book, God willing, *Di Volgare Eloquenza;* (3) Because this form of the title is confirmed by Boccaccio, G. Villani, Lionardo Bruni, and Trissino.

APPENDIX II

Stanzas of Canzoni illustrating the Rules given in II. 12 and 13

No. 1. Stanza referred to above, II. 12 : 24-29*n*.

First Foot

Amor, che nella mente mi ragiona
Della mia donna disiosamente,
Move cose di lei meco sovente
Che l' intelletto sovr' esse disvia.

Second Foot

Lo suo parlar sì dolcemente sona
Che l' anima ch' ascolta e che lo sente
Dice, ' O me lassa! ch' io non son possente
Di dir quel ch' odo della donna mia.'

Diesis

Sirma, or Coda

E certo e' mi convien lasciare in pria
S' io vo' trattar di quel ch' odo di lei

Ciò che lo mio intelletto non comprende,
E di quel che s' intende
Gran parte, perchè dirlo non saprei.
Però se le mie rime avran difetto,
Ch' entreran nella lode di costei,
Di ciò si biasmi il debole intelletto,
E 'l parlar nostro che non ha valore
Di ritrar ciò che dice Amore.

No. 2. Stanza referred to above, II. 12: 65*n*.

First Foot

Poscia ch' Amor del tutto m' ha lasciato
Non per mio grato
Chè stato—non avea tanto gioioso,
Ma perocchè pietoso
Fu tanto del mio core
Che non sofferse d' ascoltar suo pianto;

Second Foot

Io canterò così disamorato
Contr' al peccato
Ch' è nato—in noi di chiamare a ritroso
Tal, ch' è vile e noioso,
Per nome di valore,
Cioè di leggiadria, ch' è bella tanto,

Diesis

Sirma, or Coda

Che fa degno di manto
Imperial colui dov' ella regna.
Ella è verace insegna
La qual dimostra u' la virtù dimora;

APPENDIX

Per che son certo, sebben la difendo
Nel dir, com' io la 'ntendo
Ch' Amor di sè mi farà grazia ancora.

No. 3.   Stanza referred to above, II. 13:
40-47*n*.

First Foot

Donna pietosa e di novella etate,
Adorna assai di gentilezze umane,
Era là ov' io chiamava spesso morte.

Second Foot

Veggendo gli occhi miei pien di pietate
Ed ascoltando le parole vane,
Si mosse con paura a pianger forte.

Diesis

Sirma, or Coda

Ed altre donne che si furo accorte
Di me per quella che meco piangea
Fecer lei partir via,
Ed appressârsi per farmi sentire.
Qual dicea, Non dormire,
E qual dicea, Perchè sì ti sconforte?
Allor lasciai la nova fantasia
Chiamando il nome della donna mia.

NOTE BY THE TRANSLATOR

This translation, which was first published in 1890, has been thoroughly revised in consequence of the publication by the Italian Dante Society of Prof. Rajna's edition of the original Latin text in 1896, followed by the smaller edition of the same in 1897. There are some important differences between the two editions, and where they occur, the text of the smaller edition has been followed in the translation. In the preparation of the notes considerable use has been made of Dr Paget Toynbee's Dante Dictionary, and I am also much indebted to this eminent authority for information communicated to me privately. I must further acknowledge my special obligation to E. Böhmer's monograph ' *Ueber Dante's Schrift De Vulgari Eloquentia* ' (Halle, 1868). I have in many difficult passages adopted his explanations. The notes to Rajna's larger edition, though exclusively concerned with points of textual criticism, incidentally throw light on the interpretation of the text, and I have not failed to take account of them. I have also made use of Prof. Saintsbury's most interesting chapter on Dante in the second volume of his *History of Criticism*, which contains an able and suggestive analysis of the *De Vulgari Eloquentia*.

A. G. F. H.

*** See postscript on page 427.

THE
DE MONARCHIA

BOOK I

CHAPTER I

[The author's motives and purposes in writing.]

It would seem that all men on whom the Higher Nature has stamped the love of truth must make it their chief concern, like as they have been enriched by the toil of those who have gone before, so themselves in like manner to toil in advance for those that shall be hereafter, that posterity may have of them whereby to be enriched.

Our debt to posterity

For he who, himself imbued with public teachings, yet cares not to contribute aught to the public good, may be well assured that he has fallen far [10] from duty; for he is not 'a tree by the streams of waters, bearing his fruit in due season,' but rather a devouring whirlpool, ever sucking in, and never pouring back what it has swallowed. Wherefore, often pondering these things with myself, lest I should one day be convicted of the charge of the buried talent, I long not only to burgeon, but also to bear fruit for the public advantage, and to set forth truths unattempted by others. For what fruit [20] would he bear who should demonstrate once more some theorem of Euclid; who should

Temporal monarchy strive to expound anew felicity, which Aristotle has already expounded; who should undertake again the apology of old age, which Cicero has pleaded? Naught at all, but rather would such wearisome superfluity provoke disgust.

And inasmuch as amongst other unexplored and important truths the knowledge of the temporal monarchy is most important and least explored, and (for [30] that it stands in no direct relation to gain) has been attempted by none; therefore am I minded to extract it from its recesses; on the one hand that I may keep vigil for the good of the world, and on the other that I may be the first to win for my glory the palm of so great a prize. A hard task in truth do I attempt, and beyond my strength, trusting not so much in my proper power as in the light of that giver who giveth to all liberally and upbraideth not.

2. *The Higher Nature*—Natura superior = God. Compare *Purgatorio*, XVI. 79, where God is referred to as *miglior natura*.

CHAPTER II

[All political theory and action is to be judged by its bearing upon the ultimate goal of human civilisation as a whole.]

Typical treatment First, therefore, we have to consider what the temporal monarchy means; in type to wit, and after intention. The temporal monarchy, then, which is called empire is 'a unique princedom extending over all persons in time,' or, 'in and over those things which are measured by time'; and there rise three main inquiries concerning the same: for in the first place we may inquire and examine whether [10] it is needful for the well-being of the world; in the second, whether the Roman people rightfully assumed to itself the function of monarchy; and in the third, whether the authority of the monarchy depends immediately upon God, or upon some other minister or vicar of God.

The first principle

But inasmuch as every truth which is not a first principle is demonstrated by reference to one that is, it behoves us in every inquiry to be clear as to the first principle [20] to which we are to return by analysis, in order to establish the certainty of all such propositions as may afterwards be laid down. And inasmuch as the present treatise is an inquiry, it would seem that before all else we must investigate the first principle in the strength of which what follows is to be established.

Be it known, then, that there are some things, in no degree subject to our power, about which we can think, but which we cannot do; such are [30] mathematics, physics, and divinity; but there are some which are subject to our power, and which we can not only think about, but can also do; and in the case of these the doing is not undertaken for the sake of thinking, but the latter for the former, since in such cases the doing is the goal.

Since, then, the present matter is concerned with polity, nay, is the very fount and first principle of right polities, and since all that

Speculative and practical studies concerns polity is subject to our power [40], it is manifest that our present matter is not primarily concerned with thinking, but with doing. Again, in the case of anything that is done it is the ultimate end which constitutes the first principle and cause of the whole thing, for it is that end which, in the first instance, sets the agent in motion; so it follows that the whole theory of the means which make for the end must be derived from the end itself. Thus there is one theory of cutting wood to build a house, and another to build a ship. That thing, then, if [50] there is any, which is the goal of the entire civilisation of the human race, will give us this first principle, a reduction to which will be held a sufficient explanation of everything to be proved hereafter. But it would be folly to suppose that there is a goal of this civilisation and a goal of that, but no one goal of all civilisations.

3 *After intention* — secundum intentionem = 'As God intended and meant it.' Dante's theme, then, is the temporal monarchy under its typical and ideal aspects, not as it actually exists. Hence the repeated qualifications and misgivings implied in such phrases as 'is found, *or ought to be found*, in the totality itself' (I. 6 : 25), and the insistence upon indications and limits of the divine purpose (see notes on II. 3). Thus, too (as we gather from II. 9 and *Epistola*, VI. [VII.] 3), the fact that the Roman Empire never really was universal is irrelevant so long as it can be shown that it was its divinely given mission to be universal.

44. *Finis* is translated *end* or *goal* indifferently, throughout this work.

CHAPTER III

[The goal of civilisation as a whole is discovered to be the realising of all the potentialities of the human mind; and this demands the harmonious development and co-operation of the several members of the universal body politic.]

So now we must consider what is the goal of human civilisation as a whole, which, when we see, more than half our work will be done, according to the Philosopher *Ad Nicomachum*. And to understand the point in question we must note that like as there is an end for which nature produces the thumb, and another than this for which she produces the whole hand, and again another than [10] either for which the arm, and another than all of these for which the whole man, so there is one end for which she produces the individual man, another for which the domestic group, another for which the district, another for which the city-state, and another for which the kingdom; and lastly, there is an ultimate goal for which the eternal God, by his art, which is nature, brings into being the human race in its universality. And it is this last for which we are now seeking as the [20] first principle to direct our inquiry.

Wherefore be it known in the first place that God and nature makes nought superfluous, but all that comes into being is for some function. For no created being is a final goal in the intention of the Creator, as Creator; but rather is the proper function of that being the goal. Wherefore it comes to pass that the proper function does not come into existence for the

The goal of civilisation

The sake of the being, but the latter for the sake of
potential the former.
intellect

[30] There is, then, some function proper to humanity as a whole for which that same totality of men is ordained in so great multitude, to which function neither one man nor one family, nor one district nor one city-state, nor any individual kingdom may attain. And what this function is will be obvious if the specific potentiality of mankind generally be made clear. I say, then, that no capacity which is shared by many beings [40], differing in species, is the specific capacity of any one of them. For since that which is specific constitutes a species, it would follow that one essence would be specifically assigned to several species, which is impossible. The specific capacity, then, which differentiates man is not merely *being*, taken without qualification, for this he shares with the elements; neither *compound being*, for this we find in [50] the minerals; nor *animated being*, for this is in plants; nor *apprehension*, for this is shared by the brutes; but *apprehension by means of the potential intellect*, which mode of being is not competent to any other save man, either above him or below. (For although there are other beings which have intellect, as man has, yet theirs is not potential intellect, as is man's; inasmuch as each of these beings is an intellectual species [60], and nought else; and their being is no other than the act of continuous understanding, else they were not sempiternal.) It is plain, then, that the specific potentiality of humanity as such is a potentiality or capacity of intellect.

III. THE FIRST BOOK 133

And since that same potentiality cannot all **and its**
be reduced to actuality at the same time by one **actualisa-**
man, or by any of the limited associations **tion**
distinguished above, there must needs [70] be
multiplicity in the human race, in order for the
whole of this potentiality to be actualised thereby. Like as there must be a multiplicity of
things generable in order that the whole potentiality of first matter may always be in act; otherwise we should have to grant the existence of
sejunct potentiality, which is impossible. And
with this Averroes agrees in his commentary on
the writings *De Anima*.

Moreover, the intellectual faculty of which I
am speaking deals not only with [80] universal
forms or species, but also, by a kind of extension, with particular ones. Whence it is
commonly said that the speculative intellect by
extension becomes the practical intellect, the
end of which is *doing* and *making*. And I draw
this distinction because there are things to be
done which are regulated by political wisdom,
and things to be *made*, which are regulated by
art. But they are all alike handmaids of
speculation, as the supreme function for which
the Prime [90] Excellence brought the human
race into being. And now we have already
reached a point at which that saying of the
Politics begins to be luminous: 'The intellectually vigorous have natural sway over others.'

21-29. The idea seems to be that the Creator creates
everything with a distinct reference to that which it
is to do or to be, and does not first create a thing
and then cast about for something it can do or be.
See further, lines 88-90 of this chapter, and compare

Paradiso, XXIX. 13 ff., and *note*. Perhaps the qualification 'as creator' means that when the individual is once created it then becomes an object of the divine care on its own account.

22. *God and nature makes*—'Deus et natura nil otiosum facit.' I preserve the usage of the original which here and elsewhere constructs 'God and nature' with a singular verb.

37, 38. *Specific potentiality.* In enumerating, in the order of their generality, the characteristics of any creature, the last (*ultimum*) which we reach is the one that 'differentiates' it from others of the same genus but of another species. This is well illustrated by what follows.

44. *Essence.* The essence of anything is that which constitutes our abstract conception of it, and which should be included explicitly or by implication in our definition of it. It is opposed to the concrete being (*esse*) of any individual of the kind. 'For the essence or nature of a thing comprehends only what is included in the definition of its kind as humanity [*i.e. humanness*, not what we mean by collective 'humanity'] comprehends all the things that fall under the definition of man; for it is in virtue of them that a man is man; and that is what "humanity" means; namely, that in virtue of which a man is man. But the individual material, together with all the accidents that individualise it, does not come under the definition of the kind; for this particular flesh and these particular bones, or paleness, or darkness, and such like, do not come under the definition of man. Wherefore this particular flesh and these particular bones, and the accidents which mark this particular matter, are not included in humanity; and yet they are included in that which the man is, wherefore that which the man is has in it something which humanity has not; and therefore the man is not completely identical with humanity; and humanity is indicated as the formal part of man, since defining principles have the relation of form to the individualing material' (Aquinas). Compare the distinction between *essentia* and *esse* in *Epistola*, X. § 23; and see further T. C., *Convivio*, pp. 123, 231.

53, 54. A *potential intellect* means an intellect which has capacities or possibilities in excess of its actual realisations at any given moment.

55-62. The beings meant are angels. It is a cardinal doctrine of mediæval angelology that each several angel is a distinct species. (Compare *De Vulgari Eloquentia*, I. 3: 5, 6.) This follows from the belief that an angel is pure form (as to which see T. C., *Convivio*, pp. 123, 231, and *note* on lines 66-78 below), for, since all things of the same species have the same form and are distinguished and individualised only by their material or by their accidents (T. C., *Convivio*, p. 26, and above, *note* on line 44), the distinction between two beings that are pure form must be a difference of kind or species. All angels, however, have this in common that their intellect is always all in act. Their life is therefore a continuous and uniform realisation of the whole knowledge and love of which they are capable, not (like that of man) the intermittent and variable realisation of a selection of the possibilities it contains.

66-78. The general idea is plain enough, namely, that God would have given the human mind its range of powers in vain if these powers never found their actualisations but remained perpetually in the mere state of potentiality. It is the goal of civilisation to realise all the potentialities of humanity by developing in peaceful co-operation all the several capacities of individuals, families, races, and so forth. The form of expression, however, and the reference to Averroes (compare T. C., *Convivio*, p. 296) seem to harden and narrow the conception somewhat, and to call for some detailed exposition. To begin with ' first matter.' As a statue consists of the material out of which it is made and the form which makes it what it is, so does everything consist of the form which makes it what it is, and the material out of which it is made. The marble, out of which the statue is made, itself consists of the informing principle which makes it marble (and not mud), and the matter which is informed by that principle. When we get back to *first* matter, therefore, it is not a *thing* at all (else it would have form and material and would not itself be *first* matter); yet neither is it nothing, or it would not be at all. We must therefore regard it as a naked possibility of receiving forms, *i.e.* of becoming *things*. Now this first matter need not have the form of this or that special thing, but it must always have the form of some thing, for it is incapable of existing independently, as matter sejunct from form. Or at any rate it seems perfectly clear that if any part or any aspect of this 'first matter' should actually exist objectively in the unimaginable state of 'separation' from all 'forms,' and should, therefore, never be anything actually while remaining everything potentially, it would exist in vain, which is repugnant to God and nature.

Averroes conceived in like manner a potential intellect (the *intellectus possibilis* of the Schoolmen) which he called the 'material intellect' (*intellectus materialis*), as a mere naked undividualised possibility of thought; apparently of determined quantity. And since thought is only concerned with the essential and permanent aspects of things, that is with their forms, the 'material intellect' was an abstract possibility of receiving forms. But this is precisely the definition of 'first matter'; and the question arose, in what does the material or potential intellect differ from first matter? The answer is that first matter receives forms as objects of thought and the material intellect receives them as thoughts. Both alike are reduced from potentiality to actuality by the act of a power (ultimately God), which, on the intellectual plane, is called the 'active intellect' (*intellectus agens*). The *intellectus agens* and the *intellectus materialis* are both of them impersonal, abstract, eternal principles, corresponding to active light and receptive transparency in the physical world. And just as a *thing* communicates with or participates in the material principle (first matter) and the formal principle, so an intellectual being (man) shares in, and becomes continuous with, both the receptive, or material, and the active intellect; and this in virtue of his own *intellectus passibilis*, *i.e.* intellect capable of experiencing passion (T. C., *Convivio*, p. 104) or being modified. This *intellectus passibilis* (not *possibilis*, observe) is an individual faculty and is seated in the mid-chamber of the brain. It is personal, concrete, and perishable.

Now, just as it is not necessary that this or that *thing* should exist, but it is necessary that *things* ('a multiplicity of things that can be generated') should exist, in order that the potentialities of first matter may be actualised in them, so it is not necessary that this or that man should exist, but it is necessary that *men* should exist, in order that the impersonal *intellectus materialis* should be actualised as thought by the action of the *intellectus agens*, the two meeting in individual men by continuity with their personal *intellectus passibiles*. All this, as Dante hints, is developed in the commentary on the third book of the *De Anima*. Elsewhere (in the *De Beatitudine Animæ*) Averroes goes so far as to declare that there must always be a philosopher somewhere in the world, since otherwise the *intellectus materialis* would in some sort exist, for the time being, as a naked possibility of thought, sejunct from thinking, which is as impossible as for first matter to exist sejunct from form.

78. *Faculty*. Latin *potentia*, translated elsewhere 'potentiality.'

78-82. 'Particular forms' is a somewhat unusual phrase to indicate forms as manifested in and by concrete individuals, not as abstracted and generalised by the intellect. Now it is with the generalised forms that the speculative intellect is concerned; but it is precisely with concrete individuals that we have always practically to do. Thus if in dealing practically with concrete things we understand their general aspects, and are guided by that understanding, we are recognising the general forms as manifested in the concrete individuals; and our speculative intellect, handling 'particular forms,' has 'become by extension practical.'

CHAPTER IV

[*The first requisite for the realisation of the goal of human civilisation is universal peace.*]

The blessedness of peace

It has been sufficiently shown that the work proper to the human race, taken as a whole, is to keep the whole capacity of the potential intellect constantly actualised, primarily for speculation, and secondarily (by extension, and for the sake of the other) for action.

And since it is with the whole as it is with the part, and it is the fact that in sedentary quietness the individual man [10] is perfected in knowledge and in wisdom, it is evident that in the quiet or tranquillity of peace the human race is most freely and favourably disposed towards the work proper to it (which is almost divine, even as it is said 'Thou hast made him a little lower than the angels'). Whence it is manifest that universal peace is the best of all those things which are ordained for our blessedness. And that is why there rang out to the shepherds from on high [20], not riches, not pleasures, not honours, not length of life, not health, not strength, not beauty, but peace. For the celestial soldiery proclaims, 'Glory to God in the highest; and, on earth, peace to men of good will.' Hence, also, 'Peace be with you' was the salutation of him who was the salvation of man. For it was meet that the supreme saviour should utter the supreme salutation. And likewise his disciples saw good to preserve this custom [30], and amongst them Paul, as all may see in his salutations.

Our exposition, then, has made clear what is **Peace** the better means (or rather the best) whereby **universal** the human race attains to its proper work. And thus we perceive the directest means of approach to that whereto as to their ultimate goal all our doings are directed, which directest means is universal peace. Therefore let this underlie [40] the following arguments, as that first principle which we needed (as aforesaid) for a mark, set up in advance; into which, as into the most manifest truth, whatsoever is to be proved must be resolved.

10. Compare Ecclesiasticus XXXVIII. 24 (25 in Vulg.): 'The wisdom of a learned man cometh by opportunity of leisure; and he that hath little business shall become wise.'

CHAPTER V

[Unity of direction is necessary in order to secure efficiency in collective action of any kind; therefore, since humanity as a whole can only reach its goal by collective action, it should be under the unified direction of a single authority.]

And now, to resume what we said at the outset, **The** the three main questions are raised and discussed **three** about the temporal monarchy, more commonly **questions** called the empire; concerning which, as already declared, we purpose to make inquiry, in the order indicated above, under the first principle now laid down. Let us therefore first discuss whether a temporal monarchy [10] is needful for the well-being of the world.

Unity of rule a necessity Now against its being needful there is no force either of argument or of authority, whereas most powerful and most patent arguments establish that it is. Of which let the first be drawn from the authority of the philosopher in his *Politics*. For there his venerable authority asserts that when more things than one are ordained for a single purpose, needs must one of them guide or rule, and the others be guided or ruled. And to this not [20] only the glorious name of the author, but inductive argument also forces assent.

For if we consider an individual man, we shall see that this is true of him; since whereas all his faculties are ordained for felicity, the intellectual faculty is the guide and ruler of all the others, else he cannot attain to felicity. If we consider the family, the goal of which is to prepare [30] its members to live well, there must needs be one to guide and rule whom they call the pater-familias, or his representative; according to the philosopher when he says, 'Every house is ruled by the oldest.' And it is his task, as Homer says, to rule over all the rest, and to impose laws on his housemates; whence the proverbial curse, 'May you have a peer in your house.' If we consider a district, the end of which is helpful co-operation both in persons and in [40] appliances, one must needs be the guide of the rest, whether he be imposed upon them by another or rise to eminence out of themselves, with the consent of the rest. Else not only do they fail to attain the mutual support they aim at, but sometimes when several strive for pre-eminence, the whole district is brought

V. THE FIRST BOOK

to ruin. And if we consider a city, the end of which is to live well and suitably, there must be a single rule, and this not only [50] in a rightly ordained polity, but even in a wrong one. For if it be otherwise not only is the end of civil life missed, but the very city itself ceases to be what it was. If finally we consider a special kingdom, the end of which is the same as that of the city, only with better assurance of tranquillity, there must be one king to rule and govern, else not only do they in the kingdom fail to reach the goal, but the kingdom itself lapses into ruin [60], according to that saying of the infallible truth, 'every kingdom divided against itself shall be laid waste.' If, then, this is so in these cases and in every other case in which a single end is aimed at, the proposition laid down above is true.

Now it is admitted that the whole human race is ordained for a single end, as was set forth before. Therefore there must be one guiding or ruling power. And this is what we mean by monarch or emperor. Thus it appears [70] that for the well-being of the world there must be a monarchy or empire.

Necessity of empire

34, 35. *Homer.* Here as elsewhere Dante is dependent for his knowledge of Homer upon the Latin translations of Aristotle. The words are quoted in *Pol.* I. 2 : 4, from *Odyssey*, IX. 114, 5, where the whole passage runs, 'Each of them lays down the law for his own children and wives, and they take no heed of each other.' It refers to the Cyclopes, and the last clause, had Aristotle quoted it, would have spoilt it very effectively for Dante's purpose.

37. *The proverbial curse.* Thus Bertran de Born, amongst the imprecations he calls down upon him-

self, if he is not true to his lady, says (speaking from personal experience), 'Senher sia eu d' un castel parsonier,' *i.e.* 'May I be joint lord of a castle.'

64. We have now proved, by induction, the proposition laid down, on the authority of Aristotle, in lines 16-19 of this chapter.

CHAPTER VI

[The parts exist for the sake of the whole, and the arrangement of the parts is subordinate to the arrangement of the whole. Therefore the arrangement of the parts cannot exhibit a higher order of excellence than the arrangement of the whole. But we may regard arrangement from two points of view. An institution must arrange itself with reference to its own good as an institution, and also with reference to the purpose for which it is instituted: and the latter arrangement is of the higher order of excellence. Now we have seen that the essential note of this higher order of excellence, namely unity of direction, is manifested by the several parts of human society, and therefore it must needs be manifested by the whole; otherwise the arrangement of the parts would exhibit a higher order of excellence than the arrangement of the whole.]

Partial and integral order

AGAIN, the relation of the partial order to the total order is the same as the relation of the part to the whole. Now the part is related to the whole as to its end and supreme good; wherefore also the order in the part is related to the order in the whole as to its end and supreme good. Whence we learn that the excellence of the partial order does not transcend the excellence of the total order, but

VI.   THE FIRST BOOK

rather the other way. Since, then, we may discover a twofold order in things, to wit the order [10] of the parts with reference to each other, and their order with reference to some unity which is not itself a part (for instance the order of the parts of an army with reference to each other, and their order with reference to the general), the order of the parts with reference to that unity is the superior order, as being the end of the other ; for the other exists for its sake, and not conversely. Wherefore if the essential principle of this order is to be found even in the parts of the human multiplicity, much more may we look to find it in that multiplicity or totality itself [20], by virtue of the previous syllogism; since that order, or essential principle of order, is the superior. But we find it in all the parts of the human multiplicity, as is sufficiently manifest by what has been said in the chapter which precedes this. Therefore it is found, or ought to be found, in the totality itself. And thus all the parts enumerated above as subordinate to kingdoms, together with the kingdoms themselves, should be ordered with reference to a single prince or princedom, that is the monarch or monarchy.

alike require unity of command

8-15. The illustration of the army and the general is taken from Aristotle (*Metaphysics*, XI. 10 : 1, 2).

'We are also to consider whether the nature of the universe finds its good, relative and absolute, in something separate and self-existent, or in its own inherent order, or in both, like an army. For the good of an army is both in its own order and in its general, and preponderantly in the latter ; for he does not exist for the sake of the order, but the order for his sake.'

Thomas Aquinas works this out beautifully in many passages, rightly taking 'the general' here to be equivalent to the purpose or good of the general. The army finds a certain 'good' in the mutual helpfulness and support of its parts, but the dominating 'good' for which it exists is the purpose to which the general directs it, viz., victory.

This implicit reference to the office or function whenever the official is designated runs through the whole of the *De Monarchia* and must never be lost sight of. Earthly felicity is the goal of man as an earthly being. Such felicity is attained by the free and full exercise of the faculties of man. Co-operation is needed for this, and (at least in the fallen state) regulation is needed to secure co-operation. The Roman Law is the supreme instrument for the regulation of the earthly affairs of men; and it is powerless without an efficient executive (*Purgatorio*, VI. 88, 89; XVI. 88-99). Hence subordination to the ideal emperor, as the official whose office is to execute Roman Law, is the road to felicity. This, which is the gist of the whole work, will gradually unfold itself as we read the *De Monarchia*, but III. 4 : 107-120 and III. 16 may with profit be read in advance at this point.

CHAPTER VII

[Humanity as a whole is itself but a member of the universal organism; and therefore, as each of its own members must have its unifying representative to bring it into relation with the whole, so must that whole itself, as a member of a greater whole, have its unifying representative, to bring it into relation with the universal order.]

Humanity FURTHER, the totality of men is a whole relatively to certain parts, and it is likewise a part relatively to a certain whole. That is, it is a whole relatively to special kingdoms and nations, as shown above; and it is a part relatively to the whole *a part of* universe, as is self-evident. Therefore, what *the universe* we consider a proper correspondence of the components of the totality of men to that totality itself, we should also consider a proper correspondence of the totality of men to that whole of which it, in its turn, is a component [10]. Now its parts properly correspond to it by means of having each one single principle only, as may easily be gathered from what has gone before. Wherefore it is true that it, in its turn, properly corresponds with the universe, or with its prince (who is God, and monarch in the unqualified sense), by means of having one single principle only, to wit the sole prince. Whence it follows that the monarchy is necessary to the world for its well-being.

15, 16. God is monarch *simpliciter*, *i.e.* absolutely, or without qualification (I remove the comma after *monarcha*), whereas the emperor is monarch 'in and over those things which are measured by time.' See above, 2 : 6, 7.

CHAPTER VIII

[It is God's purpose that all things should resemble himself to the utmost extent that their nature allows. Now *unity* is supremely realised in God, and the nature of humanity admits of unification. Therefore it is a part of God's purpose that humanity should resemble himself by being unified, which it can only be when subject to one prince.]

AND everything is well and best disposed which is disposed after the intention of the prime agent,

The likeness of God which is God. And this is self-evident to all who deny not that the divine excellence attains the height of perfection. It is of the intention of God that every created thing should present the divine likeness in so far as its proper nature is capable of receiving it. Wherefore it is [10] said, 'Let us make man after our image and likeness.' And although 'after our image' may not be said of things lower than man, yet 'after our likeness' may be said of all things soever, since the whole universe is nought else than a certain footprint of the divine excellence. Therefore the human race is well and best disposed when, to the measure of its power, it is likened to God. But the human [20] race is most likened to God where it is most one; for it is in him alone that the absolute principle of the one exists. Wherefore it is written, 'Hear, O Israel, the Lord thy God is one.'

But the human race is then most one when it is all united in one, which can not be save when it is subject in its totality to one prince, as is self-evident. Therefore, it is when subject to one prince that the human race [30] is most likened to God, and consequently most conforms to the divine intention; and this is being well and best disposed, as was shown at the beginning of this chapter.

Far-fetched and inconclusive as the argument of this and the following chapter may seem to the modern reader, there can be no doubt that the conception they embody dominated the medieval imagination and exercised a compelling force on political speculations.

CHAPTER IX

[Man, as the child of heaven, must imitate its unity of motion.]

LIKEWISE every son is well and best disposed when he follows the track of a perfect father, in so far as his proper nature allows. The human race is the son of heaven, which is most perfect in all its work, for 'man is begotten by man and the sun' according to the philosopher in the second *De Naturali Auditu*. Wherefore the human race is best disposed when it follows the track of heaven in so far as [10] its proper nature allows. And since the whole heaven, in all its parts, motions, and movers, is regulated by a single motion (to wit of the *primum mobile*), and a single motor, God (as human reason apprehends in philosophy with the utmost clearness), it follows, if our syllogising is sound, that the human race is then best disposed when it is ruled in its motors and motions by a single prince as single motor, and [20] by a single law as single motion. Wherefore it appears necessary to the well-being of the world that there should be a monarchy or single princedom, which is called empire. This reasoning Boethius sighed forth when he said :—

'O felix hominum genus,
Si vestros animos amor
Quo cælum regitur, regat!' [1]

The harmony of heaven

---

[1] 'Oh happy race of men, were your minds ruled by heaven-ruling love!'

An argument similar to that of this chapter, but even more fantastic, is put forward in *Convivio*, IV. 23. The speculations of the Neoplatonic and other schools of philosophy as to the emanations from the primal Being of successive orders of existence, represented by the successive heavens, each causing and dominating the order beneath it, had deeply tinged mediæval thought, and give actuality to such arguments as that contained in this chapter.

Underlying such fanciful speculations is the deeper feeling (common to systems of thought as remote from each other as Christianity and Confucianism), that the order and regularity of the heavenly phenomena show the norm and give the promise of a corresponding order and regularity in the affairs of man. This is in truth, as Dante indicates, the source alike of the sighs and of the 'consolation' of Boethius.

6, 7. 'Generat enim homo hominem et sol' (*Phys.* II. 2: 11). Aristotle, however, does not represent man as in any *specific* sense the child of the sun. He might equally well, for his purpose, have said 'generat enim equus equum et sol.' But the phrase as it stands seems to have struck the mediæval fancy, apart from its context.

CHAPTER X

[To pronounce judgment on differences that arise between politically independent powers, there must be some supreme tribunal, and therefore a supreme prince.]

The supreme earthly umpire

WHERESOEVER contention may arise there must needs be judgment, else there were an imperfection without its proper perfector; which is impossible, since God and nature fails not in things necessary. Now between any two princes, one of whom is in no way subject to the other, contention may arise, either through their own fault

X.   **THE FIRST BOOK**   149

or that of their subjects, as is self-evident. *must be*
Wherefore there [10] must needs be judgment *the sole*
between such. And since the one may not take *prince*
cognisance of what concerns the other, the one
not being subject to the other (for a peer has no
rule over his peer), there must needs be a third of
wider jurisdiction who, within the compass of his
right, has princedom over both. And such a
one will either be the monarch or not. If he
is, the proposition is established. If not,
he again will have a co-equal outside the compass
of his jurisdiction; and these two will again [20]
need a third; and so we shall either go on to
infinity (which may not be), or must come to
the first and highest judge by whose judgment
all contentions may be solved, either mediately
or immediately. And he will be monarch or
emperor. Therefore monarchy is necessary
for the world. And this reasoning was per-
ceived by the Philosopher when he said,
'Things love not to be ill-disposed; but a
multiplicity of princedoms is ill; therefore [30],
one prince.'

    Nothing could better help the student to distinguish
between the substance of the form of the *De Monarchia*,
or to free himself from slavery to words, than reflec-
tion upon this chapter. He will see that Dante's 'im-
perialism' does not mean the supremacy of one nation
over others, but the existence of a supreme law that
can hold all national passions in check; so that the
development of international law and the establish-
ment of arbitration are its nearest modern equivalents;
and the main difficulty is found in the want of any
power of compulsion by which the nations can be
made to refer their quarrels to the supreme tribunal
and accept its awards, whether it sits at Rome or
at the Hague.

30, 31. The saying is really quoted by Aristotle (*Met.* XI. 10 : 14) from Homer (*Iliad*, II. 204), but there is nothing in the Latin translation to show that it is not part of the text.

CHAPTER XI

[Justice is required for the well-being of the world. Therefore the ruler that directs human affairs should have the will and the power to execute justice. Now greed is the great foe of justice in the will; so the ruler should be free from greed. This the monarch is likely to be, for there is no margin of unattained power or wealth beyond his control, to excite his cupidity; moreover, love inspires the desire to do justice, and the monarch, having the responsible care of humanity, will be prone to love it. Moreover, as the chief earthly source of the well-being of mankind, he will take a delight in the effect of his own causal energy; he will therefore have a better will to be just than any other kind of ruler; and obviously he will have more power than any other.]

Justice MOREOVER, the world is best disposed when justice is most potent therein; whence Virgil, in praise of that age which was visibly rising in his own day, sang in his *Bucolics* :—

'*Iam redit et Virgo, redeunt Saturnia regna.*' [1]

By 'Virgin' he meant Justice, who was also called Astræa. By 'Saturnian kingdoms' he meant the best ages, which were [10] also called the golden.

[1] 'Already, too, the Virgin is returning; and Saturnian kingdoms come again.'

Justice is most potent under a monarch only, therefore for the best disposition of the world it is needful that there should be a monarchy or empire. *secured by the monarch's will*

To prove the sub-assumed, be it known that justice, in herself, considered in her proper nature, is a certain straightness or rule, rejecting the oblique on either side. And thus she is not susceptible of more and less, any more than whiteness, considered [20] in the abstract, is. For there is a class of forms of this kind subject to composition, but themselves consisting in a simple and invariable essence, as the Master of the Six Principles rightly says. Such qualities, however, are susceptible of more or less with respect to the subjects by which they are contracted, according as more or less of their contraries is mingled in the said subjects. Where, then, there is least of the contrary of justice intermixed [30], both as regards disposition and as regards operation, there justice is most potent. And then it may truly be said of her as the Philosopher says, 'Neither Hesperus nor Lucifer is so wondrous fair.' For then she is like Phœbe, gazing diametrically over against her brother from the purple of the morning calm.

As concerns disposition then, justice may sometimes find opposition in the will [40]; for, where the will is not pure from all greed, even though justice be present, yet she is not absolutely there in the glow of her purity; for she is lodged in a subject which to some extent, though it be never so little, resists her. Wherefore they are rightly rebuffed who attempt to and inspire the judge with passion. But as concerns power operation, justice finds limitation in power. For since justice is a virtue that refers to others, how can one act in accordance with her if he have not the power of rendering [50] to each what is his due? Whence it is obvious that the more powerful the just man is, the more ample will justice be in her operation.

From this exposition, then, we may argue thus: Justice is most potent in the world when it exists in the most willing and the most potent subject. The monarch alone is such a one, therefore it is only when justice exists in the monarch that she is most potent in the world. This prosyllogism [60] runs by the second figure, with intrinsic negation, and is like this: —All B is A; only C is A; therefore only C is B. That is, all B is A; nothing except C is A; therefore nothing but C is B.

The first proposition is clear from the preceding explanation. The second is demonstrated as follows, first as regards the will, then as regards the power. To prove the first point [70] we must note that greed is the chief opponent of justice, as Aristotle indicates in the fifth *Ad Nicomachum*. If greed be absolutely removed, nothing is left to oppose justice; whence it is the opinion of the Philosopher that such things as can be determined by law should in no case be left to the judge. And this for fear of greed, which readily turns the minds of men aside. Now where there is nought that can be desired, there it is [80] impossible for greed to be; for when their objects are destroyed the passions cannot persist. But the monarch has nought that he can desire, for his jurisdiction is bounded by the ocean alone, which is not the case with other princes, since their principalities are bounded by others; as for instance the King of Castile's by the King of Aragon's. Whence it follows that the monarch may be the purest subject of justice amongst [90] mortals.

to suppress greed

Moreover, just as greed, though it be never so little, clouds to some extent the disposition of justice, so does charity or right love sharpen and brighten it. In whomsoever therefore right love has the greatest power of inhering, in him justice may take the most commanding place. The monarch is such; therefore when he exists justice is most powerful, or at any rate may be so. Now, that [100] right love has the action I have said, may be shown thus. Greed, scorning the intrinsic significance of man, seeks other things; but charity, scorning all other things, seeks God and man, and consequently the good of man. And since, amongst the other blessings of man, living in peace is the chief (as was said above), and justice is the chiefest and mightiest accomplisher of this, therefore charity will chiefly give vigour to justice; and the stronger she is, the [110] more.

And that right love should inhere in the monarch most of all men is shown thus. Everything lovable is the more loved the closer it is to the lover. But men are closer to the monarch than to other princes, therefore they are most loved by him, or at least they ought to be. The first proposition is manifest if the nature of patients and agents be considered. The second *in the spirit of love* proposition is demonstrated [120] thus. Men only come into contact with other princes partwise, but with the monarch in their totality. And again, men come into contact with other princes through the monarch, and not conversely; and thus, charge of all men primarily and immediately inheres in the monarch, and in other princes only through the monarch, inasmuch as their charge is derived from that supreme charge.

Moreover, the more universal a cause [130] is the more fully has it the nature of cause; for the subordinate cause is only a cause in virtue of the superior, as is clear from the *De Causis*. And the more a cause is a cause the more does it love its effect, since such love is inherent in the cause as such. Therefore since the monarch is the most universal of mortal causes of the wellbeing of men (since the other princes, as already said, are so through him), it follows that the good [140] of men is more loved by him than by any other.

Now that the monarch has the greatest power to effect justice who doubts?—unless he be ignorant of the meaning of the word, for if one be the *monarch* he can have none to oppose him. The main sub-assumed proposition, therefore, is sufficiently expounded. Wherefore the conclusion is certain, to wit, that for the best disposition of the world it is necessary that there should be a [150] monarchy.

14. *Sub-assumed.* Dante often uses the terms 'assumed' and 'sub-assumed' [proposition] for 'major' and 'minor' [premise]. In this case the 'sub-assumed' is that 'justice is most potent under a monarch only.'

20-24. Gilbertus Porretanus (1070-1154), Bishop of Poictiers, was the author of a short treatise entitled *De sex principiis*. Aristotle in his *Categories* had enumerated ten things that can be predicated. You can predicate of anything:—(1) Its quiddity,*i.e.* what it is; (2) Its quantity, *e.g.*, how big it is or how many ; (3) Its relativity (*ad aliquid*), *e.g.*, that So-and-so is a father, or that this is the double of that (compare below, III. 12 : 44); (4) Its quality, *e.g.*, that it is pale or heavy or skilful; (5) Its action, *i.e.* what it is doing; (6) Its passion, *i.e.* what is being done to it ; (7) Its position, *e.g.*, lying or standing; (8) Its whereabouts, *e.g.*, in Thebes or Athens ; (9) Its when, *e.g.*, yesterday or to-morrow ; (10) Its habit, *e.g.*, armed or sandalled.

The first four of these 'predicaments' Aristotle worked out at length. The other six form the subject of Gilbert's treatise. It begins with the perplexing words, 'Forma est compositioni contingens, simplici et invariabili essentia consistens,' which Dante quotes. I have translated these words as I suppose Dante to have understood them, and I imagine him to mean that there are some qualities, such as gravity or levity, which are intrinsically susceptible of degree, others, such as whiteness and straightness, which are absolute. These latter cannot be more or less, intrinsically; but they may be more or less mixed. For substantial and accidental forms compare below, III. 12 : 40 ff., *note*.

It is doubtful, however, whether Dante rightly understood Gilbertus, who seems to have used 'form' as equivalent to 'predicament,' and to mean by 'composition' a concrete thing consisting of form (in the more usual scholastic sense) and matter. Albertus Magnus evidently finds this opening sentence difficult of exposition.

25, 26. *With respect to the subjects*. The *subjectum*, or thing *brought* or *thrown under* the assertion, made in a proposition, is analogous to the 'substantia' or thing that *stands under* attributes or experiences. Here, then, the subject by which whiteness is contracted is the *white thing*, the subject by which justice is contracted is the *man who practises justice*.

59-65. A prosyllogism is a syllogism the conclusion of which is one of the premises of another syllogism—in this case of the 'sub-assumed' or ' minor premise' of the syllogism in the first paragraph of this chapter.

A syllogism of the second figure is one in which the common term (in this case A) is the predicate in both premises. All syllogisms of this form must have one positive and one negative premise ; but the premises ' All B is A ' and ' only C is A ' are both in appearance positive. The negative, however, is ' intrinsic ' in the form of the subject of the minor premise ' only C.' The proposition is equivalent to ' all not C is not A,' which is a negative proposition. So at least I understand the passage.

72. The passage referred to is *Eth. Nic.* V. 4. It does not quite bear Dante out, but it establishes a special connection between one meaning of ' injustice ' and the vice of avarice.

81 ff. Aristotle (incidentally in *Eth. Nic.* VIII. 12) says something very like this. His words (as read by Dante) are : ' Non enim est rex, qui non per se sufficiens et omnibus bonis superexcellens. Talis autem nullo indiget. Utilia igitur sibiipsi quidem non utique intendet, subditis autem.' In its estimate of human nature and the motives by which it is actuated the argument seems identical with that often urged by socialists, that if adequate provision against actual want were made, the dread of poverty would cease to goad mankind, and the wolf of avarice would be slain.

The intimate bearing of all this upon the allegory of *Inferno*, I., is obvious.

126. The stress must be laid on the *collective* charge of mankind. Each monarch is only indirectly concerned with the good of other subjects than his own. Humanity *as a whole* therefore stands in immediate relation to the emperor, but only in mediated relation to the several kings.

132, 133. On the *De Causis* see *Convivio*, p. 146. Its opening words are : ' Omnis causa primaria plus est influens supra causatum suum quam causa universalis secunda.'

146, 147. *The main sub-assumed,* namely the proposition in lines 10, 11: 'Justice is most potent in a monarch only.'

CHAPTER XII

[Men are free when they can follow the goal of their own nature without being wrenched aside to serve some other purpose; and this is only the case when rulers seek to further the good of their subjects, instead of making them the slaves of their own greed. Now, as we have seen, it is only under unity of administration that rotten and tyrannical forms of government can be checked and scope be given to sound ones.]

AND the human race when most free is best disposed. This will be clear if the principle of freedom be understood. Wherefore be it known that the first principle of our freedom is freedom of choice, which many have on their lips but few in their understanding. For they get as far as saying that free choice is free judgment in matters of [10] will; and herein they say the truth; but the import of the words is far from them, just as is the case with our teachers of logic in their constant use of certain propositions, given by way of example in Logic; for instance, 'A triangle has three angles equal to two right angles.'

Therefore I say that judgment is the link between apprehension and appetite. For first a thing is apprehended, then when [20] apprehended it is judged to be good or bad, and finally he who has so judged it pursues or shuns it. If, then, the judgment altogether sets the

Freedom

secure under a monarch appetite in motion, and is in no measure anticipated by it, it is free. But if the judgment is moved by the appetite, which to some extent anticipates it, it cannot be free, for it does not move of itself, but is drawn captive by another. And hence it is that brutes cannot have free judgment because their judgments are always anticipated [30] by appetite. And hence too it may be seen that the intellectual substances whose wills are immutable, and separated souls departing from this life in grace, do not lose their freedom of choice because of the immutability of their wills, but retain it in its most perfect and potent form.

When we see this we may further understand that this freedom (or this [40] principle of all our freedom) is the greatest gift conferred by God on human nature; for through it we have our felicity here as men, through it we have our felicity elsewhere as deities. And if this be so, who would not agree that the human race is best disposed when it has fullest use of this principle? But it is under a monarch that it is most free. As to which we must know that that is free which [50] exists 'for the sake of itself and not of some other,' as the Philosopher has it in his work, *De Simpliciter Ente*. For that which exists for the sake of something else is conditioned by that for the sake of which it exists, as a road is conditioned by the goal. It is only when a monarch is reigning that the human race exists for its own sake, and not for the sake of something else. For it is only then that perverted forms of government are made straight, to wit democracies, oligarchies, and tyrannies, which force the human race [60] into slavery, (as is obvious to whosoever runs through them all), and that government is conducted by kings, aristocrats (whom they call *optimates*), and zealots for the people's liberty. For since the monarch has love of men in the highest degree, as already indicated, he will desire all men to be made good, which cannot be under perverted rulers. Whence the Philosopher in his *Politics* says, 'Under a perverted government a good man is a bad citizen, but [70] under a right one, a good man and a good citizen are convertible terms.' And such right governments purpose freedom, to wit that men should exist for their own sakes. For the citizens are not there for the sake of the consuls, nor the nation for the sake of the king, but conversely, the consuls for the sake of the citizens, the king for the sake of the nation. For just as the body politic is not established for the benefit of the laws, but the laws for the benefit of the body politic, so too they who live under the law are not ordained [80] for the benefit of the legislator, but rather he for theirs, as saith the Philosopher again in what has been left by him on the present matter. Hence it is clear that, albeit the consul or king be masters of the rest as regards the way, yet as regards the end they are their servants; and the monarch most of all, for he must assuredly be regarded as the servant of all. Hence it may begin to appear at this point how the monarch [90] is conditioned in laying down the laws by the end set before him.

The governors are servants of the governed

Therefore the human race is best disposed when under a monarchy. Whence it follows that for the well-being of the world the existence of a monarchy is necessary.

15, 16. Dante insinuates that many teachers of logic do not really understand the elementary mathematical truths which they use so freely as illustrations.

17-37. *Appetite.* The Latin *appetitus* (though sometimes used in a limited and evil sense) does not necessarily carry the limitations of the English 'appetite.' It includes any desire, however spiritual. Thus God and goodness are the supreme *appetibilia*. Compare T. C., *Purgatorio*, XVIII. : 57, *note.* This ideal relation between appetite and judgment therefore is characteristic of the freedom of heaven itself, which throws light on what is to many students the hard saying of *Paradiso*, XXVIII. 109-111, that knowledge is the primary, and love the secondary foundation of blessedness; for in the case of the angels and the blessed souls the will is perfectly free, because the appetite, or love, follows the vision of the supreme object of love. Appetite therefore is subject to judgment and is not its master.

It is interesting, however, to note that in the previous chapter (lines 91-110) the converse principle has been admitted. For the monarch's love of his people so clears his sight as to enable him to perceive the essential significance of humanity, instead of being confused by its adjuncts. 'Appetite' in a good sense therefore may after all sometimes precede and guide the judgment, though appetite, as a rule, must follow it on pain of misleading it.

31. *Intellectual substances* = angels; see above, 3: 55-59 and *note.*

42. Witte and Moore read '*sicut dixi*' = *as I have asserted it to be*, between 'is' and 'the greatest gift.' This is taken by Witte to refer to the opening words of this chapter. But the MSS of the *De Monarchia* which we actually possess read '*sicut in Paradiso Commedie jam dixi*,' or leave a space (see Witte's edition, p. 23). Of course if this were a genuine reading it would decide the question of the date of the composition of this work (see Appendix, p. 283),

and would relegate it to the last years of Dante's life. The difficulty of accepting the passage, however, is very great. Our MSS. are all of them bad. The first edition of the *De Monarchia* (Johannes Oporinus, 1559) was based on MSS. now lost, and it does not contain this reference to the *Paradiso*. Editors are agreed in rejecting it as an interpolation, and there seems to be no reason to retain the words '*ut dixi*' any more than the rest of the passage. See, on the whole question of the text, Witte's *Prolegomena* to his edition of 1874.

44. *Deities*. The original is *dii*=gods. Compare *Paradiso*, V. 123; XIII. 31; and also Psalm LXXXII. [Vulg. LXXXI.] 6; John X. 34.

49, 50. Hence the 'liberal' or 'free' arts are those which serve no practical or commercial purpose, astronomy and music for instance, but not architecture. The phrase quoted occurs in *Met*. l. 2 : 11. *De Simpliciter Ente* is only another title for the *Metaphysics*.

88-91. Compare above, 6 : 8-15*n*.

CHAPTER XIII

[No man can effectively produce a disposition in others unless he loves it for its own sake. The ruler then cannot eliminate greed from among his subjects, unless he is himself genuinely free from it and is inspired by a love of its contrary. Hence the monarch, who (as shown above) best complies with this condition, would be the best ruler.]

FURTHER, he who is himself capable of the best disposition for governing is also capable of disposing others best. For in every action the chief intent of the agent, whether acting by necessity of nature or by choice, is to unfold its

The disposition

own likeness; wherefore every agent, in so far as it acts, finds delight therein. Because, since everything that exists desires its own being, and by acting [10] the agent's being is in a certain measure expanded, delight of necessity follows; for delight always attaches to the thing desired. Therefore nothing can act unless it already is itself that which the thing acted upon is to become. Wherefore the Philosopher in his work *De Simpliciter Ente* says, 'Everything which is reduced from potentiality to actuality is reduced thereto by something which is already in actuality what that other is to become,' for if anything attempted to act under other conditions the attempt would be vain. And thus [20] may be refuted the error of such as think that by saying well and doing ill they can inform others with life and morals, not perceiving that the hands of Jacob were more persuasive than his words, albeit the former urged what was false, the latter what was true. Whence the Philosopher *Ad Nicomachum* says, ' For in what concerns passions and actions words are less convincing than deeds.' Hence also it was said from heaven to the sinner [30] David, ' Wherefore dost thou tell of my righteousness?' As much as to say, 'In vain dost thou speak, so long as thou thyself art other than that which thou speakest.' Hence we gather that he who would dispose others best must himself be best disposed.

But the monarch alone is he who is capable of being best disposed to rule. Which is thus shown: a thing is prepared for any habit or operation with ease and perfection proportioned

XIII. THE FIRST BOOK

to the absence within it [40] of anything to counteract such preparation. Whence they who have never been taught anything, come more easily and perfectly to the habit of philosophical truth than they who have been taught too early and are imbued with false opinions. Wherefore Galen well saith that such need double time for acquiring knowledge. Since, then, the monarch cannot have any occasion for greed, or at any rate can of all men have [50] least occasion thereto, as has been shown above (the which is not the case with the other princes), and since greed, in its turn, is the sole corrupter of judgment and impeder of justice, it follows that the monarch is capable either of the absolutely good disposition for governing, or at least of a higher degree thereof than others; because he amongst all others is capable of the highest degree of judgment and justice. Which two things are the chief ornaments of a legislator and an executor of law, as that most holy king [60] testified when he requested of God the things meet for a king and a son of a king. 'God!' he said, 'give thy judgment to the king and thy justice to the king's son.' *most potent in the monarch*

It is therefore rightly said, when said in the sub-assumed, that the monarch alone is he who is capable of the best disposition for ruling. Therefore the monarch alone is capable of disposing others best. Whence it follows that for the best disposition of the world [70] monarchy is necessary.

CHAPTER XIV

[Though the one supreme ruler must have no peer (for a duplication of his office would be superfluous), he must have subordinates to attend to details and to adapt the general principles of which he is the guardian to the varying requirements and circumstances of different peoples and states.]

Unity in principle AND it is better that what is capable of being done by one should be done by one than by more than one. Which is thus shown forth. Let A be the one by which a thing can be done, and let A and B be the more than one by which, in like manner, the same thing can be done. If then that same thing which is brought to pass by A and B, can be brought to pass by A alone, B is called in in vain, because nothing follows from its being called in, inasmuch as that same thing was taking [10] place before by the sole agency of A. And since every such calling in is otiose or superfluous, and everything superfluous is repugnant to God and nature, and everything repugnant to God and nature is bad (as is self-evident), it follows not only that it is better for it to be done by one if it can be, than to be done by more than one, but further that it is good for it to be done by one, and bad absolutely for it to be done by more than one.

Moreover, a thing is reckoned better for being [20] at a less distance from the best; and the end has the characteristic of best. But being done by one is less distant from the end, therefore it is better. And that it is less distant is

XIV   THE FIRST BOOK   165

shown thus : Let C be the end, A the being **Diversity** done by one, A and B the being done by more **in application** than one. It is manifest that the way from A through B to C is longer than straight from A to C. But the human race can be ruled by one supreme prince who is the monarch.

Whereanent, doubtless, we should note that [30] when we say the human race can be ruled by one supreme prince we are not to be so understood, as that every petty decision of each municipality (since even the bye-laws sometimes leave us in the lurch and themselves need direction, as is clear from the Philosopher in the fifth *Ad Nicomachum*, in his commendation of *epyekia*) could issue from him immediately. For nations, kingdoms, and cities have their special conditions [40] which ought to be regulated by different laws. For a law is a rule to direct life. And naturally the Scythians who live outside the seventh clima, and experience great inequality of days and nights, and are oppressed by an almost intolerable chill of frost, must needs be regulated in a different way from the Garamantes who live under the equinoctial circle and always have the light of day equal in length to the darkness of night, and because of the excessive [50] heat of the air cannot endure to be covered with a superfluity of garments. But it must be thus understood, that the human race in those things which are common, and are inherent in all, should be ruled by him, and guided by his common rule to peace. And this rule or law, the particular princes ought to receive from him, as the practical intellect receives the major proposition from the speculative [60] intellect, and adds

The prince and his deputies under it the particular proposition which is properly its own, and so proceeds to the particular practical conclusion. And not only is this possible to one; but it must of necessity flow from one, that all confusion concerning universal principles may be removed. And thus Moses writes in the Law that he himself did; for joining to himself the chiefs of the tribes of the sons of Israel, he relegated to them the inferior judgments, reserving to himself alone [70] the higher and more general; which more general judgments the chieftains made use of throughout their tribes according as they were applicable to each of them.

Wherefore it is better for the human race to be ruled by one than by more than one, and therefore by a monarch who is one single prince; and if better then more acceptable to God, since God always wills the better. And since when there are only two alternatives better [80] and best are the same, it follows that between 'one' and 'more than one' not only is 'one' more acceptable to God, but most acceptable. Whence it follows that the human race is best disposed when it is governed by one. And thus for the well-being of the world it is necessary that there should be a monarchy.

1-28. This is a specimen of the abuse of formal logic, which has brought undeserved discredit on mediæval thought and reasoning generally. It is obvious that it is a mere manipulating of symbols and machinery, and does not in any way advance the thought.

29-73. It is interesting to note that the systems of law annually issued, by which justice was administered in the Italian commonwealths, were avowedly based on Roman law, with such modifications or supplements as were judged necessary under the special conditions. This serves further to emphasise the fact that what Dante has in his mind when he speaks of the empire, is the enforcing of the general principles of justice embodied in the Roman law.

38. *Epyckia.* This is one of the Greek words that found their way into the Latin translations of Aristotle and were more or less cruelly mauled by the scribes. It represents ἐπιείκεια, and means 'equity.'

43. That is beyond 50° 30' north latitude. See *De Vulgari Eloquentia*, I. 8 : 3, *note*.

CHAPTER XV

[Unity, the principle of good in general, is the principle of concord (the uniform motion of many wills) in particular. Now well-regulated society must obviously be concordant, and therefore possessed by unity of will, which is only possible under a unified directing power.]

FURTHER, I affirm that 'being' and 'oneness' and 'goodness' are related in steps of priority according to the fifth sense of *prius*. For 'being' naturally precedes 'oneness' and 'oneness' naturally precedes 'good'; for that which is most existent is most one, and what is most one is most good. And the further anything is removed from the supremely existent the further is it removed from being one, and therefore from being good. Therefore [10] in every kind of things, that is best which is most one, as saith the Philosopher in his work *De Simpliciter Ente*. Whence it comes about that 'being one' is seen to be the root of 'being good,' and 'being many' the root of 'being

Being, unity, and excellence

Harmony bad.' Wherefore Pythagoras in his Correlations places 'unity' on the side of good, and 'plurality' on the side of evil, as we see in the first *De Simpliciter Ente*. Hence it may be [20] seen that sinning is naught else than despising and departing from 'unity' and seeking multiplicity. And this the Psalmist perceived when he said, 'They are multiplied in the fruit of corn and wine and oil.'

It is clear, then, that everything which is good, is good in virtue of consisting in unity. And since concord, as such, is a good, it is manifest that it consists in some [30] unity, as in its proper root. Which root we shall discover if we consider the nature or meaning of concord. For concord is a uniform movement of more wills than one. By which account it is seen that the unity of wills which is indicated by uniform motion is the root of concord or indeed is concord itself. For just as we should call a number of clods concordant because they all agree in descending [40] towards the centre, and a number of flames concordant because they all agree in ascending to the circumference, did they do this of their own will, so we call a number of men concordant because they are simultaneously moved in respect to their volitions towards a single thing; which thing is formally present in their wills, like as a single quality, to wit gravity, is formally present in the clods, and another single quality, to wit levity, in the flames. For the volitional virtue is a certain potentiality, but the kind of the apprehended good [50] is its form, the which form, like other such, being one in itself, is multiplied after

XV THE FIRST BOOK

the multiplicity of the matter that receives it, just like 'soul' and 'number' and other forms subject to composition.

of human wills under a prince

This being premised in order to establish the major premise we are about to lay down, let us proceed thus to our thesis. All concord depends on unity in wills. The human race when best disposed is [60] a concord. For as a single man when best disposed both as to mind and body is a concord, and so also a house, a city, and a kingdom, so likewise is the whole human race. Therefore the human race when best disposed depends upon a unity in wills. But this unity cannot be unless there is one will dominating and ruling all the rest to oneness; inasmuch as the wills [70] of mortals, because of the seductive delights of youth, have need of a directive principle, as the philosopher teaches in the last *Ad Nicomachum*. Nor can that one will exist unless there be a single prince of all, whose will may be the mistress and ruler of all others. Now if all the above deductions are sound, which they are, it is necessary for the best disposition of the human race that there should be a monarch [80] in the world, and therefore for the well-being of the world that there should be a monarchy.

1-24. *The fifth sense of prius.* Aristotle, in the *Catagories*, lays down five ways in which priority may be predicated. The fifth applies to such cases as this: If it is true that a man is in a certain place, then the statement that he is in that place is also true. And if the statement is true then the fact is true. But although each truth involves the other, yet the truth of the fact is in a certain sense *prior* to the truth of the statement.

Dante here maintains that existence and unity, and unity and goodness, reciprocally imply each other, but that causally existence has the precedence of unity and unity of goodness. There are several possible lines of thought and speculation which may be in his mind. In *Met.* I. 1 : 5 (to which Dante seems to be referring) Aristotle declares that experience of a number of special instances of a thing does not constitute knowleage, for which it is necessary that we should perceive the connecting principle that makes them a unity. We may suppose, then, that truth is progressively attained when multiplicity yields to unity in our thoughts. In like manner in our pursuit of every kind of good, or blessedness, we are distracted by inconsistent aims (dissipated in pursuit of 'corn and oil and wine,' losing the unity of our purposes and our own unity) because we do not see the essential unity of all real blessedness and goodness, and therefore seek it in its accidents rather than in its substance; 'goodness' then attaches to things in virtue of their essential unity, and 'badness' in virtue of their distracting diversity. Again, it is only in their unity that things really exist—Man, in the unity of body and soul, for example, or the one body in the unity of the many members. The final vision of the *Paradiso* in which the whole universe is perceived as a unity, and therefore in its intensest reality, or existence, is the apotheosis of this conception. Existence, then, involves unity, as unity involves goodness. Both members of the gradation, existence and unity, unity and good, are elaborately worked out by Boethius in the third book of the *Consolatio.*

22-24. Psalm IV. 7 (in Vulg. IV. 8), 'A fructu frumenti, vini, et olei, multiplicati sunt.'

48-54. The power of willing is a potentiality, the special volition is an act. The volition then has form and material. The volitional power is the material (which can only be *informed* by the desire for some real or supposed good); the kind or species of good sought (which gives the volition its special character) is its form. If, then, a number of wills act concordantly, the volitions are one in form, but many in individualisation by the numerical plurality of the material informed.

54. *Other forms subject to composition.* Compare above, chap. 11 : 20-23 and *note.* Angels are forms not subject to composition, hence the qualification.

55-60. The syllogism to which Dante proceeds runs thus: 'All harmony depends on unity of will; the human race in its right condition is a harmony, therefore the human race in its right condition depends on unity of will.' The object of the preceding argument has been to establish the major premise of this syllogism.

CHAPTER XVI

[All these arguments are confirmed by the fact that the Incarnation took place under the peaceful rule of the monarch Augustus. But distracted man refuses to tend his sick reason, speculative and practical, or his sick affections, by ministering these truths to them.]

ALL the reasons set forth above are confirmed by a memorable experience; namely, of that state of mortal things which the Son of God, when about to become man for man's salvation, either awaited, or, when he would, produced. For if we go through all the states and periods of man, even from the fall of our first parents, which was the point at which we turned aside on our wanderings [10], we shall find that the world was never quiet on every side except under divus Augustus, the monarch, when there was a perfect monarchy. And that in truth the human race was then blessed in the tranquillity of universal peace is witnessed by all the historians, witnessed by illustrious poets. To

The birth of Christ

under the empire this the scribe of the gentleness of Christ has likewise deigned to bear witness; and finally Paul has called that most happy state the 'fulness of time' [20]. Verily the time and all temporal things were full, for no ministry to our felicity was then vacant of its minister.

But what the state of the world has been since that seamless garment first suffered rending by the nail of covetousness we may read—would that we might not also see! O race of men in what storms and losses, in what shipwrecks must thou needs be tossed, so long as, transformed into a beast of many heads, thou [30] strivest after many things! Thou art sick in either intellect, sick in affection. Thou dost not minister to the higher intellect by reasonings that cannot be gainsaid, nor to the lower by the aspect of experience, nor even to thy affection by the sweetness of divine persuasion, when there sounds to thee through the trumpet of the Holy Spirit, 'Behold how good and how pleasant it is for brethren to dwell together in unity.'

18. *Fulness of time*, taken by Dante as a direct reference to the temporal power. Compare above, chap. 2: 5-7.

BOOK II

CHAPTER I

[How the author came to understand the meaning of Roman history; how the scornful pride of his freshly acquired knowledge gave place to the longing to spread its blessings, for the instruction of princes and for the freedom of the peoples; which must be brought about by the demonstration of the divine right of Roman rule.]

'WHEREFORE have the nations raged and the peoples meditated vain things? The kings of the earth have arisen and the princes have gathered together against the Lord and against his Christ. Let us burst their chains and cast their yoke from us.' *The Roman people*

As, when we cannot win to the face of the cause, we are wont to marvel at an unaccustomed effect, so when we have learned the cause do we look down with a kind of derision upon such as [10] are still lost in wonder. Time was that I, too, marvelled that the Roman people had been raised to supremacy on the terrestrial globe, with none to resist. For it was my thought, as I looked upon the surface only, that they had gained it by no right but merely by force of arms. But now that I have pierced with the eyes of my mind to the marrow of it, and have seen by most convincing signs that it

held sway was divine providence which effected [20] this,
not by my wonder has vanished, and a certain derisive
force contempt comes in its place when I understand how the nations muttered against the pre-eminence of the Roman people, when I see the peoples meditating vain things, as I myself was once wont to do; when, moreover, I see the grievous sight of kings and princes agreeing in this alone, to oppose their Lord and his anointed Roman prince. Wherefore, in derision, touched with a certain grief, I may take up, on behalf of [30] the glorious people and of Cæsar, the words of him who cried on behalf of the prince of heaven, 'Wherefore have the nations raged and the peoples meditated vain things? The kings of the earth have arisen and the princes have gathered together against the Lord and against his Christ.'

Yet natural love suffers not derision to endure, but (like the summer sun which scatters the mists of morning, and rising in his brightness shoots forth his rays) prefers to put derision [40] aside and pour forth the light of instruction; wherefore, to break the chains of the ignorance of such kings and princes, and to show that the human race is free from their yoke, I will exhort myself, as I follow on with the most holy prophet, and will add the words that next follow, to wit: 'Let us burst their chains and cast their yoke from us!'

And these two things will be sufficiently accomplished if [50] I carry out the second part of my present purpose, and make manifest the truth concerning the question now in hand. For if it shows that the Roman empire existed

I. **THE SECOND BOOK** 175

by right, not only shall I clear away the cloud **but of** of ignorance from the eyes of the kings and **right** princes who usurp to themselves the public government, as they falsely suppose that the Roman people did, but all mortals will recognise that they are free from the yoke of these [60] usurpers.

Now the truth concerning this question may be shown not only by the light of human reason but also by the ray of divine authority. And when these two unite in one, needs must heaven and earth consent together. Wherefore leaning upon the confidence afore noted and trusting to the testimony of reason and authority, I proceed to the solution of the second question.

To understand the point of view from which Dante's arguments throughout this book are urged we must keep constantly in mind the parallelism between the spiritual and temporal power, between the history of Palestine and the history of Rome, between their outcomes in the gospel and the system of Roman law respectively. The Roman empire existed for the elaboration and promulgation of Roman law, as the chosen people for the preparation of the gospel. Thus the proof that the Roman people were specially appointed by God for this purpose and were specifically protected by him in its execution, carries with it the permanent authority of Roman law, and of its appointed guardian, just as the miracles of the Old Testament are taken as giving divine authority to the gospel dispensation and to its ministers. Hence the logical hiatus between the proof of the mission of Rome to rule the world, and the obligation of the Italian cities to obey the nominee of the German electors, if it does not disappear, is at anyrate notably reduced; and the slenderest links of legal fiction (as that the Roman people had deputed their right to the electors, and so forth) might bridge over the chasm even to such a powerful intellect as Dante's. Granted that an institution has divine authority, arguments will always be found (and accepted) for believing that those who are *de facto* entrusted with its administration are divinely authorised. See further the *note* on chap. 3 of this book.

49. *These two*, that is, enlightening the ignorant rulers and freeing those enslaved..

65. *The confidence afore noted.* See I. 1 : 35-39.

CHAPTER II

[Since all good exists primarily in the mind of God, the norm of justice or right is to be found in his will; and since the will of God is in itself invisible, we must be content, in tracking it out, with such degree of certainty as the nature of the case allows.]

Principle of inquiry WHEREAS we have inquired concerning the truth of the first matter in dispute with such adequacy as the subject-matter allows, the truth of the second now presses for inquiry—to wit, whether it was by right that the Roman people acquired for itself the dignity of empire; and the first step of this investigation is to ascertain that truth to which the arguments of the present investigation must be reduced [10] as to their proper principle.

Be it known then that like as art exists in three grades—in the mind of the artificer, in the instrument, and in the material informed by art—so too we may regard nature in three grades. For nature is in the mind of the first mover, which is God, and further in the heaven as in the instrument by means of which the likeness of the eternal excellence is spread over fluctuating [20] matter. And as when the artificer is perfect and the instrument is in perfect order, any flaw that may occur in the form of art must be imputed to the material alone, so, since God realises the supreme perfection, and his instrument, the heaven, falls no way short of its due perfection (as is evident from our studies in philosophy concerning the heaven), it remains that whatsoever flaw there is in things below is a [30] flaw on the part of the material submitted to the action of God and the heaven, and is beside the intention both of God as the active principle of nature, and of the heaven; and that whatsoever good there is in things below, since it cannot come from the matter itself, which only exists as potentiality, must come primarily from the artificer, God, and secondarily from heaven, which is the instrument of that divine art which men commonly call nature.

The divine will

Hence it is clear that right, since it is [40] a good, exists, primarily, in the mind of God. And since everything that is in the mind of God is God (according to that word 'What was made was life in him'), and since God supremely wills himself, it follows that right is willed by God, inasmuch as it is in him. And since in God the will and what is willed are identical, it follows further that the divine will is right itself, and hence it follows again that right as manifested in things is nought else than the similitude of the divine will [50]. Whence it comes to pass that whatever is not consonant with the divine will cannot be right, and whatever is consonant with the norm of right the divine will is right. Wherefore to ask whether anything takes place by right, though the words differ, is yet nought else than to inquire whether it takes place according to what God wills. Let this, then, be our underlying principle: that whatever God wills in the society of men [60] is to be regarded as true and pure right.

Moreover we must remember that, as the philosopher teaches in the first *Ad Nicomachum*, 'Certainty is not to be looked for in the same degree in every case, but according as the nature of the subject admits of it.' Wherefore it will be sufficient ground for the arguments to proceed on, under the principle we have reached, if we investigate the right of that glorious people [70] by the aid of manifest signs and the authorities of the sages. In sooth the will of God is in itself invisible, but the invisible things of God are understood and perceived by means of things which are made. For though the seal be hidden yet does the wax stamped by it yield patent knowledge of it, hidden though it be. Nor is it marvellous if the divine will must be sought through signs, since even the human will is no otherwise perceived than by signs, save to the man himself who wills.

27, 28. *Our studies*, etc. It was an established principle, often appealed to by Thomas Aquinas, that the heavens 'pati non possunt defectum.' Probably Dante means by *ut ex his patet quæ de cælo philosophamur*, 'as we learn when studying the *De Cælo*.'

32. *God as the active principle of nature*. I have paraphrased *Dei naturantis* = 'God naturing,' where 'naturing' is a transitive participle. Compare above, l. 1 : 2*n*.

39. *Right.* See first note on chap. 5 below (p. 193).

42, 43. Note the peculiar form of the citation (John I. 3). Dr Moore says that Augustine twice cites the words in the same way.

45-47. God as the supremely existent is the supremely unified being (compare i : 15 above); and distinctions which exist in other beings are lost in him. Thus there is no distinction between his desire and the thing he desires; consequently if the thing he desires is justice, his desire or will is itself justice.

50, 53. Compare *Paradiso*, XIX. 88.

CHAPTER III

[The claim of the Roman people to universal empire is justified by their nobility, inherited from Æneas.]

I AFFIRM, then, with respect to this matter, that Nobility it was by right and not by usurpation that the Roman people vindicated to itself the office of monarch, which is called empire, over all mortals. And the first proof thereof is this: It was meet for the noblest people to be set above all others. The Roman people was the noblest. Therefore it was meet for it to be set above all others. The assumed is proved by reason [10]: since honour is a reward of virtue and promotion is honour, promotion is a reward of virtue. But it is clear that men are ennobled by merit of virtue, their own to wit, or that of their forebears. For nobility is 'virtue and ancient wealth' according to the Philosopher in the *Politics*; and according to Juvenal—

'*Nobilitas animi sola est atque unica virtus*,'[1]

[1] 'Virtue is the sole and only nobility of mind.'

of Æneas which two opinions refer to two kinds [20] of nobility, to wit, a man's own and that of his forebears.

Therefore the reward of promotion is meet for the noble, by virtue of the cause of nobility; and since rewards ought to be commensurate with merits, after that word of the gospel, 'with what measure ye mete it shall be measured to you again,' it is fitting that the most noble should be the most pre-eminent. Now the sub-assumed is supported by the testimony of the ancients. For our divine poet Virgil, throughout the *Æneid* [30] testifies, for an everlasting memorial, that the glorious king Æneas was the father of the Roman people. And Titus Livius, the choice scribe of the feats of the Romans, bears witness with him, in the first part of his volume, which takes its start from the capture of Troy. And this unconquered and most pious father was of such nobility, both on account of his own conspicuous virtue, and on account of his progenitors and his consorts (all [40] whose nobility by hereditary right devolved upon him), that I should never be able to set it forth at length, 'sed summa sequar vestigia rerum.'[1]

With respect, then, to his own proper nobility, listen to our poet when he introduces Ilioneus, in the first, uttering this entreaty:—

'*Rex erat Æneas nobis, quo iustior alter
Nec pietate fuit, nec bello maior et armis.*'[2]

Hear him again in the sixth, where, speaking

[1] 'But I will follow the main track of events.'
[2] 'Æneas was our king, than whom no other was more just in piety, nor greater in war or arms.'

III. THE SECOND BOOK 181

of the dead Misenus, who had been [50] in **by**
Hector's service in war, and after Hector's **descent**
death had given himself to the service of Æneas,
he says that this Misenus 'had followed no
lesser fortunes'; instituting a comparison between
Æneas and Hector, whom Homer glorifies above
all others, as the Philosopher tells us in what
he writes 'on morals to be shunned,' *ad
Nicomachum*.

But as concerns his hereditary nobility, we
find that each several portion of the tripartite
[60] world had ennobled him both with an-
cestors and with consorts.

For Asia had ennobled him with his more
immediate ancestors as Assaracus and the others
who ruled over Phrygia, a region of Asia, whence
our poet in the third :—

'*Postquam res Asiæ Priamique evertere gentem
Immeritam visum Superis.*'[1]

Europe again ennobled him with his most ancient
ancestor, to wit, Dardanus. Africa again en-
nobled him with his most ancient ancestress,
Electra to wit, born of King Atlas [70] of
great name. Even as our poet bears witness
of them both in the eighth, where Æneas says
thus to Evander :—

'*Dardanus Iliacæ primus pater urbis et auctor,
Electra, ut Graii perhibent, Atlantide cretus,
Advehitur Teucros ; Electram maximus Atlas
Editit, æthereos humero qui sustinet orbes.*'[2]

[1] 'When the gods had seen good to overthrow the affairs of Asia and the race of Priam, undeserving of such fate.'
[2] 'Dardanus, the first father and author of the city

and by wedlock Now, that Dardanus drew his origin from Europe our bard sings in the third when he says :—

[80] '*Est locus, Hesperiam Graii cognomine dicunt,
Terra antiqua, potens armis atque ubere glebæ.
Œnotrii coluere viri, nunc fama minores
Italiam dixisse ducis de nomine gentem.
Hae nobis propriæ sedes ; hinc Dardanus ortus.*'[1]

And that Atlas was from Africa, a mountain therein, called by his name, is witness; and that it is in Africa Orosius thus tells us in his description of the world : 'Now its farthest limit is Mount Atlas, and the islands which they call the [90] Fortunate.' By 'its' he means 'Africa's,' for thereof was he speaking.

And in like manner I find that he was ennobled by wedlock. For his first wife, Crëusa, daughter of King Priam, was of Asia, as may be gathered above from what has there been said. And that she was his wife our poet bears witness in the third, where Andromache questions the father, Æneas, about his son, Ascanius, thus :—

of Ilium, sprung, as the Greeks tell, from Atlas' daughter Electra, comes sailing to the Teucri. To Electra the mighty Atlas gave being, who bears the orbs of heaven on his shoulder.'

[1] 'A place there is—Hesperia the name given it by the Greeks—an ancient land, mighty in arms and in fertility of soil. Œnotrian swains tilled it; and now fame goes that later generations have called the nation Italy, from their leader's name. This is our proper seat, for hence sprang Dardanus.'

[100] '*Quid puer Ascanius? superatne, et vescitur aura,*
Quem tibi iam Troja peperit fumante Creusa?'[1] with three princesses

His second wife was Dido, queen and mother of the Carthaginians in Africa. And that she was his wife our same poet chants in the fourth, for he says of Dido:—

'*Nec iam furtivum Dido meditatur amorem,*
Coniugium vocat; hoc prætexit nomine culpam.'[2]

The third was Lavinia, the mother both of the Albans and Romans, daughter and [110] heir alike of King Latinus, if the testimony of our poet be true in the last, where he introduces the conquered Turnus, beseeching Æneas thus in supplication:—

'*Vicisti; et victum tendere palmas*
Ausonii videre. Tua est Lavinia coniux.'[3]

Which last wife was of Italy, the noblest region of Europe.

This, then, being noted in evidence of the sub-assumed, who is not satisfied that [120] the father of the Roman people, and therefore that people itself, was the noblest under heaven? or who will fail to note the divine predestination in that twofold concourse of blood from every

[1] 'What of the boy Ascanius? does he survive? is he pastured by the breeze? whom Crëusa brought forth to thee, when Troy was already smouldering?'
[2] 'Nor is it furtive love that Dido henceforth contemplates. She calls it wedlock, and under this name shields her fault.'
[3] 'Thou hast o'ercome! The Ausonians have seen me stretch forth my hands, a vanquished man. Thine is Lavinia to wife.'

several portion of the world upon a single man?

The whole argument of this chapter should be compared with such points as the emphasis laid in the book of Genesis upon the purchase by Abraham of the cave of Machpelah for hard cash, evidently recorded as giving the Israelites a claim to Palestine; or again, with the contention in the epistle to the Hebrews that the superiority of the New over the Old Dispensation is proved by Abraham, the father of Levi, giving tithes to Melchisedec, the representative of Christ. It is the kind of argument that depends for its value entirely upon the antecedent conviction that the series of events in question was expressly intended by God to be significant; that it constitutes in fact a kind of divine cipher which challenges us to discover its message by noting every minutest indication, and endeavouring to divine its import. This antecedent conviction was in Dante's mind with respect to Roman history, just as clearly as it was in the mind of the writers of the New Testament with respect to Israelite history, and he argued as men have always (and quite reasonably) argued in matters as to which they held it.

9. The assumed, *i.e.* major premise.

15, 16. *Politics*, IV. 8: 9. It is important to note that Dante cannot have had this passage in his mind, and therefore had not probably read it, when he wrote the fourth book of the *Convivio*. See T. C., *Convivio*, p. 427.

18. *Nobility of mind.* The passage is taken from Juvenal, VIII. 20. But it runs:—

'Tota licet veteres exornent undique ceræ
 Atria, nobilitas sola est atque unica virtus.'

Dante has added the 'animi,' which (as Dr Moore points out) helps to bring out his contrast between the two kinds of nobility. He doubtless quoted from memory.

27. *The sub-assumed, i.e.* the minor premise, 'the Roman people was the noblest.'

41, 42. *Æneid*, I. 342. But the true reading is *fastigia* = 'summits' or 'heads.' It is not Dante's custom

IV. THE SECOND BOOK

to incorporate a direct quotation as part of his own expression of his thought, as he does here.

56. *On morals to be shunned,* that is to say in the seventh book of the *Ethics,* the opening passage of which contains the celebrated division of 'morals to be shunned,' referred to in *Inferno,* XI. 82, 83. Compare T. C., *Inferno,* pp. 393, 394.

101. *Æneid,* III 339, 340. Apparently Virgil left the second line incomplete 'Peperit fumante Crëusa' was one of the attempts made to fill it in. 'Obsessa est enixa Crëusa' was another, less poetical but in better accord wlth Virgil's narrative.

CHAPTER IV

[The Roman right to rule further proved by the testimony of miracle.]

MOREOVER, that which is helped to its own per- **Miracles** fection by the support of miracles is willed by God and consequently comes to pass by right. And that this is true is evident; for as Thomas says in his third *Contra Gentiles,* 'A miracle is that which takes place through divine agency, beside the order commonly instituted in things.' Whence he himself proves that it is competent to God alone to work [10] miracles. And this is confirmed by the authority of Moses in the passage which tells how, when it came to making lice, Pharaoh's magicians—making essay of natural principles in the way of art, and failing therein—exclaimed, 'It is the finger of God.' If, then, a miracle is the immediate operation of the first agent, without the co-operation of second agents (as the said Thomas in his book above cited sufficiently proves), it follows that, when *confirmed the power* portents are worked in favour of aught, it is impious to deny [20] that that which is so favoured is provided by God, as well pleasing to him. Wherefore the pious course is to accept the contradictory, namely: The Roman empire was helped to its perfection by the support of miracles. Therefore it was willed by God, and consequently was and is by right.

But that God did show forth miracles to perfect the Roman empire is proved by the witness of illustrious authors [30]. For when Numa Pompilius, the second king of the Romans, was sacrificing, after the manner of the Gentiles, Livy, in his first part, testifies that a shield fell down from heaven into the city chosen of God. Which miracle Lucan calls to mind in the ninth of the *Pharsalia,* in describing the incredible violence of the south wind to which Lybia is subject; for he says :—

' *Sic illa profecto*
Sacrifico cecidere Numæ, quæ lecta iuventus [40]
Patricia cervice movet ; spoliaverat Auster,
Aut Boreas populos ancilia nostra ferentes.' [1]

And when the Gauls, who had already captured the rest of the city, trusting to the darkness of the night, were secretly creeping up to the Capitol, which alone remained to avert the final extinction of the Roman name, Livy and many illustrious writers bear concordant

[1] ' By such means, surely, dropped down to Numa, as he sacrificed, those shields which chosen youths shake on patrician neck. Auster or Boreas had spoiled the peoples who bore the shields that were ours.'

witness that a goose, never seen there before, of Rome
chanted the approach of the Gauls, and waked
the guards to defend the Capitol. Of which
[50] thing our poet was mindful when he de-
scribed the shield of Æneas in the eighth; for he
sings thus :—

> '*In summo custos Tarpeiæ Manlius arcis*
> *Stabat pro templo, et Capitolia celsa tenebat,*
> *Romuleoque recens horrebat regia culmo.*
> *Atque hic auratis volitans argenteus anser*
> *Porticibus, Gallos in limine adesse canebat?*' [1]

And when the nobleness of Rome, under
pressure of Hannibal, had fallen so low that for
the final [60] obliteration of the affairs of Rome
nought was lacking save that the Poeni should
trample on the very city, Livy, in the *Punic War*,
tells, amongst other gests, that a sudden and in-
tolerable hailstorm so dismayed them that the
victors might not follow up their victory.

And was not Clœlia's passage miraculous,
when, as Porsenna was besieging the city, she, a
woman and a captive, broke her chains, supported
by the wondrous aid of God, and swam across
the Tiber, as almost all the scribes of the affairs
of Rome [70] record to her glory?

Thus was it altogether fitting that he should
do who from eternity provided for all things in
symmetrical beauty; that he who, when visible,

[1] 'On the summit of the Tarpeian citadel Manlius
stood on guard before the temple, and held the
heights of the Capitol; while the new-reared palace
was rough with the thatch of Romulus. And here,
wrought in silver, flying about the golden porticoes,
the goose chanted of the Gauls already on the
threshold.'

was about to do miracles as testimony to things invisible, should, when invisible, do the like in testimony of things visible.

41. *Patrician neck*. The Salian priests, who performed the shield dance with the sacred shields (*ancilia*), were all patricians. Note that Lucan, who is cited by Dante as an authority for the miracle, really gives a rationalistic turn to the story. The wind tore off from other nations the *ancilia* that were by destiny the property of the Romans ('our *ancilia*') and blew them to Rome!

55. The difficulties presented by this line (*Æneid*, VIII. 654) led Heyne to doubt its authenticity. Why '*recens*'?

71-75. Before God became visible in Christ, he (himself invisible) worked miracles in favour of the visible order upheld by the empire. When on earth in the person of Christ he (himself visible) worked miracles in favour of the invisible order upheld by the Church. Such symmetries were much thought of in the Middle Ages. Anselm brings many of them forward as arguments in the *Cur Deus Homo*. His interlocutor, Boso, objects that they are like a beautiful picture painted on air or water, and require some solid surface of argument to put behind them and paint them upon.

CHAPTER V

[The public spirit manifested by the Romans is an indication that in acquiring the empire of the world they were contemplating the goal of right.]

Rome's citizens
AGAIN, whosoever purposes the good of the commonwealth, purposes the goal of right. And that this follows is shown thus: Right is 'a real and personal proportion of man to man, which, when preserved, preserves human society,

and when infringed infringes it.' (For the well-known description of the *Digests* does not tell us what the essence of right is, but describes it by declaring what it is in practice.) If, then, the above [10] definition contains a true account of what and why right is, and if the end of every society is the common good of those associated, it follows of necessity that the end of every system of right must be some common good, and that it is impossible that there should be a system of right that does not contemplate a common good. Wherefore Tully well says in the first of the *Rhetoric :* ' The laws are ever to be interpreted to the good of the commonwealth.' For if the laws are not directed to the good of those [20] under the law, they are laws in name alone and cannot be laws in fact. For laws ought mutually to bind men for common advantage, wherefore Seneca well says of law, in his book *De Quatuor Virtutibus,* ' Law is the bond of human society.' It is plain, then, that whosoever contemplates the good of the commonwealth contemplates the end of right. If, then, the Romans contemplated the good of the commonwealth, it will be true [30] to say that they contemplated the end of right.

aimed at the public good

Now that the Roman people, in subjecting the terrestrial globe to itself, did contemplate the aforesaid good, their deeds declare; for in those deeds, banishing all greed, which is ever hostile to the common weal, and loving universal peace, with liberty, that people, holy, compassionate, and glorious, is seen to have taken no thought for its own advantage so long as it might

The Roman state look to the weal of the human [40] race. Whence it is well written, 'The Roman empire springs from the fount of compassion.'

But since nought of the intention of any agent who has free choice can be known to any other than the agent himself, save by means of external signs, and since all statements are to be investigated in accordance with the nature of their subject-matter, as was said before, we shall have done enough on this point if we indicate the indubitable [50] signs of the intention of the Roman people, both in colleges and in individual persons.

As concerns colleges, which seem to be a kind of connecting link between individuals and the commonwealth, the sole authority of Cicero in the second *De Officiis* suffices: 'As long,' he says, 'as the supremacy of the commonwealth rested on benefits, not on wrongs, wars were waged either on behalf of allies or for supremacy, and the results of the wars were either mild or necessary. The senate was the port and refuge [60] of kings, of peoples, and of nations. Our magistrates and commanders sought their chief praise in defending the provinces and allies, justly and in good faith. Wherefore their rule deserved rather to be called the protection than the command of the world.' Thus Cicero.

Concerning individual persons I shall proceed summarily. Can it be said [70] that they sought not the common good, who by sweat, by penury, exile, privation of children, loss of limb, and finally by the offering up of their very lives, sought to advance the public good?

Did not that great Cincinnatus leave us a

holy example of freely laying down office at the proper term, when, having been taken from the plough and made dictator (as Livy [8c] tells), after his victory and after his triumph he restored the sceptre of command to the consuls and returned, of his own free will, to sweat at the plough-tail after his oxen? In truth Cicero, disputing against Epicurus, in what he wrote *de Fine Bonorum*, recorded to his praise this deed, when he said, 'And thus it was that our ancestors took that great Cincinnatus from his plough to make him dictator.' *Cincinnatus, Fabricius, Camillus*

[90] Did not Fabricius give us a lofty example of resisting greed when, in the fidelity that held him to the Commonwealth, poor as he was, he scoffed at the great pile of gold offered to him, and having scoffed thereat and uttered words worthy of himself, contemned and refused it? His memory, too, our poet confirmed in the sixth, when he sang:—

'*Parvoque potentem Fabricium.*' [1]

[100] Was not Camillus a memorable example to us of how to set the laws above our own advantage? For he (as Livy tells), himself under sentence of exile, had freed his fatherland from siege and had restored to Rome spoils including her own; and when the whole people called him back, he departed from the sacred city, nor returned thither until leave to reimpatriate himself was brought him by authority of the senate. And this great-souled man the

[1] 'And Fabricius, mighty on his little.'

Brutus, Mucius, the Decii, Cato

poet commends [110] in the sixth, where he speaks of '*referentem signa Camillum.*' [1]

Did not that first Brutus show us how sons and all others are to be held of less account than the freedom of the fatherland? For Livy says that, when consul, he adjudged to death his own sons for conspiring with the enemy. Whose glory is kept fresh in the sixth of our poet, when he sings of him:—

'*Natosque pater nova bella moventes* [120]
Ad poenam pulchra pro libertate vocabit.' [2]

What did not Mucius tell us we must dare for our fatherland when he had fallen upon Porsenna unawares, and then because his hand had erred, gazed upon it in the flames, while it was still his own, with the same countenance with which he might have beheld the torture of a foe? To which Livy, too, bears wondering testimony.

Next come those most sacred victims, the Decii, who for the public weal [130] laid down their devoted souls; as Livy tells, glorifying them not after their deserts but after his own powers. And that sacrifice, beyond narration, of the severest champion of true liberty, Marcus Cato. Of these the former two shrank not from the shades of death for their country's weal; and the latter, to kindle the love of liberty in the world, gave proof of how dear he held her by preferring to depart from life a

---

[1] 'Camillus bringing back the standards.'
[2] 'And his own sons, in that they stir fresh wars, shall the father call to punishment, for lovely liberty.'

free man rather than remain alive bereft of [140] liberty. Of all these the glorious means grow warm again under the voice of Tully in what he writes *de Fine Bonorum*. For Tully says of the Decii: 'When Publius Decius, the consul, first of his family, devoted himself, and with loosened rein dashed right into the ranks of the Latins, was he thinking aught of his pleasures where and when he should reap them? When he knew that he must die upon the spot and sought that death with a more burning [150] passion than that with which Epicurus held we should seek pleasure! But had that deed of his not rightly been extolled, his son, in his fourth consulship, would never have imitated it; nor would his son again, waging war, as consul, with Pyrrhus, have fallen in that battle and offered himself a third victim for the commonwealth in unbroken family succession.' And in what he wrote *de Officiis*, he said of Cato, 'The cause of Marcus Cato [160] was no other than that of the rest, who surrendered to Cæsar in Africa; but yet perchance it would have been counted a fault in the rest had they slain themselves, because their life was lighter and their ways were less austere: but since nature had given to Cato a weight of character past belief, which he had confirmed by unbroken constancy, ever remaining true to the purpose and resolve which he had taken, for him it was more fitting to die than to look upon the face [170] of a tyrant.'

The Decii and Cato

Throughout this chapter (and the whole Book) the word *jus* presents some difficulty to the translator. The German *Recht* is its exact equivalent; but we have no English word that means at once 'right,' 'code, or body of legislation,' and 'law, or justice.'

3-9. The source of this definition of *jus* has not, I believe, been identified. It was unknown to Witte. Church calls attention to Aristotle, *Eth. Nic.* V. 6, 8, ' Est ergo justum proportionale quiddam.' The description at the beginning of the *Digests*, here referred to, is ' Jus est ars boni et æqui '='Right is the art of the good and just.'

24. The work *De Quatuor Virtutibus* was ascribed to Seneca (T. C., *Convivio*, p. 185).

41. The phrase *Romanum imperium de fonte nascitur pietatis* is of unknown origin. It was current in Dante's time, and occurs in the legend of Sylvester and Constantine (to which Dante refers in *Inferno*, XXXVII. 94, and below, III. 10 : 1-6) as given in the *Legenda Aurea* (T. C., *Golden Legend*, vol. ii. p. 199).

52. *Colleges*, of course, means ' sets of colleagues,' *e.g.*, the senate, and the staff of civil administrators, or of military officers. Association in such colleges is a kind of link or step by which men are made to feel their connection with the wider fellowship of the commonwealth.

68-170. Compare *Convivio*, IV. 5. Both passages were suggested by Virgil (*Æneid*, VI. 756-853).

105. *Including her own.* He had spoiled the Gauls, who had previously spoiled the Romans. A part of the spoils therefore were the former possessions of the Romans themselves.

132-139. Compare *Purgatorio*, I. 71-75. The symbolic aspect of Cato's suicide, as a vindication of liberty, so completely overwhelmed all other considerations in Dante's mind, that he thought of him neither as guilty of the crime of self-slaughter nor as the foe of civil order as represented by the founder of the empire, Julius Cæsar, but simply as the perfect representative of the triumph of the spirit over the flesh, and the perfect vindicator of that true ' freedom ' which consists in the reason retaining the absolute sway over the appetite. Compare above, I. 12 : 17-37. Lucan's treatment of Cato in the *Pharsalia* might be quoted *in extenso* to illustrate this view. It is from these considerations that we must explain

Cato's position in purgatory, and Dante's idea that he shared in the salvation vouchsafed to Christians alone (compare *Paradiso*, XIX. 103-105).

CHAPTER VI

[The goal of right cannot really be contemplated save by those who have right on their side. Therefore the Roman people, who contemplated the goal of right, must have had right on their side.]

So now two things have been set forth: firstly, that whosoever contemplates the good of the commonwealth contemplates the end of right. Secondly, that the Roman people in subjecting the world to itself contemplated the public good. We may now argue to our thesis thus: Whosoever contemplates the end of right advances with right. The Roman people in subjecting the world to itself contemplated the end of right [10], as is manifestly proved in the foregoing chapter, by the instances cited above. Therefore the Roman people, in subjecting the world to itself, did so by right, and consequently took to itself the dignity of empire by right. *The Roman empire rests on right*

And for this conclusion to be reached from premises all of which are manifest we have to prove the proposition that whosoever contemplates the end of right advances with right. Now to make this evident we must note that [20] everything exists for the sake of some end, else it were superfluous, which may not be, as was said above. And like as every thing exists for its proper end, so every end has its proper thing whereof it is the end. Wherefore it is im-

The proper end of right possible that any two things, as two, can in their own name contemplate the same end. Else there would follow the same inadmissible result, namely, that one or the other would be in vain. Since, then, as already shown [30], there is a certain end of right, it follows that in asserting that end to exist we have asserted right to exist, since it is the proper and essential effect of right. And since it is impossible in any sequence to have the antecedent without the consequent (man, for instance, without animal), as is clear by construction and destruction, it is impossible to pursue the end of right without right, since everything stands to its proper end in the relation of consequent to antecedent. For it is impossible [40] to attain a healthy state of the members without health. Wherefore it is abundantly plain that he who contemplates the end of right must needs contemplate it rightfully. Nor does that useful rejoinder drawn from the words of the Philosopher, where he treats of *eubulia*, apply to this case. For the Philosopher says, ' But it may also happen that a sound conclusion is reached by a false syllogism, though not soundly, the middle term being equivocal.' For if a true [50] conclusion is ever drawn from false premises it is but incidentally, the truth being imported by the mere words of the conclusion; for of itself what is true never follows from what is false. But words which stand for what is true may well follow from words which stand for what is false.

And the like holds in doings. For although a thief should relieve a poor man from the proceeds of a theft, yet this is not to be called an alms, albeit it is such an action as would have **Semblance and reality** had the form of alms had it been done from the man's [60] own substance. So with the end of right. For were anything professing to be the end of right obtained unrighteously, it would only be the end of right (that is to say, the common good) in the same sense in which an offering made from ill-acquired sources is an alms. And thus, since in the proposition we are speaking of the end of right really being there, and not only appearing to be there, the objection is void. We have therefore established the point in question.

> Dante has proved that the Roman people contemplated the goal of right or justice, and has now to justify from this the inference that they had right or justice on their side. That justice is calculated to secure the end of justice is obvious, but not equally obvious that this end cannot be secured in any other way. Dante attempts to establish his point by two steps, first by showing that where the effect is the proper (that is the exclusive) result of its special cause, you can infer the presence of the cause from the effect, as surely as you can infer the presence of the effect from the cause; so that in this case you can as certainly argue that the man who contemplates the goal of right has right on his side as you can argue that if Socrates is a man, he is an animal, though the *form* of the argument if generalised would appear to involve a fallacy, like that of arguing that if Socrates is an animal he is a man. In the second place Dante argues that he has shown that the Romans really were contemplating the end of right as such, and not merely contemplating on other grounds an end which chanced to be the end of right; so that it was in truth the end *proper* to right, and only to be reached by right that they contemplated. Thus its presence really does argue the presence of right.
>
> 43 ff. The passage in Aristotle (*Eth. Nic.* VI. 10)

on εὐβουλία, or good advice, says you cannot call advice good because it happens to turn out well, any more than you can be sure that a syllogism is sound because it yields a right conclusion. Dante anticipates the possibility of its being said in like manner: 'The Roman people may have *happened* to hit the goal of right, but without any real alliance with right.' To this he replies that in that case they would no more have reached the goal of right than a thief who should give to the poor would have done an alms.

CHAPTER VII

[A public body that claims the right to exercise any function must show that it has effective power to do so. Hence when any magistracy is instituted its power to perform the duties imposed on it is considered and secured. And since nature also (not less than man but more) observes this balance between faculty and opportunity (which balance is indeed the natural foundation of all justice), it follows that there is a harmony between natural powers and natural function or vocation in every case, so that to preserve the natural order must be right. Now for the full accomplishment of all the purpose of humanity (as we have already seen) various capacities in various races and individuals are needed; and such nature in her care provides. Amongst others she provided the Roman people with a faculty for ruling, and with the balancing opportunity or duty of ruling; hence the Roman people, in subduing the world to its sway, was obeying nature, and had right on its side.]

Nature and the providence of man AND what nature has ordained, it is right to maintain. For nature in the provision she makes does not fall short of the providence of man, else the effect would surpass the cause in excel-

VII. THE SECOND BOOK

lence, which is impossible. But we perceive **Function** that when colleges are instituted, not only is **and** the order of the colleagues with respect to each **faculty** other considered by him who institutes them, but also the capacity for exercising their office. And this amounts to [10] a consideration of the limitation of the right of the college or ordered institution, for right does not extend beyond power. Therefore nature, in what she ordains, does not fall short of this provision. Whence it is clear that nature orders things with reference to their faculties, which reference is the foundation of right laid down in things by nature. Hence it follows that the natural order in things cannot be preserved without right, since the basis of right [20] is inseparably bound up with that order. Necessarily, therefore, the preservation of such order is right.

The Roman people was ordained by nature to command. Which is thus made clear: Just as he would fall short of the perfection of art who should consider the final form alone, but should take no heed for the means by which to attain to the form, so would nature if she contemplated only the universal form of the [30] divine similitude in the universe, and neglected the means thereto. But nature lacks no perfection, since she is the work of the divine intelligence. Therefore she contemplates all the means by which the final goal of her intention is approached.

Since, then, there exists a goal of the human race, which is, in its turn, a necessary means to the accomplishment of the universal goal of nature, it follows that nature contemplates it.

Diversity of gifts Wherefore [40] the philosopher does well to show in the second *De Naturali Auditu* that nature always acts with a view to the end. And since nature cannot attain this goal by means of a single man (since the operations needful thereto are many, requiring multiplicity in the operators), nature must of necessity produce a multiplicity of men, ordained for diverse operations; to which, in addition to the influence [50] from above, the virtues and properties of places here below do much contribute. Thus we see that not only individual men, but peoples, are some of them apt by nature to rule and others to be subject and to serve, as the Philosopher sets forth in what he has written *de Politicis*. And for such as these last, even as he says, it is not only expedient to be ruled, but also just, even though they be forced thereto.

And if these things are so, it is not to be doubted [60] that nature ordained in the world a place and a people for universal command; else she would have been lacking to herself, which is impossible. Now what this place and what this people were is sufficiently manifest from what has been said above and what will be said below, to wit, Rome and her citizens or people. The which our poet too has touched upon right subtly in the sixth, introducing Anchises admonishing Æneas, the father of the Romans [70], thus:—

' *Excudent alii spirantia mollius æra,*
 Credo equidem; vivos ducent de marmore vultus,
 Orabunt causas melius, cælique meatus
 Describent radio, et surgentia sidera dicent :

VII. THE SECOND BOOK 201

Tu regere imperio populos, Romane, memento ;   The
Hæ tibi erunt artes, pacisque imponere morem,   Roman
Parcere subiectis et debellare superbos.' [1]   people born to command

And the disposition of the place he subtly touches on in the fourth, when he introduces Jove discoursing to [80] Mercury concerning Æneas, after this fashion :—

' *Non illum nobis genitrix pulcherrima talem*
Promisit, Graiumque ideo bis vindicat armis :
Sed fore qui gravidam imperiis, belloque frementem
Italiam regeret.' [2]

Wherefore it has been sufficiently urged that the Roman people was ordained by nature for command. Therefore the Roman people, in subjecting the world to itself, attained to empire by right.

44 ff. Compare with this passage in particular and with the whole of this chapter, *Paradiso*, VIII. 100 ff.

---

[1] ' Others shall beat out the breathing bronze more softly, I do well believe it ! And shall draw living features from the marble ; shall plead causes better, and trace with the rod the movements of the sky, and tell of the rising stars. Roman ! do thou be mindful how to sway the peoples with command. These be thy arts ; to lay upon them the custom of peace, to spare the subject and fight down the proud.'

[2] ' Not such did his fairest mother promise us that he should be — twice rescuing him therefore from Grecian arms,—but that he should be the man to rule o'er Italy, pregnant with empires, and snorting war.'

CHAPTER VIII

[OF the judgments of God open and hidden : of judgements open to reason, and judgments open to faith ; of hidden judgments, revealed in sundry fashions; of revelation through the ordeal of combat, and the ordeal of rivalry.]

Manifest and hidden judgments AGAIN, rightly to hunt down the truth of our inquiry we must note that the divine judgment in affairs is sometimes manifest to men and sometimes hidden. And it may be manifest in two senses, that is to say discernible by reason or by faith. For there are some judgments of God to the which human reason may attain on its own [10] feet; as to this, that a man should expose himself for the weal of his country. For if the part ought to expose itself for the weal of the whole, then (since man is a certain part of the city-state, as the Philosopher shows in his *Politics*) man ought to expose himself, as the less, for the sake of his country, as the greater good. Wherefore the Philosopher *Ad Nicomachum*, 'For it is lovable [to secure a benefit] to one alone, but better and more divine [to secure it] to the people and city.' Now this [20] is a judgment of God; else human reason, in its rectitude, would not follow the intention of nature, which is impossible.

There are also certain judgments of God to which human reason, albeit unable to attain of its proper strength, is nevertheless raised by dint of faith in what is said to us in the sacred writings ; as for instance this : That no one, however perfect in the moral and intellectual virtues, both as to [30] disposition and practice, **Judg-** may be saved without faith, if he have never **ments** heard aught of Christ. For human reason of **manifest to faith or** itself cannot see that this is just, but helped by **revealed** faith it may. For it is written *ad Hebræos*, **by ordeal** 'Without faith it is impossible to please God.' And *in Levitico*, 'Any man of the house of Israel who shall slay an ox or a sheep or a goat in the camp [40], or outside the camp, and shall not bring it as an oblation to the Lord at the door of the tabernacle, shall be guilty of blood.' The door of the tabernacle is a figure of Christ, who is the door of the eternal conclave, as may be gathered from the Gospel: the slaughter of animals is a figure of human works.

That judgment of God is hidden, to which human reason can attain neither by the law of nature nor by the law of Scripture, but sometimes by special grace, which may come to pass in divers [50] ways, sometimes by simple revelation, sometimes by revelation through the intervention of some ordeal: by simple revelation in two ways, either by the spontaneous act of God, or at the instance of prayer. By the spontaneous act of God in two ways, either expressly or by a sign. Expressly, as the judgment against Saul was revealed to Samuel. By a sign, as God's judgment concerning the deliverance of the sons of Israel was revealed to Pharaoh by signs [60]. At the instance of prayer, as he knew who said in the second *Paralipomenon*, 'When we know not what we should do, this only have we left, to turn our eyes to thee.'

Judgment by lot and by contest By the intervention of ordeal in two ways: either by lot or by contest [*certamen*]. For the word 'to contend' [*certare*] is derived from 'making certain' [*certum*]. The judgment of God is sometimes revealed to man by lot, as appears in the substitution of Matthias, in the *Acts of the Apostles* [70]. By contest the judgment of God is revealed in two ways, either by clash of strength, as when a pair of champions contend (which kind are called combatants), or by the strife of rivals, each of whom strains to get first to some mark, as happens in the contests of athletes running for a prize. The first of these ways was figured amongst the Gentiles in that [80] combat between Hercules and Antæus, of which Lucan makes mention in the fourth of the *Pharsalia* and Ovid in the ninth *De Rerum Transmutatione*. The second was figured amongst them by Atalanta and Hippomenes, in the tenth *De Rerum Transmutatione*.

Neither should it be overlooked that, in these two ways of contending, it so stands that in the one they who contend may impede each other without wrong, to wit the [90] champions in a combat; but in the other not. For athletes should not foul one another, albeit our poet seems to have thought otherwise in the fifth when he makes Euryalus receive a prize, whereas Tully in the third *De Officiis* more rightly disallows it, herein following the opinion of Chrysippus; for he says: 'Chrysippus declares with the neatness that so often distinguishes him, *He who runs a course should strive and strain with his utmost force to* [100] *win, but should in no wise trip him up with whom*

he is contending.' And now, having made these *On foul-*
distinctions, in this chapter, we may draw two *ing an ad-*
effective arguments for our thesis from them; *versary*
to wit, one from the ordeal of athletes and
another from the ordeal of champions; the
which I will follow out in the next following
chapters.

61. *Paralipomenon,* i.e. *Chronicles.*

CHAPTER IX

[The judgment of God as to the empire of the world
was revealed in the failure of all other attempts
to gain it, to which history testifies, and the
success of the Romans, which is vouched by the
authority of pagan and Christian scriptures.]

THAT people, then, which prevailed when all were *Aspirants*
contending for the empire of the world, pre- *to empire*
vailed by divine judgment. For since the settle-
ment of the universal contention must engage
God's care more deeply than the settlement of
a particular contention, and since in certain
particular contentions the divine judgment is
asked by the athletes, according to the well-
known proverb, 'To whom God has made the
grant, to him let Peter add the blessing,' there
is no doubt but that success amongst the athletes
contending for [10] empire of the world must
have followed the judgment of God. Now it
was the Roman people which prevailed when
all were striving for empire; which will be
manifest if we consider the athletes, and consider

Ninus, also the prize or goal. The prize or goal was
Vesoges, supremacy over all mortals, which is what we
Cyrus mean by empire. But this befell to none save
to the Roman people, which people was not [20]
only the first but the only one to reach the goal
of the contest, as will immediately be shown.

For the first amongst mortals who panted after
this prize was Ninus, King of the Assyrians; and
though, together with the partner of his bed,
Semiramis, he strove in arms for the empire of
the world, through the course of ninety years and
more (as Orosius reports), and subdued all Asia
to himself, yet were not the western parts of the
world ever subject to them [30]. Of these
two, Ovid makes mention in the fourth, where
he says *in Pyramo* :—

' *Coctilibus muris cinxisse Semiramis orbem ;* ' [1]

and below :—

' *Conveniant ad busta Nini lateantque sub umbra.*' [2]

Secondly, Vesoges, King of Egypt, aspired to
this prize; and although he harried south and
north in Asia (as Orosius records), yet never did
he secure the half part of the world. Nay [40],
rather, nigh midway between the starters and
the goal, he was flung back from his rash emprise
by the Scythians.

Next, Cyrus, king of the Persians, attempted
the same; who having destroyed Babylon and
transferred the empire thereof to the Persians,
ere he had made trial of western regions, laid

---

[1] 'Semiramis girt the circle with walls of brick.'
[2] 'They are to meet at the tomb of Ninus, and are to lie concealed beneath the shade.'

down his life and his project together at the hands of Tamiris, queen of the Scythians.   **Xerxes, Alexander**

But after these, Xerxes, son of Darius, and [50] King of the Persians, invaded the world with so great multitude of nations, and with so great might that he spanned with a bridge the passage of the sea that parts Asia from Europe betwixt Sestos and Abydos; of which marvellous work Lucan was mindful in the second of the *Pharsalia*, for there he sings:—

'*Tales fama canit tumidum super æquora Xerxem
   Construxisse vias*';[1]

Yet finally miserably repelled from his [60] attempt, he failed to attain the prize.

Besides these, and after them, Alexander, the Macedonian king, drawing nearest of all to the palm of monarchy, forewarned the Romans by his ambassadors to surrender to him; but or ever their answer came, as Livy tells us, he collapsed in mid-course, in Egypt. Concerning whose tomb, which is in those parts, Lucan bears witness in the eighth, inveighing [70] against Ptolemy, King of Egypt, saying:—

'*Ultima Lageæ stirpis perituraque proles
Degener, incestæ sceptris cessure sorori,
Quum tibi sacrato Macedo servetur in antro.*'[2]

'O thou depth of the riches both of the wisdom and knowledge of God,' who would

---

[1] 'Such paths, fame chants, proud Xerxes paved across ths seas.'

[2] 'Last and expiring offspring of the stock of Lagus! Degenerate, and soon to yield the sceptre to thine incestuous sister; although the Macedonian be guarded by thee in the consecrated cave!'

Rome alone attains not lay his hand upon his mouth before thee! For, as Alexander strove to trip up his Roman rival in the course, thou—that his rashness might proceed [80] no farther—didst snatch him from the contest.

But that Rome attained the palm of so great a prize is proved by many testimonies. For our poet says in the first:—

' *Certe hinc Romanos olim volventibus annis,
Hinc fore ductores, revocato a sanguine Teucri,
Qui mare, qui terras omni ditione tenerent.*' [1]

And Lucan in the first:—

' *Dividitur ferro regnum, populique potentis
Quæ mare, quæ terras, quæ totum possidet orbem* [90]
Non cepit fortuna duos.' [2]

And Boethius in the second, discoursing of the prince of the Romans, speaks thus:—

' *Hic tamen sceptro populos regebat
Quos videt condens radios sub undas
Phœbus extremo veniens ab ortu,
Quos premunt septem gelidi triones,
Quos notus sicco violentus æstu
Torret, ardentes recoquens arenas.*' [3]

---

[1] 'Verily as years roll on, hence shall spring the Romans; hence the leaders, from the blood of Teucer that lives again, who shall hold sea and land in all-embracing sway.'

[2] 'The kingdom is cleft by the sword, and the fortune of the mighty race that holds possession of the sea, the lands, ay, the whole orb, was too narrow to contain two men.'

[3] 'He ruled under his sceptre the peoples whom Phœbus sees as he plunges his rays beneath the waves,

IX. **THE SECOND BOOK** 209

This witness too does Luke [100], the scribe the prize of Christ, who speaketh all things true, uphold sought in that part of his discourse: 'There went out by all an edict from Cæsar Augustus that the universal world should be enrolled.' In which words we may clearly learn that the universal jurisdiction of the world then pertained to the Romans.

From all which things it is manifest that when all were contending for empire of the world the Roman people prevailed. Therefore it was by divine judgment that it so prevailed; and [110] therefore it obtained such empire by the divine judgment; which is to say that it obtained it by right.

31. *In Pyramo.* That is to say 'in the passage concerning Pyramus.' The mode of citation is the same as that in Luke xx. 37, where Moses is said to have called the Lord the God of Abraham, 'in the Bush.'

32. *Orbem.* So Witte reads, without noting any variant. But the usual text in Ovid (*Met.* IV. 58) gives *urbem*; and so Dr Moore reads here.

40. *The starters.* Dante uses the word *athlothetæ*, which he got from the Latin translation of Aristotle (*Eth. Nic.* I. 4, 5). It means the judges of the contest who sat at that end of the stadium from which the competitors started and to which they also returned. But from the context, and from the commentary of Thomas Aquinas, Dante would understand them to be the starters only, and would suppose that the race was run to the other end of the course.

65. *In Egypt.* Alexander really died in Babylon. Now Cairo was called Babylon in mediæval times, and Dr Moore suggests a confusion between the two Ṛ ˙ lons on Dante's part. It is a fact, however, that ₐₗ.ₑxander's tomb was in Alexandria. Perdiccas was

---

and as he rises in extremest east; whom the seven chill oxen press, whom the mighty south wind scorches with heat, baking the burning sands.'

possessed of his body, and on an expedition to Egypt he was robbed of it by Ptolemy Lagi, who placed it in a tomb in Alexandria. Perhaps we need go no further than to suppose that Dante took for granted that Alexander had died where he was buried.

66. *As Livy tells us.* There is no such statement in Livy. On the contrary he says (IX. 18) that he does not suppose the Romans had ever heard of Alexander. Dante seems almost to use 'Livy' as a general term for Roman history, much as we call geometry 'Euclid.' On the sources of this particular story, see Witte's edition of the *De Monarchia*, p. 71.

CHAPTER X

[The ordeal of single combat when duly safeguarded may be held to reveal the judgment of God.]

The Ordeal
MOREOVER, what is acquired by ordeal is acquired by right. For wheresoever human judgment is at fault, either because it is involved in the darkness of ignorance or because there is no presiding judge, then, lest justice should go to lea, we must have recourse to him who so loved her as himself to meet her claim with his own blood, in death. Hence the psalm [10], 'Just is the Lord, and deeds of justice hath he loved.' Now this is what takes place when by the free assent of either side, not in hatred but in love of justice, the divine judgment is sought through means of mutual clash of strength, alike of mind and body. Which clash, since it was first tried in the single combat of one to one, we call *duellum*.

But we must ever take heed that like as, when it is a question of war, all means should first [20] be tried in the way of award, and only in the last resort should the way of battle **Its formal** be tried (as Tully and Vegetius agree in saying, **charac-** the one *in Re Militari*, the other *in Officiis*), **teristics** and like as in medical treatment, everything else should be tried before steel and fire, and they only in the last resort; so when every other way of finding judgment in a dispute has been exhausted, we are to recur in the last instance to this remedy, forced by a [30] kind of compulsion of justice.

There are, then, two formal characteristics of the ordeal; one that has just now been spoken of; the other that was touched upon above, to wit that the contenders or champions should enter the palæstra, not in hate or love, but in sole zeal for justice, with common consent. And therefore Tully spoke well in dealing with this matter, for he said: ' But wars, the aim of which is the crown of empire [40], should be waged less bitterly.'

But if the formal characteristics of the ordeal are preserved (else were it no ordeal) they who, under compulsion of justice, are gathered together by common consent in zeal for justice—are they not gathered together in the name of God? And if so, is not God in their midst, since he himself promises as much in the gospel? And if God is present, is it not impious to think that justice may succumb?—justice whom [50] he so loves as is forenoted above! And if justice cannot succumb in ordeal, is not that which is acquired by ordeal acquired by right?

This truth even the Gentiles recognised before the trumpet of the gospel had sounded, when they sought judgment from the fortune of

Its validity recognised by Pyrrhus ordeal. Whence that Pyrrhus who was ennobled by the character of the Æacidæ, as well as by their blood, when the legates of the Romans came to him [60] concerning the redemption of captives, answered well:—

> '*Nec mi aurum posco, nec mi pretium dederitis ;*
> *Non cauponantes bellum, sed belligerantes,*
> *Ferro, non auro, vitam cernamus utrique.*
> *Vosne velit, an me regnare Hera, quidve ferat sors,*
> *Virtute experiamur. Et hoc simul accipe dictum :*
> *Quorum virtuti belli fortuna pepercit,*
> *Eorundem me libertati parcere certum est.*
> *Dono ducite.*' [1]

[70]. Thus Pyrrhus. By Hera he meant fortune, which agency we better and more rightly call the divine providence. Wherefore let the champions beware of taking up a cause for a price; since then it should not be called an ordeal but a mart of blood and unrighteousness. Nor in such case are we to think of God as the present judge, but rather that ancient foe who had stirred up the strife. If they would be champions, and not hucksters [80] of blood and of unrighteousness, let them ever have before their eyes, as they enter the palæstra, that

---

[1] 'Neither do I ask for gold nor shall ye render me a price. Not as hucksters of war, but as warriors, with steel and not with gold let us decide the issue of life to either side. Whether Hera will have you or me to rule, or what fate has in store, let us assay in valour. And take this word as well: whose valour the fortune of war hath spared, their liberty have I decreed to spare. Take them for naught.'

THE SECOND BOOK

Pyrrhus who fighting for empire so despised gold as we have said. *Weak instrument strong in God*

But if, against the truth that we have shown, the wonted point be urged concerning the inequality of men's strength, let the objection be refuted by the victory which David won over Goliath. And if the Gentiles should seek another instance let them refute it by the victory of Hercules over Antæus. For it were a foolish thing [90] indeed to hold that the strength which God sustains is weaker than a chance champion.

It has now been sufficiently shown that what is acquired by ordeal is acquired by right.

31. *Formal characteristics*, *i.e.* features which make an ordeal what it is, and not a mere brute struggle for mastery. It is the observance of these conditions that gives the 'form' of ordeal to the conflict (T. C., *Convivio*, pp. 123, 231.)

63-69. The lines are by Ennius. Dante found them quoted by Cicero, in the passage of the *De Officiis* referred to in line 24 of this chapter (1 : 12).

CHAPTER XI

[The Roman Empire was established by a series of conflicts, which were sometimes actually single combats and sometimes essentially of the nature of single combat.]

But the Roman people acquired empire by single combat as is proved by witnesses worthy of faith. And the exposition of this will not only make the present matter plain, but will also show that at every turning-point, from the early *Single combats of Rome*

Turnus, the Curiatii times of the Roman Empire, the issue was determined by single combat.

For at the first when the matter of contention was about the abode of father Æneas, who was the first father of this [10] people, Turnus the king of the Rutuli being his opponent, a single combat was finally accepted by the common consent of the two kings as a means of inquiring into the divine will, as is sung in the last of the *Æneid.* In which contest such was the clemency of the victorious Æneas, that had he not spied the belt of which Turnus had stripped Pallas when he slew him, he the victor would have granted both life and [20] peace to his conquered foe, as the last verses of our poet testify.

And when two peoples had sprung up in Italy from the same Trojan root, the Romans to wit and the Albans, and long contention had been between them for the ensign of the eagle and the household gods of the Trojans and the honour of principality, finally, by common consent of those concerned, to solve the debate [30], three brothers Horatii on the one side and as many brothers Curiatii on the other, fought in the sight of kings and people, who gazed in suspense on either side. Then it was that the three Alban champions and two of the Romans being slain, the palm of victory went over to the Romans under king Hostilius. And this Livy has minutely set forth in the first part, and Orosius too bears witness with him.

Then with the observance of every right [40] of war, they fought for empire with neighbouring peoples, with the Sabines and with the

XI. THE SECOND BOOK

Samnites, under the form of ordeal, albeit with a multiplicity of combatants, as Livy tells. And in this method of conflict with the Samnites fortune, so to speak, almost repented her of what she had begun, which Lucan takes as an illustration thus, in the second :—

The Samnites, Pyrrhus, Hannibal

> '*Aut Collina tulit stratas quot porta catervas,*
> *Tunc quum pæne caput mundi rerumque potestas* [50]
> *Mutavit translata locum, Romanaque Samnis*
> *Ultra Caudinas superavit vulnera furcas.*' [1]

But when the strifes among the Italians were settled, and the contest for divine judgment had not yet been fought out with the Greeks and the Carthaginians, both the one and the other of whom pretended to empire, then Fabricius on the Roman side and Pyrrhus on the Greek contended for the glory of empire with a multitude of soldiery ; and it fell to Rome. Again, when Scipio for the Italians and Hannibal [60] for the Africans waged war under form of ordeal, the Africans fell before the Italians as Livy and the other writers of Roman affairs frame to bear witness.

Who, then, is so dull of mind as not by this time to see that by right of ordeal the glorious people gained for itself the crown of the whole world? Truly might a Roman have said what the apostle saith to Timothy, 'There is laid up

---

[1] 'Or as many heaps of slain as pressed upon the Colline Gate, what time the headship of the world and sway of things all but passed over and transferred its site, and the Samnite broke the record of Roman wounds, beyond the measure of the Caudine Forks,'

Roman supremacy established by right for me a crown [70] of righteousness'; laid up, to wit, in the eternal providence of God. Now let presumptuous jurists see how far they stand below that watch-tower of reason whence the human mind surveys these principles; and let them hold their peace, content to set forth counsel and judgment after the meaning of the law.

And now it has been shown that the Roman people acquired empire by single combat. Therefore it acquired it by right, which [80] is the main proposition of the present book.

Hitherto this proposition has been established by arguments which find their chief support in the principles of reason; but from this point forward it must be demonstrated once again from the principles of Christian faith.

42. *Ordeal.*—The word here and in some other passages of this chapter translated 'ordeal' is *duellum*, elsewhere translated 'single-combat.'

17. *Pallas.*—One of the most pleasing episodes of the *Æneid* tells how Æneas sought aid from Evander, the Greek king of the city occupying the future site of Rome. Evander's son, Pallas, led the auxiliaries and was slain by Turnus.

51. The passage occurs in the *Pharsalia*, II. 134-138. Dante read *superavit* in line 138, where the modern editions have *speravit*. The whole passage needs some explanation. In the second or 'great' Samnite war, B.C. 336-304, at the Caudine Forks, the Roman army surrendered to Caius Pontius, B.C. 321, under conditions which were afterwards disgracefully repudiated by the senate. Long afterwards in the Social War, B.C. 90-89, various Italian nations, including the Samnites, waged war with Rome to obtain the franchise. They established the head-quarters of their confederation at Corfinium (to which, therefore, the domination of the world was within a tittle of

XII. THE SECOND BOOK

passing over). They were defeated, however, though many of their claims were conceded. In B.C. 82, during the civil wars of Rome after the death of the great Marius, when Sulla was opposed by the younger Marius and others, the Samnites were still a formidable power on the Marian side. Sulla defeated Marius at Sacer Portus and shut him up in Præneste. Telesinus the Sabine general attempted to relieve him, and failing in this, made a swoop upon Rome and almost effected an entrance at the Colline Gate. He is 'the Samnite' to whom Lucan refers as (according to the true reading) 'hoping to eclipse the slaughters of the Caudine Forks.'

71. The *jurists* here referred to are obviously the Decretalists, or interpreters of canon law, not the commentators on the *Corpus Juris*, *i.e.* Justinian's code of Roman or civil law. See below, III. 3: 92-124.

CHAPTER XII

[To these arguments from reason must be added arguments from revealed Christian truth. And these latter must be urged all the more because the chief opponents of the empire are the clergy, who profess most zeal for the Christian faith, although in fact their zeal is but selfishness, which is reacting on the influence and resources of the church, which they meanwhile abuse. To proceed, then, to the argument; any one who voluntarily obeys a command sanctions its justice. Christ obeyed the decree of Augustus as to the enrolment of the citizens of the world, which Augustus would have had no right to issue had he not been the rightful ruler of the world. Therefore Christ sanctioned the claim of Augustus to the rightful sovereignty of the world.]

FOR they have been the first in murmuring and meditating vain things against the Roman prince- *False zeal*

Greed of the clergy — dom who call themselves zealots for the Christian faith; nor have they any pity on the poor of Christ. And not only are these defrauded in the revenues of the churches, but the very patrimony of the church herself is daily plundered, and she impoverished, while they who make a show of justice, shut out him who should put justice into [10] execution.

Nor is such impoverishment without the judgment of God, since the resources of the church are neither turned to the succour of the poor whose patrimony they are, nor are held in gratitude from the emperor who offers them. Let the same return whence they came. They came well, they return ill; for though well given they have been badly held. What is that to such pastors? What if the substance of the church is flowing away, as long as the [20] properties of their own kin are swelling? But perchance it were better to pursue our subject, and in devout silence await the succour of our Saviour.

I say, then, that if the Roman empire was not of right, then Christ, by his birth, presupposed a wrong. The consequent is false, therefore the contradictory of the antecedent is true, for contradictories may be deduced from each other in the counter sense.

[30] The falsity of the consequent need not be demonstrated to believers; for if a man is a believer, he grants that it is false, and if he grants it not he is not a believer; and if he is not a believer this present argument is not pursued for him.

The sequence I thus demonstrate: Whosoever

observes an edict by choice, urges its justice by so doing; and since deeds are more persuasive than words (as the philosopher holds in the last [40] *Ad Nicomachum*), he urges it more potently than if he approved it in word. But Christ, as Luke, his scribe, bears witness, chose to be born of a virgin mother under edict of the Roman authority, in order that the Son of God, made man, might be enrolled as a man in that unique register of the human race. Now this was observing the edict. Or perchance it were more reverent to suppose that that decree was issued by Cæsar at the divine suggestion in order that he who had been awaited so [50] many ages in the society of mortals might himself register himself amongst mortals.

Christ sanctioned the Roman authority by His birth

Christ, then, gave assurance by deed that the edict of Augustus, who exercised the authority of the Romans, was just; and since jurisdiction is implied in the just issuing of an edict, it follows that he who sanctioned the edict as just also sanctioned the jurisdiction whence it emanated, which jurisdiction, however, was unjust unless it was of right.

And note that the argument [60] adopted to refute the consequent, although it derives its formal validity from one of the loci, yet when reduced, shows its force by the second figure, just as the argument from the assertion of the antecedent shows its force by the first. For it is thus reduced: Every unjust thing is urged unjustly; Christ urged nothing unjustly, therefore he did not urge anything unjust. From the assertion of the antecedent, thus: everything unjust is urged unjustly [70]; Christ

Locus and syllogism urged something unjust, therefore he urged it unjustly.

15-18. *Let the same, i.e.* the resources just spoken of, namely, the temporalities of the pope. Let them go back to the emperor, who in the person of Constantine gave them in good faith, though they have been used so ill. Compare the last lines of the next chapter.

24-29. If such a connection can be established between two propositions as to show that the second necessarily follows from the first, the relation is called a sequence (*consequentia*,) the first proposition being the antecedent and the second the consequent. When such a sequence is established, the falsity of the consequent involves the falsity of the antecedent, and the truth of the antecedent involves the truth of the consequent; but you cannot argue from the falsity of the antecedent to the falsity of the consequent, nor from the truth of the consequent to the truth of the antecedent.

In the present case, then, the falsity of the consequent, 'Christ by his birth presupposed a wrong,' —which will be universally admitted amongst Christians—involves the falsity of the antecedent, 'The Roman empire was not by right.'

Again, 'contradictories' are pairs of propositions so related to each other that they cannot both be true and cannot both be false (compare *Paradiso*, VI. 21). They are either of the form 'all A is B' and 'some A is not B,' or of the form 'no A is B' and 'some A is B.' In the case of 'singular' propositions the contradictory of an assertion is the simple negation, and the contradictory of the negation is the assertion; if, then, 'the Roman empire was not by right' is false, which it is, then its contradictory, 'the Roman empire was by right,' is true.

35. *The sequence I thus demonstrate, i.e.* 'I thus prove that if the Roman empire was not by right, it really does follow that Christ by his birth presupposed a wrong.'

59-71. Dante says that the argument has formal validity 'per aliquem locum.' *Locus* is a technical term and describes certain forms of argument, the first of them being the *locus medius*, which (as Petrus Hispanus declares in the fifth of his ' libelli,' see *Paradiso*, XII. 135) argues from terms which partly coincide with those in which the question is formulated, and partly differ from them, 'for instance, if the question is whether justice is good, and the proof is given that a just man is good and therefore justice is good.' Dante here declares that though formally the argument owes it validity to this *locus medius*, yet it can be thrown into sound syllogistic form. By the *locus medius* we may argue that because Christ did not urge anything unjustly (which is axiomatic) he did not urge anything unjust. But we may if we like begin with the formal declaration, 'It is impossible to urge anything unjust except by urging unjustly.' Then, making this our major premise, we go on the minor, 'Christ urged nothing unjustly,' and draw our conclusion, 'Therefore he urged nothing unjust.' This is a syllogism of the second figure in which the common term is in the predicate of both propositions. If you preferred to put the thing into the shape of *reductio ad absurdum* on the supposition that the first term of the sequence (see above, lines 24-29) is true, then it would run—' No one can urge an unjust thing without urging it unjustly. Christ (on the supposition that the Roman empire did not exist by right) urged an unjust thing, therefore he urged it unjustly, which is absurd ; and this is a syllogism of the first figure.'

CHAPTER XIII

[Moreover, the rightful authority of the Roman empire is essential to the whole scheme of salvation. For the sin of Adam was the sin of collective human nature, and therefore justice could only be vindicated by the punishment of collective human nature. Now human nature was collectively present in Christ; but a penalty, however justly deserved, is not a punishment, which vindicates the demands of justice, unless inflicted by a duly authorised official. The penalty of death was inflicted on Christ by Pilate; therefore, had Pilate not had authority over the whole of human nature, he would not have been able to pronounce valid judicial sentence (the execution of which would vindicate justice) upon human nature. And we should therefore still be sons of wrath because of our fallen nature.]

Roman authority an essential moment in the scheme of salvation

AGAIN, if the Roman empire was not of right, the sin of Adam was not punished in Christ. But this is false, therefore the contradictory of that from which it follows is true. The falseness of the consequent appears thus: Since by the sin of Adam we all were sinners, for the Apostle says, 'As by one man sin entered into this world, and, through sin [10] death, so death entered into all men, inasmuch as all sinned,' if satisfaction for that sin had not been wrought through the death of Christ, we should still be sons of wrath by our nature, to wit, our corrupted nature. But this is not so, since the Apostle *Ad Ephesios*, says, when speaking of the Father, ' Who predestined us to adoption to himself as sons, through Jesus Christ, according to the purpose of his will, to the praise and [20] glory of his grace, with which he favoured us in his beloved Son, in whom we have redemption by his blood, remission of sins, according to the riches of his glory which superabounded in us.' And Christ himself, too, enduring punishment done upon himself, says in John, ' It is finished'; for where it is finished nought remains to be done.

Formal characteristic of a judicial sentence

And to establish this congruity be it known that [30] punishment does not simply mean penalty inflicted on him who worked the wrong, but penalty so inflicted by one who has penal jurisdiction. Wherefore unless the penalty be inflicted by a qualified judge it should not be looked upon as a punishment, but rather as itself a wrong. Wherefore that Hebrew said to Moses, ' Who ordained thee a judge over us?'

If, then, Christ had not suffered under a qualified judge, that suffering would not have been [40] a punishment. And the judge could not have been qualified had he not had jurisdiction over the whole human race; since it was the whole human race that was to be punished in that flesh of Christ, who, as the prophet saith, was bearing or sustaining our griefs. And Tiberius Cæsar, whose vicar Pilate was, would not have had such jurisdiction unless the Roman empire had been of right.

This is why [50] Herod, though not knowing what he did (any more than Caiaphas when he spoke truth concerning the heavenly decree), sent back Christ to Pilate to be judged, as Luke tells us in his gospel. For Herod did not represent Tiberius under the ensign of the eagle or the ensign of the senate, but he was a king appointed by him to a special kingdom,

Christ sanctioned the Roman authority by his death and he ruled under the ensign of the kingdom committed to him.

So let them cease to reproach the Roman [60] empire who feign themselves to be sons of the church, when they see that the Bridegroom, Christ, thus confirmed it at either limit of his warfare. And now, I take it, it has been sufficiently shown that the Roman people acquired to itself the empire of the world by right.

Oh blessed people! Oh glorious thou, Ausonia! had he who enfeebled thy empire either ne'er been born, or ne'er been misled by his own pious purpose.

This singular and (as far as I know) original theory of Dante's is presupposed in the great passage on the redemption in *Paradiso*, VII. It amounts to nothing less than a declaration that the sentence of death pronounced by Pilate upon Christ, so far as it was a sentence upon human nature collectively present in him, was a just sentence, pronounced by a duly authorised official. The supplementary doctrine, that so far as the death of Christ was the work of the Jews, and was wrought on the whole person of Christ, it was the supreme outrage, is developed in the *Paradiso*, but not in this passage.

29. *To establish this congruity.* In the Latin *propter convenientiam.* 'Convenientia' is equivalent to the 'consequentia' or 'sequence' of the last chapter (12 : 35). Dante is to establish that the validity of the cancelling of Adam's sin really is dependent on the right of the Roman empire. See above, lines 1-3.

51. *Caiaphas.* See John XVIII. 14.

54-58. Herod, then, did not represent the universal power of Rome, and therefore he had no jurisdiction over universal human nature, in Christ. Pilate had.

66-69. *I.e.* 'Would that Constantine had never been born, or had never been betrayed by his mistaken piety unto giving the pope his temporalities.' Compare *Purgatorio*, XXXII. 124-129; *Paradiso*, XX. 55-60, etc.

BOOK III

CHAPTER I

[The third question still remains, whether the authority of the Roman monarchy was derived direct from God or is dependent on the papacy.]

'HE shut the mouths of the lions, and they hurt me not; for righteousness was found in me in his sight.' In the beginning of this work it was proposed to inquire into three questions in such fashion as their subject-matter would allow. And in the foregoing books I believe the task has been sufficiently accomplished with respect to the first two of them. It now remains to treat of the third. And since the truth [10] about it cannot be laid bare without putting certain to the blush, perchance it will be the cause of some indignation against me. But since Truth from her immutable throne demands it, and Solomon too, as he enters the forest of the Proverbs, teaches us (by saying that he himself will do it) to meditate upon the truth and abjure the impious man, and the Philosopher, teacher of morals, urges us to sacrifice friendship for truth, therefore I take courage from the above words of [20] Daniel, wherein the divine power, the shield of such as defend the truth, is proffered;

Truth demands undivided allegiance

Relation of pontiff and prince
and, putting on the breastplate of faith, according to the admonition of Paul, in the warmth of that coal which one of the seraphim took from the celestial altar and touched the lips of Isaiah withal, I will enter upon the present wrestling ground, and by the arm of him who delivered us from the power of darkness by his blood, in the sight of all the world will I hurl the impious and the liar out of the ring [30]. What should I fear, since the Spirit, coeternal with the Father and with the Son, says by the mouth of David, 'The just shall be had in everlasting remembrance. He shall not be afraid of an evil report'?

The present question, then, concerning which we are to make inquiry, lies between two great lights, to wit the Roman pontiff and the Roman prince; and we are to ask whether the authority of the Roman monarch, who is monarch of the world by [40] right, as proved in the second book, is immediately dependent upon God; or rather on some vicar or minister of God, by whom I understand the successor of Peter, who in very truth bears the keys of the kingdom of heaven.

14. *Forest.* The original word is 'sylva,' which was used for a 'store' or 'miscellaneous collection.'

CHAPTER II

[The fundamental truth which underlies the arguments of this book, is that what is repugnant to the intention of nature is against the will of God.]

FOR the discussion of the present question we must lay down some principle (as we did in the former cases) the virtue of which shall inform the arguments for disclosing the truth. For unless the principle be first laid down, to what profit can even he who speaks the truth labour?—since the principle alone is the root of the intermediary propositions which are to be laid down.

The divine will and the trend of nature

Therefore let this irrefragable truth be set down [10] at the outset, to wit that God diswills that which is repugnant to the intention of nature. For if this were not true its contradictory would not be false, namely, that God does not diswill what is repugnant to the intention of nature. And if this be not false, neither are its consequences. For in the case of necessary sequences it is impossible that the consequent should be false if the antecedent is not.

[20] But from 'not diswilling' one of two things necessarily follows, either 'willing' or 'not willing,' just as from 'not hating' follows of necessity either 'loving' or 'not loving' (for 'not loving' is not 'hating,' any more than 'not willing' is 'diswilling,' as is obvious); therefore if these things are not false, neither will it be false that 'God wills what he does

Goal, path, and impediment

not will,' the falsity of which cannot be transcended.

Now that this assertion is true [30] I thus set forth: It is manifest that God wills the goal of nature, else the heavens would move in vain, a thing not to be uttered. If God willed an impediment to the goal he would will the goal of the impediment, else he would will in vain. And since the goal of the impediment is that the impeded thing should not be, it would follow that God wills the goal of nature not to be, which we began by saying he did will to be.

But if God did not will the impediment [40] of the goal, in so far as he did not will it, it would follow from his not willing it that he cared not at all whether the impediment were or were not. But he who cares not about an impediment cares not about the thing which it may impede, and consequently has it not in his will. And what one has not in his will he wills not. Wherefore if the goal of nature may be impeded (which it may), it follows of necessity that God does not will the goal of nature, and hence [50] follows as before that God wills what he does not will. That principle, then, from the contradictory of which such absurd consequences follow, is itself most true.

---

22. *Not willing*, in the sense of not exercising the will on the subject at all; neither willing nor diswilling.

29. *This assertion*, viz., that it follows from either of the two alternatives ('God wills,' and 'God does not will what is repugnant to the intention of nature') that 'God wills what he does not will.' Each alter-

native is dealt with separately in one of the two following paragraphs.

39-42. By hypothesis God does not diswill it; therefore, if he does not will it either, he must be indifferent to it.

CHAPTER III

[The contention that the empire is dependent on the church is opposed not so much ignorantly as factiously; for though the pope and certain other pastors may be sincere, yet the majority of those who take this view are instigated thereto by their greed, their ignorance, and their arrogance. For the refutation of all these the distinction must be borne in mind between the secondary authority of the decretals and the primary authority of the Old and the New Testaments, the decrees of the councils, and the writings of the great Fathers. With those who are wilfully factious, however, the author will not argue, but only with those who are open to conviction.]

ON the threshold of this investigation we must note that the truth about the first question required explanation rather to remove ignorance than to quell contentiousness; whereas the investigation of the second question is concerned equally with ignorance and contentiousness. For there are many things of which we are ignorant, but on which we do not dispute; for instance, the geometrician knows not how to square the [10] circle, but does not dispute thereon; and the theologian knows not the number of the angels, yet does not dispute about it; nor does the Egyptian know aught of the

Ignorance and contentiousness

Ignorance, sincere or contentious civilisation of the Scythians, but he does not therefore dispute as to their civilisation.

Now the truth of this third question has to deal with such contentiousness that whereas in other cases ignorance is wont to be the cause of contentiousness, here it is rather contentiousness which is the [20] cause of ignorance. For to men whose wills insist on flying ahead of the inspection of their reason it ever befalls that if their affections are wrong they put the light of reason behind their backs, and are led like blind men by their affections, while obstinately denying that they are blind. Whence it comes right often to pass not only that falsehood has a patrimony of her own, but that many [of her subjects] issuing from her boundaries o'errun the encampments of others, and there, understanding naught themselves are [30] naught understood, and thus stir the wrath of some, the indignation of others, and of certain the laughter.

Well, then, there are three classes of men who chiefly fight against the truth which we are seeking.

For the supreme pontiff, the vicar of our Lord Jesus Christ and successor of Peter (to whom we owe not what is due to Christ but what is due to Peter), in zeal perchance [40] for the keys, together with certain pastors of Christian flocks, and others who, I believe, are moved solely by zeal for mother church, oppose the truth which I am about to demonstrate; perhaps, as I have said, in zeal and not in insolence.

But there are others, whose stubborn greed has put out the light of reason, who declare

themselves sons of the church, whereas they are **The de-**
of their father the devil, who not only stir up **cretalists**
contentiousness with respect to this question, but
hating the very name of the most [50] sacred
princedom, would impudently deny the first
principles of the former investigations and of
this.

There is also a third set whom they call the
Decretalists, strangers and ignorant in every
kind of theology and philosophy, who carp at
the empire, laying all their weight upon their
Decretals (which, for the matter of that, I hold
to be worthy of reverence), and setting their
hopes, I take it, on the supremacy of the same.
And no wonder; for I have heard [60] one of
them declare and volubly maintain that the
traditions of the church are the foundation of
the faith; may which impious thought be extirpated from the minds of men by those whom
the world doubts not to have believed, before
the traditions of the church were, in Christ the
Son of God, either to come or present or having
already suffered; and believing to have hoped,
and hoping to have glowed with love, and so
glowing to have become co-heirs with him.

[70] And that such may be utterly excluded
from the present wrestling ground be it noted
that there is certain scripture, antecedent to the
church, certain contemporaneous with the church
and certain posterior to the church.

Before the church are the Old and New
Testaments, which were 'given for eternity,'
as the prophet says; for this is what the church
means when she says to the Bridegroom, 'Draw
me after thee.'

Scripture before, with, and after the church

[80] With the church came those venerable chief councils with which no believer doubts that Christ was present, since we have it that he himself, when about to ascend to heaven, said to his disciples, 'Behold, I am with you through all the days until the end of the world,' as Matthew bears witness. There are likewise the scriptures of the doctors, Augustine and others; and he who doubts that they were aided by the Holy Spirit has either never seen [90] their fruits, or if he has seen, has by no means tasted them.

After the church came those traditions which they call Decretals, which, indeed, though they are to be revered because of the apostolic authority, should indubitably be held inferior to the fundamental scripture, since Christ blamed the priests for the contrary. For when they asked him, 'Why do your disciples transgress [100] the tradition of the elders?' (for they neglected the washing of hands), Christ, as Matthew testifies, answered them, 'And why do ye transgress the commandment of God for the sake of your tradition?' Wherein he sufficiently indicates that the tradition was of less account.

But if the traditions of the church are subsequent to the church, as has been set forth, then of necessity authority accrues not to the church from the traditions, but to the [110] traditions from the church. And they who have naught save the traditions to allege must be shut out, as already said, from this wrestling ground. For they who are pursuing this truth must proceed, as they track it, on ground of those scriptures from which the authority of the church flows. *Insincere and sincere opponents*

These, then, being thus excluded, we must likewise exclude others, who, though covered with the feathers of crows, yet prank themselves as white sheep in the flock of the Lord. These are the sons of impiety who, that they may follow up [120] their own infamies, prostitute their mother, drive out their brethren, and will not hear of a judge. For why should arguments be sought for them when their greed prevents them from seeing even the first principles?

Wherefore there remains only the struggle with those who are led by a certain zeal towards mother church to overlook the precise truth which we are investigating. And with them, relying upon the reverence which a dutiful son owes to his father, which [130] a dutiful son owes to his mother, I—in duty towards Christ, in duty towards the church, in duty towards the pastor, in duty towards all who profess the Christian religion—enter in the cause of truth upon the contention of this book.

73-78. The references are to Ps. CX. 9 (in the English versions, CXI. 9), 'Mandavit in æternum testamentum suum' (where Dante applies *testamentum* to the Old and New Testaments), and to *Song of Solomon* I. 3, allegorically interpreted of the church.

92-124 The reader may be startled by the 'Protestant' tone of this passage, which seems to treat the church as having completed her authoritative utterances during the period of the earlier councils and of the great Fathers. We must be careful, however, not so to read the passage as to make it prove too much. Dante's expression *after the church*, cannot possibly be taken to mean that in the age of the Decretals, the church had passed away and was no longer on earth. And, again, since the councils and the works of the early Fathers were themselves subsequent to the institution of the church, neither can we understand *after the church* to mean 'after the institution of the church.'

We must suppose, then, that the difficulty arises from Dante using concurrently (and perhaps welding together in his mind) two 'ways of saying *prius*' (see above, I. 15 : 3 and *note*), namely, the first two ways enumerated by Aristotle (*Cat.* 11) ; temporal and causal priority to wit. The scriptures of the Old and New Testaments are 'prior' to the church in both senses (though it is difficult to understand how Dante can have regarded the formal institution of the church as later than the composition of the Pauline Epistles, for instance). The great councils and the early fathers accompany the church in time, but continue the process of laying her foundations. The Decretals, on the other hand, do not either lay or strengthen the foundations of the church, but are themselves amongst her expressions or utterances, under her institutional aspect. They are of the nature, therefore, of a task that the church has to undertake, because of the fallen state of man (compare lines 107-124 of the next chapter), rather than a part either of her credentials or of the essential revelation conveyed through her. The church, then, is causally prior to the Decretals. And also, in a secondary sense, her great formative period, as a matter of fact, was temporally prior to the era of the Decretals, though (as Dante would doubtless hold) her authority to deal formatively with doctrinal truth remains unimpaired, should occasion arise for its exercise.

That Dante's respect for the Decretals was sincere is testified by the place assigned to Gratian (*Paradiso*, X. 104), who compiled his *Decretum* in the twelfth century; but his contempt for the Decretalists appears not only from this passage but from *Paradiso*, IX. 133-135 ; XII. 83, and the *Epistle to the Italian Cardinals*, lines 111-121. See page 335 of this volume.

CHAPTER IV

[The arguments for the dependence of the empire are drawn from scripture and from certain transactions between popes and emperors. And first, from the dependence of the moon (supposed to represent the empire) upon the sun (supposed to represent the church) for her light. Twofold confutation of this argument: first, by showing that the sun and moon do not represent the church and the empire, and second, by showing that if they did the analogy would still fail at the point required for the argument.]

Now those for whom the whole disputation that follows will be conducted assert that the authority of the empire depends upon the authority of the church, as the inferior artisan is dependent on the architect; and thereto they are moved by sundry adverse arguments which they draw from sacred scripture, and from certain things done alike by the supreme pontiff and by the emperor himself; though they strive also to gain some support from reason.

Argument from the sun and moon

[10] For they say firstly, following the scripture of *Genesis,* that God made two great luminaries, a greater luminary and a lesser luminary, that the one might rule over the day and the other the night. And these they have been accustomed to understand as spoken allegorically of those two regimens, to wit the spiritual and the temporal. Thence they argue that like as the moon, which is the lesser luminary, has no light save as she receives it from the sun, so neither has the temporal [20]

On formal and material refutation regimen any authority save as it receives it from the spiritual regimen.

To refute this and their other arguments, be it noted that as the Philosopher has it in what he writes *de Sophisticis Elenchis*, 'the refutation of an argument is the exposure of an error.' And since the error may be in the matter and may be in the form of the argument, there are two ways of going wrong, by making either a false assumption or a bad [30] syllogism. Both which the Philosopher objected to Parmenides and Melissus, saying, 'For they lay down what is false, and syllogise wrongly.' And here I use 'false' in a wide signification, including the improbable, which, when the matter is only one of probability, has the nature of falsehood. If, however, the error is formal, then he who would disarm the conclusion must do it by showing that the due form of the syllogism has not been observed. Whereas if the error is in [40] the matter it is either because the assumption is absolutely false or because it is relatively false; if absolutely, the refutation proceeds by destroying the assumption, if relatively, by drawing a distinction.

Noting this, be it observed, for the better understanding of the refutation of this point and of others to be dealt with hereafter, that there are two ways of going wrong as to the mystic sense, either by looking for it where it is not or by [50] taking it as it ought not to be taken. Concerning the first, Augustine says in the *City of God*, that 'not everything which is told as having happened is to be taken as being significant; but for the sake of that which is significant that which is not significant is also added. Only with the ploughshare is the earth cleft, but in order for this to be done the other parts of the plough are also [60] needed.'

On the error of excess in allegorising

On the second point, the same Augustine says in his *Christian Doctrine*, speaking of him who should find in the scriptures something other than he who wrote them really says, that 'It is the same mistake as one should make who should quit the way but should come by a circuitous route to the place whereto the road leads'; and he adds 'that the error of such an one should be pointed out to him for fear lest his habit of leaving the path should carry him into cross roads and wrong ones.' Then he points out the reason why we should be careful to avoid this error as to the [70] scriptures, saying, 'Faith will totter if the authority of the divine scriptures is shaken.' But I say that if such mistakes are made in ignorance they should be pardoned after careful correction, just as we should pardon one who should be scared by a lion in the clouds. But if the mistakes are made on purpose we must deal with such as go thus astray no otherwise than with tyrants who follow not the public laws for the common advantage [80] but strive to wrest them to their own.

Oh, the supreme crime, though it were but in dreams, of abusing the intention of the eternal Spirit! For the sin is not against Moses, not against David, not against Job, not against Matthew nor Paul, but against the Holy Spirit who speaks in them. For though the scribes of the divine utterance be many, one is he who dictates to them, even God [90]; who has deigned to set forth his will to us by the pens of many writers.

Anachronism of the argument materially

This being premised, I go on to speak to the matter introduced above, by way of negation of that saying of theirs that those two luminaries typically import these two regimens, wherein lies the whole strength of their argument. But it may be shown in two ways that this interpretation of the passage can by no means be defended. First, since such [100] regimens are certain accidents of man himself, God would seem to have followed a perverse order in producing the accidents before their proper subject, and to say this of God is absurd. For those two luminaries were produced on the fourth day, and man on the sixth day, as may be seen in the text.

Moreover, since those regimens exist to direct men to certain ends (as will be shown below), if man had remained in the state [110] of innocence in which he was made by God he would have had no need of such directive regimens. Such regimens, then, are remedial against the infirmity of sin. Now since on the fourth day not only was man not sinful but man was not at all, to produce remedies would have been superfluous, which is counter to the divine excellence. For a physician were foolish to prepare a plaster to apply to the future [120] abscess of one as yet not born. It must not be said, then, that on the fourth day God made these two regimens; and consequently Moses cannot have meant what they make out that he did.

But even if we allow this false statement we may disarm it by the method of distinction.

And this is a gentler way of proceeding with an adversary, for it does not show that he is uttering an absolute falsehood, as the method by destruction does [130]. I say, then, that although the moon has no abundant light save as she receives it from the sun, it does not therefore follow that the moon herself is derived from the sun. Wherefore be it known that the existence of the moon is one thing, her virtue another, and her operation yet a third. As to her existence the moon is in no way dependent on the sun, neither is she with respect to her virtue, and not absolutely with respect to her operation; for her motion is derived from her proper mover, and her influence [140] from her proper rays. For she has a certain light from herself as is manifest in her eclipse. But with respect to her better and more virtuous operation she does receive something from the sun, to wit, abundance of light by the receipt of which she operates with more virtue.

Its formal invalidity

In the same way, then, I affirm that the temporal power does not receive its being from the spiritual, nor its virtue, which is its authority; nor even its efficiency absolutely. But it does receive [150] therefrom the power of operating with greater virtue, through the light of grace which the blessing of the supreme pontiff infuses into it, in heaven and on earth. And, therefore, the argument erred in form, for the predicate in the conclusion is not a term of the major, as is obvious; for it runs thus: 'The moon receives light from the sun, which is the spiritual regimen. The moon is the temporal regimen. Therefore the temporal regimen

Residuum of truth receives authority from the spiritual regimen.' [160]. Now the term in the major is 'light,' but in the predicate of the conclusion they substitute 'authority,' which two things are diverse both in their subject and their sense, as we have seen.

44. *Distinction* is the technical term for the process of *distinguishing* between the sense in which you must understand the term of a proposition in order that it may be true, and the sense in which you have to take it in order to make it support your conclusion.

63-72. The extracts given by Dante are scarcely intelligible as they stand, but the whole passage in the *De Doctrina Christiana* (i. 41) is very striking. Augustine is speaking of a man who misinterprets scripture, but in such a way as to derive lessons from it profitable for building up love to God and one's neighbour. Such a man reaches the goal, as one might do who had wandered from the way and yet reached the place to which the way led. But such a one must have his error shown him, and must be warned that if he takes to dealing arbitrarily with scripture he will become opinionative and will cease really to follow its lead and submit himself to it. And if this habit grows upon him he will be lost 'for we walk by faith not by sight; and faith will totter if the authority of the divine scriptures be shaken, and if faith totters love herself languishes, for if any one has fallen from faith he must of necessity fall from love, for none can love what he does not believe to exist'; and so forth.

100. The regimens being relations and not independent substances or existences, can only exist in an 'underlying something,' *i.e.* their proper *subject*.

107-120. From this important passage we gather that man restored to the state of Eden would not need ecclesiastical, any more than he would need imperial guidance or authority. Hence Virgil 'crowns *ana mitres*' Dante at the entrance of the Garden of Eden (*Purgatorio*, XXVII. 142, see 'Note on Dante's Purgatory,' T. C., *Purgatorio*, pp. 432 ff.).

V. THE THIRD BOOK

139. *Her proper mover, i.e.* the angel who 'by understanding' moves the proper sphere of the moon, whose rotation is from west to east, and whose period is a month. Compare *Convivio*, II. 6. In a sense the other angels, who confer its other motions (such as that corresponding to the proper motion of the stars) upon the moon might be called her 'proper' movers, for a special angel presides over each; but in using the singular Dante is clearly thinking especially of the angel who confers her most conspicuous proper motion (*i.e.* her monthly motion) on the moon.

163. *Subject, i.e.* in the things to which they respectively pertain as 'accidents.'

CHAPTER V

[It is further argued that Levi's seniority to Judah implies the authority of the priesthood over the empire. But, granted that the significance of Levi and Judah is as supposed, the authority in question is not the same thing as seniority, nor is it necessarily involved in it.]

Argument from Levi and Judah

They also draw an argument from the text of Moses, saying that from the loins of Jacob flowed the type of these two regimens, to wit, Levi and Judah, the one of whom was the father of the priesthood, and the other of the temporal regimen. Then they argue from them thus: 'As Levi was related to Judah so is the church related to the empire. Levi preceded Judah in birth, as is evident [10] in the text, therefore the church precedes the empire in authority.'

This is easily indeed refuted; for the assertion that Levi and Judah, the sons of Jacob,

Its formal invalidity represent those regimens I might refute as before by denying it; but let it be granted; yet when they infer in their argument that as Levi was first in birth so the church is first in authority, I say, as before, that the predicate of the conclusion is one [20] and the major term is another; for authority is one thing and nativity another, both in subject and sense. Therefore there is an error in form. And it runs like this: 'A preceded B in C; D is in the same relation to E that A is in to B; therefore D preceded E in F,' whereas F and C are different.

And if, by way of rejoinder, they should say that F follows from C, that is to say authority from seniority, and that the consequent may be [30] substituted in an inference for the antecedent (as animal for man), I reply that it is false; for there are many seniors by birth who not only do not precede those younger than themselves in authority but are preceded by them; as is evident when bishops are younger in years than their arch-presbyters. And thus the objection is seen to err in alleging as a cause what is not a cause.

20. *The major term* is the one which, in a syllogism of the first figure, is the predicate alike of the major premise and of the conclusion. It is so called because it embraces the middle term, which itself embraces the subject of the minor premise. Thus in 'All A's are B, all C's are A, therefore all C's are B,' B is the major term because it has a wider range than A, the middle term, whereas C has a narrower range than A and is therefore the minor term. In the case in point, Dante shows that the syllogism runs: 'The relation of Judah to Levi is the relation of *seniority*. The relation of the church to the empire

is the relation of Judah to Levi. Therefore the relation of the church to the empire is the relation of *authority;* which is, of course, a false syllogism, for the 'predicate of the conclusion' (authority) differs from the 'major term' (seniority).

29-31. In virtue of such a 'sequence' (*cf.* II. 12: 24-29 *note*) as 'If he is a man he is an animal' we may speak of 'man' as the antecedent and 'animal' as the consequent; and in such a case if your syllogism justified the conclusion 'therefore he is a man,' you would be at liberty to substitute 'therefore he is an animal,' since 'animal' is involved in 'man.' In like manner if it could be shown that priority of authority was a legitimate 'consequent' of priority of birth, then the syllogism drawn out in the last note would be sound. Dante proceeds to show that this is not so.

36. *Objection.* In Latin *instantia,* the technical term for a 'rejoinder,' by which the refuted party seeks to disarm the refutation. Cf. *De Aqua et Terra,* § 17: 1 *note.*

CHAPTER VI

[From Samuel's deposing Saul it is argued that the vicar of God can give and take away temporal authority. But Samuel was not the vicar of God but his express emissary *ad hoc ;* and an express emissary may do things (within his express commission) that a vicar might not do in the exercise of his general discretion.]

FROM the text of the first book of Kings they allege the election and deposition of Saul. And they say that Saul, the king on the throne, was deposed by Samuel who was exercising the office of God, as commanded, which is obvious in the text. And hence they argue that as that vicar of God had authority to give and take

Argument from Samuel and Saul

Ambassador and vicar away the temporal regimen and transfer [10] it to another, so now, too, the vicar of God, the priest of the universal church, has power to give and take away and also to transfer the sceptre of the temporal regimen. Whence it would undoubtedly follow that the authority of the empire would be dependent in the way they affirm.

And on this we must say (denying their assertion that Samuel was the vicar of God), that it was not as vicar that he acted, but as [20] a special ambassador *ad hoc* or as a messenger bearing an express mandate of God, which is obvious from the fact that he did and reported that alone which God had said.

Wherefore be it known that it is one thing to be a vicar, another to be a messenger or minister, as it is one thing to be a teacher and another to be a translator. For a vicar is one to whom jurisdiction, according to law or according to his [30] discretion, has been granted; and therefore within the limits of the jurisdiction granted him he can execute the law or enforce his own will in a matter of which his lord has no knowledge at all. The messenger, on the contrary, as messenger, cannot do this; but as the hammer works in the virtue of the smith alone, so does the messenger in his will alone who sends him. It does not follow, then, that if God did this through [40] his messenger Samuel therefore the vicar of God may do it. For God has done, is doing, and shall do, many a thing through the angels which the vicar of God, the successor of Peter, could not do.

Wherefore their argument draws an inference

VI. THE THIRD BOOK

from the whole to the part and is constructed **An argu-**
like this: 'Man can hear and see, therefore the **ment a**
eye can hear and see,' which does not hold. **fortiori**
But it would hold negatively, thus: 'Man
[50] cannot fly, therefore man's arms cannot fly.'
So here 'God (as Agatho held) cannot by his
messenger make things that have taken place, not
have taken place, therefore neither can his vicar
do so,' would hold.

28. The vicar may be empowered simply to administer existing law, or to deal on his own discretion with cases not provided for by the law; but in either case he may deal with matters of which his principal has no direct cognisance; whereas the ambassador can do nothing except by direct reference to his principal, and with his direct sanction. Just as the translator must have direct sanction from his author for everything he says, whereas the teacher expounds and applies the laws of his science or the results of his own reflection and insight without needing to refer at every step to the direct sanction of his authorities. In a sense, then, it might seem that the vicar has wider discretion and authority than the nuncio; but on the other hand since the principal acts direct through the nuncio he may empower the latter to do things for which no vicar as such could possibly be competent. Hence God's messenger may be directly commissioned to do things beyond the authority of any vicar. He is merely the translator of the divine words, and as such, though he has no authority himself, he is the channel of the supreme authority.

52, 53. This opinion of Agatho (or more properly, Agathon), is recorded by Aristotle, *Eth. Nic.* vi. 26.

CHAPTER VII

[It is argued that since God has power over temporal as well as spiritual things so has his vicar. But it does not follow that the authority of the vicar is co-extensive with that of the principal, and it is obvious that in the case of the pope it is not so. Nor indeed can the principal in any case depute the whole of his authority; for the prime source of authority, on which the prince himself is dependent, is of larger scope than his authority itself, and therefore he cannot create an authority the peer of his own.]

Christ's supremacy THEY also allege the oblation of the Magi, from the text of Matthew, saying that Christ received both frankincense and gold to signify that he was lord and ruler of both temporal and spiritual things; whence they infer that the vicar of Christ is lord and ruler of the same, and therefore has authority over both.

In answer to this I admit the text and sense [10] of Matthew, but what they attempt to infer therefrom is faulty in the term. For they syllogise thus: 'God is lord of spiritual and temporal things. The supreme pontiff is the vicar of God. Therefore he is lord of spiritual and temporal things.' Now both the propositions are true, but the middle is changed and the argument has four terms, which violates the syllogistic form, as is clear from what is written *De Syllogismo* [20], in general. For God, who is subject of the major premise, is one, and the vicar of God, who is the predicate in the minor, is another.

And should any one insist on the equivalence

of vicar the insistence is futile, for no vicariate, *does not* divine or human, can be equivalent to the primal *imply that* authority, as is easily seen. For we know *of his* that at any rate with respect to the workings of nature the successor of Peter is not equipotential with the divine authority [30]; for he could not make earth go up or fire come down, in virtue of the office committed to him. Nor is it possible that God should commit all things to him, since God could not in any way commit the power of creating, nor of baptising either, as is plain to proof; albeit the Master has said the contrary in the fourth.

We also know that no man's vicar as vicar is [40] equivalent to the man himself, because no one can give what is not his. Now the princely authority is only the prince's to use, for no prince can confer authority upon himself. He may accept or resign the office; but he cannot make another the prince; for the creation of a prince does not depend on the prince. And if this is so it is manifest that no prince can substitute for himself a vicar equivalent to himself. Wherefore [50] the objection has no weight.

19. *De syllogismo simpliciter*, that is the 'Prior analytics.'

23. *Insist on the equivalence of 'vicar,'* Lat., 'Instaret de vicarii æquivalentia,' *i.e.* found a rejoinder on the equivalence of the term 'vicar' to the term 'God.' Compare above, 5 : 36*n*.

37. *The Master*, *i.e.* the *Magister Sententiarum*, Peter Lombard. (Compare *Paradiso*, X. 107, and *note.*) He says that Christ deputed the *ministry* of baptising to his servants, but retained the *power* of baptising to himself, though he might have deputed

that too. Dante denies this. The 'power' in question is the power of remitting sins by baptism.

CHAPTER VIII

[From the power of binding and loosing conferred by Christ upon Peter, it is argued that his successor has power to bind and loose the authority of temporal monarchs. But that power was implicitly limited by the reference to heaven, and it has therefore no application to temporal things.]

The power to bind and loose THEY also allege from the text of the same that word of Christ to Peter, 'And whatsoever thou hast bound on earth shall be bound in heaven also, and whatsoever thou hast loosed on earth shall be loosed in heaven also.' And they gather from this text of Matthew, and likewise from the text of John, that the same was said to all the apostles. Whence they argue that, by concession of God, the successor of Peter [10] can both bind and loose everything; and hence they infer that he can loose the laws and decrees of the empire, and bind laws and decrees for the temporal regimen; from which what they assert would really follow.

We must proceed against this by distinction, applied to the major of the syllogism they employ. For their syllogism runs: 'Peter had power to loose and bind all things. Peter's successor has whatsoever Peter had. Therefore Peter's [20] successor has power to loose and bind all things.' Whence they infer that he has power to loose and bind the authority and decrees of the empire.

I grant the minor, but the major only with a *subject* distinction. And therefore I say that this *to quali-* sign of universality 'all,' which is implied in *fication* 'whatsoever,' never distributes beyond the scope of the term distributed. For if I say 'every animal runs,' the distribution of 'every' covers all that is included [30] under the genus 'animal.' But if I say 'every man runs,' then the universal qualification only distributes over what is covered by this term 'man.' And when I say 'every grammarian' the distribution is still further contracted.

Wherefore we must always consider what it is which the universal qualification has to distribute, and when we do so we shall easily see how far the distribution extends, on [40] considering the nature and scope of the distributed term. Wherefore when it is said 'Whatsoever thou hast bound,' if this 'whatsoever' were to be taken absolutely their contention would be true, and he would not only be able to do what they assert, but to loose a wife from her husband and bind her to another while the first still lived, which he by no means can. He would also be able to absolve me while I am not penitent, which even God himself could not do.

[50] Since this, then, is so, it is manifest that the distribution in question is not to be taken absolutely, but relatively to something. And to what it is relative is sufficiently evident when we consider what it was that was being granted to him, in connection with which that distributive qualification was added. For Christ says to Peter, 'I will give thee the keys of the kingdom of heaven,' that is, 'I will make thee doorkeeper

and limited to spiritual things of the kingdom of heaven.' Then he adds, 'And whatsoever,' that [60] is 'everything which,' that is 'everything which has reference to that office' thou shalt have power to loose and bind. And thus the sign of universality which is implied in 'whatsoever' is restricted in its distribution by the office of the keys of the kingdom of heaven. And taken thus the proposition under discussion is true; but absolutely it clearly is not so. And therefore I say that although Peter's successor can loose and bind within the requirements of the office committed to Peter, yet it does not [70] follow from that that he can loose or bind the decrees of the empire, or the laws, (as was their contention) unless it could be further proved that this concerns the office of the keys; and the contrary of this will be shown below.

1. *The same*, *i.e.* Matthew (as in the preceding chapter). See *Matthew* XVIII. 18 (*John* XX. 23).

24. *Distinction.* See above, chap. 4: 44*n*. Also compare *Paradiso*, XIII. 109, and the whole argument that leads up to it.

CHAPTER IX

[It is further argued that the two swords (which Peter said he had) are authority over spiritual and over temporal things. But it is clear from the text that if that had been Peter's meaning he must have misunderstood the words of Christ, to which he was answering; for these words refer to the real necessity of protecting themselves which the disciples would now experience when he left them. And in the next place it is unlike the frankness and impetuosity which all the Gospels assign to Peter to speak otherwise than directly and simply; and finally, if after all Peter's words had an allegorical meaning, it would be better to regard the two swords as the sword of words and the sword of deeds by which the disciples of Jesus were to set the world in commotion.]

THEY also take that word in Luke which Peter utters to Christ when he says, 'Lo here are two swords,' and they say that by those two swords the two regimens aforesaid are meant; and since Peter said they were where he was, that is with him, they argue that, in authority, those two regimens abide with Peter's successor. *The two swords*

[10] And we must proceed against this by denying the sense on which the argument is built; for they say that those two swords which Peter produced import the two aforesaid regimens, which must be flatly denied, in the first place because such an answer would not have agreed with the meaning of Christ, and secondly because Peter, after his impulsive manner, answered merely to the obvious aspect of things.

Now that his answer would not have agreed [20] with the meaning of Christ will be manifest

to be taken literally if we consider the words that precede and the occasion of the words. For it must be borne in mind that this saying was on the day of the supper, wherefore, higher up, Luke begins thus: 'Now the day of unleavened bread was come, on which the passover must needs be slain'; and at this supper Christ had already spoken of his approaching passion in which he must be parted from his disciples. It must [30] also be noted that when those words were spoken all the twelve disciples were together; whence, shortly after the words just quoted, Luke says, 'And when the hour was come he lay down to meat and the twelve apostles with him.' And thence without a break in the conversation he comes to these words, 'When I sent you forth without scrip and purse and sandals, was aught lacking to you? And they said, no. Wherefore he said to them: But now whosoever has [40] a scrip let him take it, and likewise his purse; and whosoever has not a sword, let him sell his coat and buy one.' Wherein the meaning of Christ is clear enough, for he did not say 'buy (if ye have them not) two swords' but rather 'twelve,' since it was to the twelve disciples that he said 'let him who has not buy,' that each of them might have one. And he said this, moreover, forewarning them of the oppression and contempt that was to come upon them [50]; as though he should say, 'As long as I was with you ye were received. Now ye will be chased away. Wherefore it behoves you to make ready even those things which I erst forbade you, for there is need.' Therefore if the answer of Peter, made to those words, had borne the meaning they assign to it, in accordance with it would at any rate not have corresponded to the meaning of Christ; and Christ would have rebuked him for it, as he often did when he answered beside the mark. Here, however, he did not so, but acquiesced [60], saying to him 'it is enough,' as though he should say, 'I mention it, because of your need; but if you cannot have one each, then two may suffice.'

And that Peter, after his manner, spoke to the obvious meaning, is supported by a consideration of that hasty and unconsidered forwardness of his, to which he was urged not only by the sincerity of his faith but, I take it, by a certain guilelessness and simplicity of nature. All the scribes of Christ bear witness to this forwardness of his [70]. Matthew writes that when Jesus had asked the disciples, 'Whom say ye that I am?' Peter answered before all, 'Thou art the Christ, the son of the living God.' He writes further that when Christ said to his disciples that it behoved him to go to Jerusalem and suffer many things, Peter took him, and began to rebuke him, saying, 'Far be it from thee, Lord, this shall not be to thee,' to whom Christ, turning, said [80] in rebuke, 'Get thee behind me, Satan.' He also writes that on the mount of transfiguration in the sight of Christ, of Moses and of Elias, and of the two sons of Zebedee, he said, 'Lord, it is good for us to be here. If thou wilt, let us make here three tabernacles, one for thee, one for Moses, and one for Elias.' He also writes that when the disciples were in a boat, at night time, and Christ was walking on

Peter's abrupt simplicity the water, Peter said [90], 'Lord, if it be thou, bid me to come to thee upon the water.' He also writes that when Christ declared beforehand that his disciples should be offended in him, Peter answered, 'Though all should be offended in thee, yet will I never be offended,' and afterwards, 'Though I must die with thee, yet will I not deny thee,' and to this Mark is co-witness. And, in addition, Luke writes that Peter had also said to Christ [100] a little before the words we have quoted about the swords, 'Lord, I am ready to go with thee both into prison and unto death.' John tells of him that when Christ would wash his feet, Peter said, 'Lord, dost thou wash my feet?' and after, 'Thou shalt never wash my feet.' He says also that he smote the servant of the minister with his sword, which likewise all four [110] concordantly recount. John also says that he went straight in when he came to the tomb, seeing the other disciple lingering at the entrance. He says again that when Jesus was on the sea-shore, after the resurrection, as soon as Peter heard that it was the Lord, he cast his coat around him, for he was naked, and threw himself into the sea [120]. Finally, he says that when Peter saw John he said to Jesus, 'Lord, and what shall this man do?'

It is well to draw out this whole list of passages concerning our archimandrite, to the praise of his guilelessness; and they clearly show that when he spoke about the two swords, he was answering Christ with a simple purport.

But if, after all, those words of Christ and Peter are to be taken typically, they must not be applied [130] to the point which these of whom I speak would have, but must be taken to refer to that sword of which Matthew writes as follows: 'Think not that I am come to send peace upon the earth. I am come not to send peace, but a sword; for I am come to set a man against his father,' and the rest. And this, indeed, comes to pass both in word and deed; wherefore Luke said *ad Theophilum* 'What Jesus began to do and to teach.' Such was the sword which Christ bid [140] them buy, and which Peter answered was already there twofold. For they were ready both for words and deeds, whereby to do what Christ declared that he himself had come to do with the sword, as we have shown.

or else as signifying words and deeds

This chapter has a special interest as showing how keen and sound a critic Dante could be when his mind was turned in that direction, and how entirely capable he was of sweeping away allegorical subtleties and taking the plain sense of the text when it suited him.

7, 8. *In authority*—*i.e.* the practical exercise of them might be deputed, but the authority remained with the pope.

138. *Ad Theophilum*—*i.e.* in the Book of Acts.

CHAPTER X

[Passing from scriptural arguments to appeals to history and reason, we first encounter the claim based on the donation of Constantine to Sylvester, by which temporal authority was conferred upon the church in the West. But the emperor had no power to give such a gift; for the appointed officer cannot annul or prejudice the office to which he is appointed. Moreover, rending the empire would be counter to human justice, as may be gathered from the whole preceding argument. And the emperor cannot have the right to destroy that on which the empire rests. Nor has an executive officer any power to limit or contract his own jurisdiction. Again, even if the emperor had had power to make the grant, the church would have had no power to receive it; for it would have been clean against the evangelic command. All this, however, is not to be understood as precluding the church from holding, under the emperor, a certain patrimony, to be administered for the poor.]

Constantine and Sylvester IT is further urged by some that the Emperor Constantine, when cleansed of his leprosy at the intercession of Sylvester, who was then supreme pontiff, granted the seat of empire, to wit Rome, to the church, together with many other dignities of the empire. Whence they argue that no one can assume those dignities thenceforth except he receive them from the church, whose they say they are. And from this it would certainly follow [10] that the one authority is dependent on the other, as they would have it.

Having therefore set out and refuted the arguments which seemed to have their roots in

X. THE THIRD BOOK

the divine utterances, it remains to set forth and refute those which are rooted in the doings of the Romans and in human reason; the first of which is the one that stands above, the syllogism running thus: 'The things that are the church's none may have by right save from the church' [20], and this is granted. 'The Roman regimen is the church's. Therefore none may have it of right save from the church.' And the minor they prove by what has been indicated above as to Constantine.

The empire cannot alienate

This minor, then, I deny; and as to their proof, I say that it has no force, because Constantine had no power to alienate the imperial dignity, nor had the church power to receive it.

And if they persist in their objection, my contention [30] may be thus proved. No one is at liberty to do, in virtue of the office deputed to him, things that are counter to that office, else the same thing in the same capacity would be counter to itself, which is impossible. But it is counter to the office deputed to the emperor to rend the empire, since it is his office to hold the human race subject to unity in willing and diswilling, as may easily be seen in the first of this present. Wherefore to rend the empire [40] is not competent to the emperor. If therefore certain dignities were (as they say) alienated from the empire by Constantine and ceded to the power of the church, the seamless tunic was rent, which not even they durst rend who pierced Christ, very God, with the lance.

Moreover, like as the church hath its own foundation, so too hath the empire; for the nor the church receive temporal authority

foundation of the church is Christ [50], whence the Apostle, *Ad Corinthos*, 'Other foundation can no man lay than that is laid, which is Christ Jesus.' He is the rock on which the church is built; but the foundation of the empire is human right. Now I say that like as the church may not contradict its own foundation, but must ever rest upon it, according to that passage of the *Canticles*, 'Who is this that cometh up from the desert [60], flowing with delights, leaning on her beloved?' so neither may the empire do anything counter to human right. But it were counter to human right should the empire destroy itself. Therefore the empire may not destroy itself. Since, then, to rend the empire were to destroy it (inasmuch as the empire consists in the unity of universal monarchy), it is manifest that he who wields the authority of the empire may not rend [70] the empire. And that it is counter to human right to destroy the empire is manifest from what has gone before.

Moreover, every jurisdiction is prior to its judge, for the judge is appointed to the jurisdiction, and not conversely. But the empire is a jurisdiction embracing every temporal jurisdiction in its scope, therefore it is prior to its judge, who is the emperor, because the emperor is [80] appointed to it, and not conversely. Whence it is clear that the emperor, as emperor, cannot change it, since it is the source of his being what he is. Now I say thus: Either he was emperor when he is said to have made the grant to the church, or he was not. And if not, it is obvious that he had no power of making grants with respect to the empire. If he was, then, since such a grant was to the prejudice of his jurisdiction, **because** he, as emperor, had no power to make it. **of their**

[90] Further, if one emperor had power to **inherent** tear never so little a piece from the jurisdiction **nature** of the empire, so on the same showing had another also. And since the temporal jurisdiction is finite, and any finite thing can be used up by finite subtractions, it would follow that the prime jurisdiction might be reduced to nothing, which is contrary to reason.

And again, since he who 'confers' is in the relation of agent, and he on whom 'it is conferred' in the [100] relation of patient (as the philosopher has it in the fourth *Ad Nicomachum*), in order for a grant to be legitimate there must be the due disposition not only of him who grants but of him to whom the grant is made. For it seems that the acts of the agents inhere in a suitably disposed patient. But the church was entirely undisposed for receiving temporal things, in virtue of express prohibitive command, as we learn from Matthew, thus: 'Possess not gold [110] nor silver, nor money in your girdles, nor purse for your journey,' and the rest. For, although we find in Luke a relaxation of the precept with respect to certain things, yet nowhere have I been able to find that permission was given to the church, after that prohibition, to possess gold and silver. Wherefore if the church had no power to receive, then even if Constantine, as far as he was concerned, had power to give, still the action was impossible because the [120] patient had not the due disposition. It is evident, therefore, that neither could the church receive by way of possession, nor could the other grant

Patrimony of the church by way of alienation. The emperor, however, had power to depute a patrimony or the like to the guardianship of the church, the superior dominion always remaining intact, its unity not admitting of division. The vicar of God, too, might receive, not as possessor, but as dispenser of the fruits for the poor of Christ, on behalf of the church [130]; as it is known the apostles did.

1-6. The Donation of Constantine, which Bryce calls the most stupendous of all the mediæval forgeries, makes Constantine declare that he had been told he could be cured of his leprosy by bathing in the blood of infants. He had collected a number of children for the purpose, but was so touched by the tears of their mothers that he abandoned the project. He was then cured by Sylvester and converted to Christianity by the miracle. After rehearsing all this Constantine goes on, in the most extravagant terms of submission and humility, to declare himself anxious to withdraw from Western Europe in order to leave the pope in the full and undisturbed possession of the authority which he now confers upon him. Dante does not challenge the authenticity of this document (though the phrase in lines 84, 85, ' when he *is said* to have made the grant,' might seem to imply some reserve) but disputes its validity, as he frequently deplores its results. Compare *Inferno*, XIX. 115-117; *Paradiso*, XX. 55-60, and many other passages.

7. *Dignities.* The word has a technical sense, and is nearly equivalent to ' privileges.' In church affairs a ' dignity ' is defined as ' a benefice that carries administration, together with jurisdiction, over ecclesiastical matters.'

104, 105. *Inhere, i.e.* are already there in potentiality and by implication.

CHAPTER XI

[A further argument is drawn from the conferring of the imperial dignity upon Charles the Great by Pope Hadrian. But we might equally well argue from Otto's deposition of Benedict and appointment of Leo to the papacy that the emperor is supreme over the church.]

THEY further say that pope Hadrian summoned Charles the Great to his aid and the church's, because of the wrongs wrought by the Lombards in the time of Desiderius, their king; and that Charles received from him the dignity of the empire, notwithstanding that Michael was the ruling emperor at Constantinople. Wherefore they say that all who have been emperors of the Romans after him are [10] themselves advocates of the church, and by the church must be called to office. And from this, too, that dependence which they wish to prove would follow.

Abuse cannot establish right

And to invalidate this, I say that their contention amounts to nothing; for the usurpation of a right does not create a right. Else in the same way it might be shown that the authority of the church depends upon the emperor, since the emperor Otho restored pope Leo, and deposed [20] Benedict and carried him off into exile in Saxony.

6. *Michael.* Constantius Copronymus, not Michael, was emperor at the time (Witte).

9-11. The original is 'et ipsi advocati ecclesiæ sunt et debent ab ecclesia advocari.' I have not been able to preserve the play upon words.

CHAPTER XII

[The appeal to reason still remains to be dealt with. They argue that there cannot be two supreme individuals of the same kind. The pope and the emperor are both men, and therefore one must be supreme. Obviously the pope cannot be the inferior, therefore he must be supreme over the emperor. But papacy and empire are accidents, not substances; and they do not determine any genus or species. As men, indeed, pope and emperor are of the same kind, and must alike be referred to the standard specimen of their kind, namely that man, whoever he may be, who is the best man. But as pope and emperor they are not beings of one kind at all, but beings standing in two different kinds of relationship; and if those two relationships are to be referred to one supreme or standard relationship, it must be sought in God, or in some abstract form of relationship under God.]

The pope alleged to be the standard man BUT their argument from reason is this. They take their first principle from the tenth of the *First Philosophy*, and say that all things which are of one kind are reduced to the unit which is the measure of all that come under that class. But all men are of one kind; therefore they must be reduced to the unit, as measure of them all. And, since the supreme pontiff and [10] the emperor are men, if that conclusion is true they must be reduced to the unit man; and since the pope must not be reduced to any other, it remains that the emperor, together with all others, must be reduced to him, as the measure and norm. Whence again their contention follows.

To refute this argument, I say that when they

declare that all things which are of one [20] kind ought to be reduced to some unit of that kind which is the standard therein, they say true. And in like manner they say true when they say that all men are of one kind. And they likewise draw a true conclusion when they infer from this that all men must be reduced to a standard unit in their kind. But when from this conclusion they draw the further inference about the pope and emperor, they fall into a fallacy *secundum* [30] *accidens*.

Substance and relation

To demonstrate which, be it known that it is one thing to be a man and another thing to be pope. And in like manner it is one thing to be a man and another to be emperor; just as it is one thing to be a man and another to be a father and master; for a man is such in virtue of a substantial form from which he acquires his species and genus, and by which he is brought under the [40] predicament of substance. But a father is such in virtue of an accidental form, or relation, from which indeed he acquires a species and genus, in a sense, but is brought under the class *ad aliquid*, or relativity. Otherwise, since no accidental form exists in itself, apart from the foundation of the substance that underlies it, everything would be reduced to the predicament of substance; and this is false. Since, then, pope and emperor are [50] such in virtue of certain relations (to wit their popedom and empiry, which are relations, the one coming under the scope of paternity and the other under the scope of dominion), it is clear that pope and emperor, as such, must come under the predicament of relation, and are consequently

The standard man to be reduced to something which exists under that class.

Wherefore I maintain that the standard to which they [60] must be reduced as men is one, and that to which they must be reduced as pope and emperor another. For as men they have to be referred to the best man, whoever that may be; who is the standard and idea of all others, so to speak; that is, to him who is most supremely one in his own kind, as may be gathered from the last *Ad Nicomachum*. In so far, however, as they are relative (which they obviously are) they must either be reduced one to the other (if the one [70] is subordinated to the other); or they must be of the same species, in virtue of the nature of their relation; or there is some third thing to which they must be reduced as to common unity. But it cannot be said that one is subordinated to the other; for in that case one could be predicated of the other, which is false; for we do not say that the emperor is pope, nor the converse. Nor can it be said that they are of the same species, since the meaning of 'pope' [80], as such, is one, and of 'emperor' another. Therefore they must be reduced to something in which they will find their union.

As to which, be it known that as relation is to relation so is related thing to related thing. If therefore the papacy and the empiry, being relations of superposition, are to be reduced to the disposition of superposition, from which disposition, together with their differentiating specialities, they are derivatives, the pope and [90] emperor being relative, will have to be

XII. THE THIRD BOOK

referred to some unity in which that disposition **and the** of superposition is found, its very self, without **standard** further differentiating specialities. And this will **relation** be either God himself in whom all disposition is universally united, or some substance inferior to God, in which the disposition of superposition is particularised by its differentiating speciality from 'disposition' in its generality. And thus it is clear that the pope and [100] emperor, as men, must be reduced to one unit, but as pope and emperor to another; and thus we have elucidated the appeal to reason.

Some light will be thrown on the ideas that underlie this very unsatisfactory chapter by a study of *De Vulgari Eloquentia*, I. 16, where the same principles are more happily and more intelligibly applied.

1-3. Aristotle, *Met.* ix. (in Latin translations x) 1, 8, and 12: 'Unity is, primarily, the first measure of every kind of thing, and most properly of quantity,' and again, 'Now in all these [length, weight, velocity] there is a certain indivisible unit which is the measure and norm.' What Aristotle means is simply that if two magnitudes of the same kind are to be compared, they must be expressed in the same unit. But to the mediæval imagination the words evidently suggested an inherent supremacy in the unit, so that it became the normal standard of reference, by conformity to which a thing rises in dignity and significance.

The whole argument and its refutation will therefore run as follows—Everything that can be predicated falls under one of the classes known as 'predicaments,' of which 'substance' is one, 'relation' another, position' a third, and so forth. That is to say, we may predicate of Socrates that he is a man, in which case what we predicate is a 'substance,' or that he is a father, in which case it is a 'relation,' or that he is here, in which case it is a 'position,' and so forth. Now every 'predicament' (*e.g.*, *substance*, or *position*), is itself a supreme genus or kind, containing under it subordinate genera and species and individuals. Every species or genus has its proper norm or standard, by comparison with which all individuals in it must be ideally judged; while practically they are subordinate to the actual individual that comes nearest to that standard. Now the pope and the emperor are men, and must therefore be ideally subordinated to the one ideal man, and practically to his nearest earthly realisation,—viz., the pope. To this Dante replies that, *in their manhood* they must be subordinated to the most ideal *man* ('whoever that may be,' says Dante, implying that it does not follow, and is not probable that the pope *as a man* will be that person); but in their popedom and empiry they are not self-existent or substantial, but related or accidental, and therefore their popedom and empiry comes not under a sub-genus of the supreme genus 'substance,' but a sub-genus of the supreme genus *ad aliquid*, or 'relation.' The sub-genus in question is that of *authority* or *superposition*, under which they are co-ordinate.

29, 30. That is to say they fall into the fallacy of applying to the subject in its accidental capacity that which was truly asserted of it only in its substantial capacity. It is as if we were to argue 'the cobbler Martin is good, therefore Martin is a good cobbler.'

33 ff. A substance is a thing that exists in itself, such as a man or a chair. An accident is that which exists only as an experience, quality, or capacity of a substance, such as love, ruddiness, skill. A substantial form, then, is that in virtue of which a substance is itself and not some other substance (*e.g.*, a man, and not an angel), whereas an accidental form is that in virtue of which an accident is itself and not some other accident (love, for instance, and not hate, or ruddiness, and not paleness). On forms in general, see T.C., *Convivio*, pp. 123, 231.

63. The passage from the *Eth. Nic.* (x. 5, 10) is much to the purpose. Aristotle is discussing the standard to which we are to refer when tastes and opinions differ, and says, 'It seems that in all such things we must take the opinion of the worthy man;

and if this is right, as would seem, then virtue and the good man, as such, are to be taken as the standard in each case, and we are to consider those things pleasures which he would regard as such, and those things pleasant in which he would delight.' For the phrase 'most supremely one in his own kind,' compare above, I. 15: 1 ff. *note.*

73. If the one relation is a special case of the other (as 'fatherhood' is a special case of 'blood-relationship') we shall be able to predicate one of the other (as 'a father is a blood-relation'). If they are individual cases of one specific (not generic) relationship, they must have the same definition, for individuals cannot be defined, a definition being constitutive of a species. If neither of these cases meets the facts, it remains that they are specific relations capable of being brought under a generic relation in which they find their unity, and from which they are derived as special cases, differentiated severally by their specific differences or differentiating specialities.

CHAPTER XIII

[After refuting the opposing arguments, we must proceed to the positive demonstration of the independence of the empire. This independence, then, is manifest from the fact that before the church was an actual institution at all Christ himself, the apostle Paul, and the angel that appeared to him, all implicitly or explicitly acknowledged the authority of Cæsar. Further, if Constantine had not authority over the temporalities, his grant to the church is void, and her claim unjust.]

HAVING set forth and refuted the errors on which they chiefly rely who say that the authority of the Roman prince depends on the Roman pontiff, we must return to the demonstration of the truth

Negative and positive proof

Independence of the empire vouched by Christ and Paul as to this third matter which was laid down for discussion from the beginning. And this truth will be sufficiently unfolded if I show, under the principle of inquiry which we have laid down, that the said [10] authority depends immediately upon the summit of all being, which is God. And this will be shown if we either disprove the church's authority over it (since no other is even alleged), or prove by direct demonstration that it depends immediately on God.

Now that the authority of the church is not the cause of the imperial authority is thus proved. If, while one thing does not exist or [20] is not exercising its virtue, another thing has its full virtue, the first thing is not the cause of that virtue. But when the church did not exist, or was not exercising its virtue, the empire had its full virtue. Therefore the church is not the cause of the virtue of the empire, and not of its authority either, since its virtue and authority are the same. Let the church be A, the empire B, the authority or virtue of the empire C. If when A does not exist, C is in B, it is impossible [30] that A can be the cause of C being in B; since it is impossible for the effect to precede its cause. Further, if, when A is not in action C is in B, then of necessity A is not the cause of C being in B; for it is necessary for the production of an effect that the cause (especially the efficient cause of which we are speaking) should first be in action.

The major proposition of this demonstration is explained by the terms; the second [40], Christ and the church confirms, Christ by his birth and death as set forth above, the church when Paul in

Authority of Constantine

the Acts of the Apostles says to Festus, 'I stand at the judgment seat of Cæsar where I must be judged'; and also when the angel of God says to Paul a little after, 'Fear not, Paul. It behoves thee to stand before Cæsar.' And below Paul says again to the Jews in Italy, 'Now when the Jews opposed [50] I was compelled to appeal to Cæsar, not as having aught of which to accuse my nation, but that I might snatch my soul from death.' But if Cæsar had not already possessed authority to judge temporal things, neither would Christ have supported his claims, nor would the angel have announced those words, nor would he who said, 'I desire to be released and to be with Christ' have appealed to a judge who was not competent.

[60] And if Constantine had not possessed authority over the patronage of the Church, what he deputed to her from the empire he could not have deputed of right, and thus the church would be wrongfully enjoying that grant, since God will have offerings without spot, according to that of Leviticus, 'every offering which ye shall bring to the Lord shall be without leaven'; which precept, though it seems to address those who grant [70], nevertheless consequentially applies to those who receive. For it were foolish to suppose that God would have that to be received which he forbids to be offered— as indeed in that same book the command is given to the Levites, 'Pollute not your souls nor touch ought of theirs, lest ye be unclean.' But to say that the church thus wrongfully enjoys the patrimony deputed her is most unseemly; therefore that is false from which it follows.

40   Dante constructs 'Christ and the Church' with a singular verb, as he also does 'God and nature.' Compare above, I. 3 : 22.

61. *Patronage.* Lat. 'patrocinium,' the same word that is translated 'guardianship' above, 10 : 124. Constantine placed a certain patrimony (*patrimonium*) under the guardianship, or patronage (*patrocinium*) of the church, which he could not have done legally unless that patronage was subject to regulation by him. The argument (if I rightly understand it) is hardly convincing. You may legally make a gift to a person or an object over which you have no kind of legal control.

CHAPTER XIV

[Again, it can be shown, by exhaustive examination of the possible sources from which the church could have derived her authority over the emperor, that no such authority exists.]

Exclusion by exhaustive examination

FURTHER, if the church had power to give the Roman prince his authority, she would either have it from God, or from herself, or from some emperor, or from the universal consent of mortals, or at least the majority of them. There is no other crevice through which this power could have flowed to the church. But she has it not from any of these. Therefore she has not the said [10] power at all.

Now that she has it not from any of these is shown as follows. If she had received it from God, it would have been either by divine or by natural law (for what is received from nature is received from God, though the proposition cannot be converted). But it is not by natural law; for nature imposes laws only on her own effects, since God cannot he insufficient where he produces aught into [20] being without secondary agents. Wherefore since the church is not an effect of nature but of God, who says, 'On this rock will I build my church,' and elsewhere, 'I have finished the work thou gavest me to do,' it is manifest that nature did not give laws to her. **of all possible sources of church authority**

But neither is it by divine law, for every divine law is held in the bosom of the two Testaments. In which bosom [30] I cannot find that anxiety or care concerning temporal things was commended to the priesthood, either former or latter. Nay, rather I find that the former priests were expressly excluded therefrom, as is plain from those of God *Ad Moysen*, and the like of the latter priests by those of Christ *Ad Discipulos*. But they could not have been relieved of this care if the authority of the temporal regimen had been derived from the [40] priesthood, since at any rate anxiety would press upon them concerning due provision in granting the authorisation, and afterwards in continuous watching lest he whom they had authorised should wander from the path of right.

Now that she did not receive it from herself is easily shown. There is nought that can give what it has not got. Wherefore everything that effects anything must already be in act that which it contemplates effecting, as is seen in what is written *De Simpliciter Ente*. But it is clear that [50] if the church gave herself that virtue she cannot have had it before she gave it; and thus she would have given herself what she had not got, which is impossible.

over the empire And that she did not receive it from any emperor is sufficiently plain from what has been set forth above.

And that she had it not from the consent of all, or of the majority of men, who doubts? since not only all the Asiatics and Africans [60] but the greater part of those dwelling in Europe would repudiate the thought. Nay! it is wearisome to bring proofs of things absolutely manifest.

27-29. Note again Dante's marked scripturalism.

34 ff. *Those of God, etc.* In the Latin, 'Per ea quæ Deus ad Moysen' and 'Per ea quæ Christus ad discipulos.' These references are in the form of quotations in which 'Deus' and 'Christus' are the authors and *Ad Moysen* and *Ad Discipulos* the titles of the works. Compare 'ex ultimis ad Nicomachum,' 'Lucas ad Theophilum,' and so forth.

CHAPTER XV

[Further proof that it is formal, or essential, to the nature of the church, not to exercise temporal authority.]

The formal nature of the church AGAIN, that which is against the nature of anything is not in the number of its virtues, since the virtues of each thing follow its nature, for the attainment of its end. But virtue to authorise rule over our mortality is contrary to the nature of the church. Therefore it is not of the number of her virtues.

To prove the minor be it [10] known that the nature of the church is the form of the church. For though nature is predicated of material and of form, yet it is more properly **revealed** predicated of form as is shown in the *De Naturali* **in the life** *Auditu*. But the form of the church is no other **of Christ** than the life of Christ, embraced both in his words and in his deeds. For his life was the idea and exemplar of the church militant, especially of pastors, and most of all of the supreme pastor, whose it is to feed the lambs [20] and sheep. Whence he himself in John, when bequeathing the form of his life, says, 'I have given you an example that as I have done to you so should ye also do.' And specifically to Peter when he had committed to him the office of pastor, as we learn from the same source, he said, 'Peter, follow thou me.' But Christ in the presence of Pilate renounced any such regimen as that in question. 'My kingdom,' said he, 'is not of this world. If my kingdom were [30] of this world, my servants would fight that I should not be given over to the Jews. But now my kingdom is not hence.'

Which is not so to be understood as though Christ, who is God, were not lord of this kingdom; since the Psalmist says, 'For the sea is his and he made it. And his hands established the dry land'; but that as the exemplar of the church [40] he had no charge of this kingdom. As though a golden seal were to say of itself, 'I am not the standard in any class,' which saying would not hold concerning it in as far as it is gold, since as gold it is the standard in the class of metals; but it holds concerning it in so far as it is a definite stamp capable of being received by impression.

It is therefore the formal principle of the

excludes temporal authority church to say and to feel that same. And to say [50] or feel the opposite is obviously counter to its form, or to its nature, which is the same thing. Whence we gather that the power of authorising this kingdom is counter to the nature of the church, for contrariety in an opinion or a saying follows from contrariety in the thing said or opined; even as truth or falsehood in speech is caused by the being or non-being of the thing, as the teaching of the *Predicaments* shows us. It has therefore been [60] sufficiently shown by the preceding arguments, which lead to an incongruity, that the authority of the empire by no means depends on the church.

49. *That same*, i.e. 'My kingdom is not of this world.'

54-59. To exercise authority over the temporal rule is counter to the form of the church; for if it were not so, neither would the corresponding expressions, opinions, and feelings be counter thereto, which we have seen they are.

58, 59. *The Predicaments.* See above, I. 15 : 1-3*n*.

CHAPTER XVI

[It has been shown that the empire is not dependent on the church, and though it is a safe inference that it is directly dependent upon God, yet so far it has been an inference only. A more direct proof may now be attempted. Man, as sharing in the nature alike of corruptible and incorruptible things, has, alone of all beings, two ends or goals of life; namely, the temporal exercise of the moral and intellectual virtues, and the eternal fruition to which he is led by the exercise of the theological virtues. And though philosophy and revelation are inherently adequate guides to these two goals, yet fallen man needs practical directive powers to keep him from wandering out of the true path, and to preserve him in the ways of freedom and of peace. And since this preservation of peaceful order in the affairs of earth is the object of temporal government, and is in its essence a preservation of the harmony between the ruling heavens and the obeying earth, the power to exercise it can, by its very nature, only be rightly conferred by him to whom the whole system of celestial relations is a present fact. It follows, then, that God alone elects the Roman emperor; and those German princes who are called 'electors' are but heralds who proclaim the divine will; that is if they can so keep their minds clear of sordid interests as to be able clearly to perceive it. Finally the whole argument of this work must be understood as establishing the independence of the empire only, not its strict co-equality with the papacy, for the representative of the eternal life may naturally expect some reverential deference from the representative of temporal life.]

ALTHOUGH in the preceding chapter it has been shown by reduction to an incongruity that the authority of the empire is not caused by the

Positive proof

of the co-ordinate authority authority of the supreme pontiff, yet it has not been altogether proved that it depends immediately on God, save by consequential inference; for the consequential inference is that if it does not depend on the vicar of God it depends on God. And, therefore, for the perfect [10] establishment of the proposition, we must prove by direct demonstration that the emperor or monarch of the world is in immediate relation to the Prince of the universe, who is God.

Now to understand this be it known that man alone of beings holds a mid-place between corruptible and incorruptible; wherefore he is rightly likened by the philosophers to the horizon which is between two hemispheres. For man [20], if considered after either essential part, to wit soul and body, is corruptible if considered only after the one, to wit the body, but if after the other, to wit the soul, he is incorruptible. Wherefore the Philosopher says well of the soul (in that it is incorruptible), in the second *De Anima*, ' And it alone is capable of being separated from the corruptible as perpetual.'

[30] If man, then, is a kind of mean between corruptible and incorruptible things, since every mean savours of the nature of the extremes, it is necessary that man should savour of either nature. And since every nature is ordained to a certain end it follows that there must be a twofold end of man, so that like as he alone amongst all beings partakes of corruptibility and incorruptibility, so he alone amongst all beings should be ordained for two final goals, of which [40] the one should be his goal as a corruptible being, and the other as an incorruptible.

XVI.   THE THIRD BOOK

of church and empire

That unutterable providence, then, has set two ends before man to be contemplated by him; the blessedness, to wit, of this life, which consists in the exercise of his proper power and is figured by the terrestrial paradise, and the blessedness of eternal life, which consists in the fruition of the divine aspect, to which [50] his proper power may not ascend unless assisted by the divine light. And this blessedness is given to be understood by the celestial paradise.

Now to these two as to diverse ends it behoves him to come by diverse means. For to the first we attain by the teachings of philosophy, following them by acting in accordance with the moral and intellectual virtues. To the second by spiritual teachings [60] which transcend human reason, as we follow them by acting according to the theological virtues; faith, hope, to wit, and charity. Now albeit these ends and means are made plain to us, the one by human reason (which the philosophers have wholly brought to our knowledge), the other by the Holy Spirit (which hath revealed the truth that is beyond our nature, but yet needful to us, by means of the prophets and sacred writers and by Jesus Christ the Son of God co-eternal with the said Spirit, and by his [70] disciples), yet would human greed cast them behind were not men, like horses going astray in their brutishness, held in the way by bit and rein.

Wherefore man had need of a twofold directive power according to his twofold end, to wit, the supreme pontiff, to lead the human race, in accordance with things revealed, to eternal life; and the emperor, to [80] direct the

under God human race to temporal felicity in accordance with the teachings of philosophy. And since none, or few (and they with extremest difficulty) could reach this port, were not the waves of seductive greed assuaged and the human race left free to rest in the tranquillity of peace, this is that mark on which he who has charge of the world and is called the Roman prince should chiefly fix his mind, to wit, that [90] on this threshing floor of mortality life should be lived in freedom and in peace. And since the disposition of this world follows the disposition that inheres in the circulation of the heavens, in order to accomplish this end, namely, that the charters which conduce to liberty and peace should be applied by the ruler in question with due reference to time and place, it is needful that they should be dispensed by him who looks upon the whole disposition of the heavens presently. And that is he only who so preordained that disposition that by it [100] he in his providence might weave all things together, each in its due order.

But if this be so, God alone chooses, he alone confirms, since he hath no superior. Whence we may further gather that neither they who now are, nor such others of any kind as have ever been called the electors, should so be called; but rather should they be reckoned the heralds of divine providence. Whence it comes to pass that they [110] to whom is granted the honour of making the proclamation, are subject from time to time to dissent; because either all or some of them are clouded by the mists of greed, and discern not the face of the divine dispensation.

Thus, then, it is plain that the authority of the temporal monarch descends upon him without any mean from the fountain of universal authority. Which fountain, one in the citadel of its simplicity, flows into manifold channels out of the abundance of its excellence. *Conclusion and qualification*

[120] And now already methinks I have sufficiently reached the mark I set before myself. For the truth of that question has been searched out in which was asked whether the office of monarch were necessary to the well-being of the world, and of that in which was asked whether the Roman people acquired empire for itself by right, and also of that last question in which was asked whether the monarch's authority depended from God, or immediately from some other. The truth concerning which last [130] question is not to be received in such narrow sense as that the Roman prince is subordinate in naught to the Roman pontiff; inasmuch as mortal felicity is in a certain sense ordained with reference to immortal felicity. Let Cæsar, therefore, observe that reverence to Peter which a first-born son should observe to a father, so that illuminated by the light of paternal grace he may with greater power irradiate the world, over which he is set by him alone who is ruler [140] of all things spiritual and temporal.

The student cannot study this chapter too carefully. It may be regarded as the key to the whole structure of the *Comedy*.

46. *Power*. The original is *virtus*, in the sense, I take it, of 'faculty,' 'power,' or 'attribute'; but here the other meaning of 'virtue' is, of course, entirely germane to the context also.

75 ff. Compare above, 4: 107 ff.

105 ff. The tradition that the office of emperor of Rome was elective was still living. In theory the Roman people were the electors; but whether the German princes, technically called 'electors,' or any older and more popular body should be, or should at any time have been, regarded as the electing college, the only true elector was God. It was the function of his earthly agents to learn and to proclaim his will.

APPENDIX

BOCCACCIO, in his *Life of Dante*, after giving some account of the *Comedy*, and of why it was written in the vernacular, continues, 'In like manner this excellent author, on the coming of the Emperor Henry VII., made a book in Latin prose, called *Monarchia*, which is divided into three books after the three points which he therein determines. In the first he proves, by logical disputation, that for the well-being of the world the empire is a necessity; and this is the first point. In the second he shows, by historical arguments, that Rome attained to the imperial title by right, which is the second point. In the third, he proves, by theological arguments, that the authority of the empire proceeds direct from God, and not through the mediation of any vicar of his, as it seems the clergy would have it; and this is the third point. This book was condemned several years after the author's death by messer Beltrando, cardinal of Poggetto,[1] and papal legate in the parts of Lombardy, pope John XXII. being in the chair. And the reason was because Lewis, duke of Bavaria,

[1] So Boccaccio, but the title is incorrect. Bertrand du Poïet (who was a Frenchman) was created Cardinal with the title *di S. Marcello* in 1316 (Ricci). He was afterwards Cardinal Bishop of Ostia.

chosen king of the Romans by the electors of Germany, came to Rome for his coronation against the pleasure of the said pope John, and being in Rome, he made a minor friar, called brother Piero della Corvara, pope, in violation of the ordinances of the church, and he made many cardinals and bishops; and there he caused himself to be crowned by this pope. And a question as to his authority rising up in many cases, he and his followers having come upon this book, began to make use of many of the arguments it contained, in support of his authority and of themselves; whereupon the book, hitherto scarcely known, became very famous. But afterwards, when the said Lewis was gone back to Germany, and his followers, especially the clergy, had come to their fall and were dispersed, the said Cardinal, with none to gainsay him, seized the aforesaid book, and condemned it publicly to the flames, as containing heresies. And in like manner he was bent on dealing with the bones of the author, to the eternal infamy and confusion of his memory, had it not been opposed by a valiant and noble cavalier of Florence, by name Pino della Tosa, who was then at Bologna, where this thing was being discussed; and with him in this was messer Ostagio da Polenta, both of whom had much power with the aforesaid cardinal.'

It is impossible to say whether Boccaccio had any independent grounds for asserting that the *De Monarchia* was written in connection with Henry VII.'s expedition, or whether it is merely a conjecture suggested by the appropriateness of the subject to the occasion. Accordingly his statement has never been regarded by modern critics as closing the question as to the date of the composition of this, in many respects, most important of Dante's minor works.

Three opinions have been earnestly advocated in recent times on the internal evidence; and against all of them weighty objections may be urged. There is indeed a passage in our existing manuscripts which if genuine, as it stands, would decide the question, and would relegate the composition of the poem to the very last years of Dante's life. In I. 12: 42, the manuscripts give a direct reference to the *Paradiso*, 'sicut dixi in Paradiso commedie' (see note on the passage, above, p. 160); but critics are almost unanimous in regarding this as an interpolation, in spite of the difficulty of explaining its occurrence in manuscripts which have not been shown to have any connection with one another. It is indeed almost impossible to believe that Dante 'on this occasion only' has obliged us with a cross-reference, leaving us to find our own way in so many other cases. And if this piece of evidence is ruled out of court, we may proceed to examine the three chief contentions on their own merits.

1. Witte argued for an early date, before Dante's exile. This is supported by the absence of any reference at all to the author's banishment, in which respect this work stands in marked contrast with the *De Vulgari Eloquentia*, the *Convivio*, and the *Epistles*. And it certainly seems difficult to think of Dante allowing such a passage as II. 5: 103 to pass his pen without some

betrayal of personal feeling, if he were indeed in exile at the time of writing. It is further urged that after the issue of the Papal Bull *Unam Sanctam* in 1302, Dante could not well have omitted all direct reference to it, while speaking of the subject as one that had never yet been treated. And further, unless this work had preceded the *Convivio*, in which he speaks of himself as already famous, he could hardly have used the language of the opening chapter of book I., implying that he has still to win his spurs.

Now these are weighty considerations; but a careful study of the internal relations between the *Convivio* and the *De Monarchia* seems to prove conclusively that the *Convivio* was written first. The whole system of the *De Monarchia* in relation to church and state and the active and contemplative life is far more mature than that of the *Convivio*; again a large part of the argument in the fourth book of the *Convivio* would be destroyed by a reference to a certain passage in Aristotle (*Pol.* iv. 8, 9); and special attention is drawn to this very passage in *De Monarchia*, II. 3 : 15-17. The maturity of the *De Monarchia*, if it were an early work, would in any case be astounding; but if the relative crudity of the *Convivio* (with its apparent ignorance of *Pol.* iv. 8, too) is to intervene between the *De Monarchia* and the *Comedy*, we are in face of a veritable psychological monstrosity. Note, too, that the difficulty is not relieved by any reference in the *Convivio* to a fuller treatment elsewhere (parallel to the reference in *Convivio*, I. 5 : 66-69 to the fuller treatment of the subject in the *De Vulgari Eloquentia*, compare T. C., *Convivio*, p. 424), such as we might have expected had the *De Monarchia* been already written and had the treatment of the theme in the *Convivio* been a loose and popular summary of what had been elaborated in that work. Arguments *e silentio*, however, are notoriously unsafe, so that too much stress must not be laid on this point.

The priority of the *Convivio* to the *De Monarchia* is defended at somewhat greater length in the appendix to the T. C., *Convivio*, pp. 425-427.

These objections appear to be conclusive against the priority of the *De Monarchia* to the *Convivio* and therefore against the early date of the former.

2. The second opinion agrees substantially with Boccaccio's statement, namely, that the work was written in connection with Henry's expedition into Italy, or rather, perhaps, in anticipation of it. In favour of this it may be urged that no one could doubt the propriety of the occasion for the production of a manifesto on the relations of church and state, and that the friendly attitude which Clement at first assumed to Henry might explain the moderation of Dante's references to the pope in III. 3 : 36-44. (Compare III. 16: 129-140.) The opening of book II.(with the reading now generally adopted) might in this case be taken as a direct reference to the election of Henry (1308), and his expected intervention in Italian affairs, and to the mutterings of an opposition which Dante did not at the moment wish to magnify. The passage as to the electors and their function in III. 16 : 104 *sqq.* would also have its special

appropriateness. This date would, further, agree with the priority of the *Convivio* in point of time, which, as we have seen, there is the strongest reason for asserting. The absence of any reference to a formal or virtual vacancy of the imperial office (such as we find in *De Vulgari Eloquentia*, I. 18 : 19 *sqq*., 44 *sqq*., and *Convivio*, IV. 3 :' 38 *sqq*.) would be fully accounted for if Henry was already elected. And again, with quite trivial exceptions the scheme presupposed or briefly enunciated in the great political letters is in closest harmony with the scheme of the *De Monarchia*, as might naturally be expected in documents of the same period. Indeed, the letters seem almost to assume that a formal exposition of the author's views is already accessible.

Against this may be urged in the first place the absence of all reference to the author's exile; and next the fact, that although the underlying scheme of thought is identical in the *De Monarchia* and in the *Epistles*, yet the tone and temper is startlingly different. The academic calm of the *De Monarchia*, and the absence of any direct reference to current political topics, is entirely remote from the prophetic furor of the *Epistles* and their direct advocacy of Henry's claims.

These arguments are very formidable, and were an alternative hypothesis open, they might be regarded as decisive. But considering the great difficulties that beset us in any case, the line of minimum critical resistance appears to be indicated by a hint dropped by Lionardo Bruni in his *Life of Dante*. Having spoken of the failure of the attempt of the exiles to regain admission to Florence by force of arms, Lionardo continues: 'This great hope having failed, Dante thought fit to waste no more time but departed from Arezzo and took his way to Verona. Here he was very courteously received by the lords della Scala and remained with them some time utterly humbled, seeking by good offices and good demeanour to gain the grace of permission to return to Florence by the spontaneous recall of the government of the place. And to this intent he laboured much, and wrote repeatedly not only to individual citizens in the government but to the people also. And amongst the rest was a long letter that begins, *Popule mi quid feci tibi?* Now while he was thus hoping for a return by way of pardon, the election of Henry of Luxemburg as emperor took place; and first his election and then his expedition threw all Italy into a fever of expectation. Whereon Dante was unable to hold his purpose of awaiting grace, but exalting himself with disdainful mind, began to revile them who were in possession of the city, calling them infamous and evil, and threatening them with the punishment they deserved at the hands of the emperor, from which, he said, it was evident that they could have no escape.' Are we at liberty to suppose that, when Henry was already elected, and was projecting his expedition to Italy with the sanction of the pope, Dante at first thoroughly retained his self-possession and took the opportunity of writing his philosophical treatise on the foundations of imperial authority, by way of preparing the minds of the Italians for the great reconciliation and reorganisation which he anticipated, carefully abstaining from unnecessarily exasperating references of any kind, even to the suppressing of all mention of his own exile?

The emotional tension of the *De Monarchia* is indeed high. One can feel the passion that lies behind it; but the expression is deliberately calm.[1] One can imagine that in presence of the almost Messianic hopes kindled in Dante's bosom by Henry's election, under the prophetic 'burden' of the belief that he was himself called to do something essential towards preparing the paths for the political redeemer (compare *Epist.* vii. 45, 46), together with the stern self-suppression needful for the carrying out of his task in the way in which he conceived it, Dante may, for a season, have regarded all his youthful work (including the *Canzoni*, over which he had lingered for so many years with affectionate pride) as mere trifling, and may have thought of himself as still liable to be called to account for the hidden talent (*De Monarchia*, I. 1).

If this comes at all near the truth it is easy to understand that when Henry was actually on the march it became impossible to maintain the tone of academic reserve any longer. And

---

[1] Indeed, this self-suppression characterises the treatise even in matters that have no reference to politics, as one may see, for instance, by comparing the reference to the exclusion of the virtuous heathen from heavenly bliss in II. 8 : 32 with the corresponding passage in the *Paradiso* (Canto xx.).

indeed it would now be senseless and inopportune. The prophetic fervour, then, broke out undisguised, in the great proclamation and appeal to the princes of Italy, *Epistola* v. But when the Italian cities, one after another, refused, as it appeared to Dante, the things which made for their peace, when Florence headed the resistance to the Lord's anointed, and Henry himself, lingering over secondary tasks, allowed the evil to gather head, then at last we see the volcano of Dante's indignation in eruption, and we have the two terrible letters to the Florentines and to Henry (*Epistolæ*, vi. vii.).

I fully admit that all this is in a measure special pleading. It is an attempt to meet the objections to assigning the date of (say) 1309 to the composition of the *De Monarchia*, which would hardly be accepted as satisfactory were there any natural escape; and I merely put it forward as a tentative suggestion towards the solution of a question admittedly beset with difficulties.

3. The third opinion is that the *De Monarchia* was composed in the last years of Dante's life, contemporaneously with the *Paradiso*. In support of this view may be urged the very close parallels of thought and even of expression between the two works, together with the general detachment and serenity of the *De Monarchia*.[1]

Against this it may be urged that it seems quite impossible to believe that Dante, at the same time that he was speaking and thinking of

[1] Generally speaking no stress is laid by the advocates of this opinion upon the direct citation of the *Paradiso* in our existing manuscripts (I. 12 : 42).

the *Comedy* in the way indicated by the opening of the twenty-fifth canto of the *Paradiso* and by the correspondence with Del Virgilio (see below, pp. 371-385) could also be speaking of himself as one that had as yet made no contribution to the public weal, in payment for all he had received (*De Monarchia*, I. 1). And further, the later years of Dante's life seem to furnish no special occasion for the production of what after all seems to announce itself as an 'occasional' writing, in spite of its breadth of treatment and weight of argument. And finally, the general tone of the work and the impression it produces are as far removed as possible from that of a philosophical postscript to the documents of Dante's actual controversies. If we compare it, from this point of view, with the echoes of his political hopes, (the rumblings of the volcano, still glowing but no longer in eruption), which we find in the later cantos of the *Purgatorio* and in the *Paradiso* (*Purgatorio*, XX. 10-15; XXXIII. 40-45. *Paradiso*, XXX. 133-148 etc.), we shall hardly be inclined to regard them as all belonging to the same emotional stratum of Dante's life.[1] Nor would it be easy to understand the absence of any direct reference to Henry's reign if the work were contemporary with the *Paradiso*.

My conclusion, then (though given merely provisionally and with full consciousness of the difficulties that surround it), is, that the *De Monarchia* was written about the year 1309, and that in it we

[1] As to ecclesiastical affairs, the contrasted tone (though it may be felt) is not nearly so marked. Compare, for instance, *De Monarchia*, II. 12: 18 *sqq.* with *Paradiso*, XXII. 82-84.

APPENDIX

first find in its full maturity the general conception of the nature of man, of government, and of human destiny, which was afterwards transfigured, without being transformed, into the framework of the 'Sacred Poem.' Thus, even in the midst of his highest hopes, Dante was already preparing that 'other path' by which, when all earthly hopes sickened, he was to reach the goal of inward peace and inward liberty which he had sought with such deep devotion.

NOTE BY THE TRANSLATOR

I have pleasure in acknowledging my obligations to F. J. Church's English translation of the *De Monarchia* (first published in 1879), and to the authoritative German translation of Oskar Hubatsch (1872).

In elucidating the numerous references to Aristotle and others, I have naturally found my starting-point in the invaluable labours of Witte and of Moore. P. H. W.

EPISTOLAE

EPISTOLA I

To the most reverend father in Christ, most beloved of their lords, to lord Nicholas, by divine compassion bishop of Ostia and Velletri, legate of the apostolic seat, and ordained by holy church pacificator in Tuscany, Romagna, the Maremma, and adjacent parts and regions, his most devoted children A. ca. and the council and whole body of the White party of Florence most devoutly and eagerly commend themselves.

1. Admonished by salutary precepts and invited by apostolic compassion, we answer, after deliberations which have been sweet to us, the purport of the sacred message which you have despatched. And should we be censured as guilty of negligence or sloth on the charge of injurious delay, let your holy discretion incline this side of condemnation; and when the numbers and weight of the consultations and correspondence which the faithful observance of the terms of our league imposes on the [10] orderly procedure of our brotherhood has been considered, as likewise the things we have in hand, if in any matter we are perchance lightly esteemed for want of due celerity, we implore the abundance of your benignity to pardon us.

Causes of delay

Reasons for war-like measures

2. As not ungrateful sons, therefore, we have inspected the letters of your compassionate paternity, which, embodying the prologue of our whole desire, at once suffused our minds with such joy as none could measure [20] either by word or thought. For that healing of our country for which we yearned with well-nigh delirious longing, the progress of your letter more than once promised under fatherly admonition. And for what else did we rush into civil war? What else did our white standards seek? And for what else were our swords and weapons reddened save that they who had hacked the civil laws at their random whim should submit their necks to the yoke of compassionate law and should be forced to observe their country's [30] peace? In truth, the lawful point of our purpose, leaping from the bowstring that we stretched, aimed, aims, and will aim, at nought save the tranquillity and liberty of the people of Florence. And if you are keeping watch on a purpose of good so absolutely acceptable to us, and are intent on bringing back our adversaries to the furrow of good citizenship, even as our sacred endeavours purposed, who shall attempt to express [40] worthy thanks to you? It is beyond either our own power, O father, or that of all the race of Florence to be found on earth. But if there is any tenderness in heaven to provide for the remuneration of such deeds, may it give you worthy rewards for clothing yourself with compassion for so great a city, and hastening to calm the impious strifes of her citizens.

3. And whereas we are urgently admonished

and required on your behalf (and in accordance **and dutiful submission**
with the purport of your own letter) by brother
L., a man of holy religion [50], urging civil
concord and peace, to cease from every assault and
practice of war and commit ourselves completely
to your paternal hands, we, as most devoted
sons to you, as lovers of peace and as righteous
men, stripping ourselves henceforth of our
swords, submit ourselves to your judgment with
spontaneous and sincere will, even as shall be
set forth in the report of your messenger, the
aforesaid brother L., and established by public
instruments formally [60] executed.

4. Therefore, with filial voice, we most
affectionately implore your most benign compassion to bedew this long harassed Florence
with the repose of tranquillity and peace; and as
a pitying father to consider us who have ever
been defenders of her people, and all who are
under our control, as commended to you; since
like as we have never ceased from the love of
our country so do we never purpose to stray
beyond the [70] limits of your precepts, but
ever, both in duty and in love, to obey all your
commands soever.

> This letter is preserved in a Vatican MS. (Palatine,
> 1729) of the close of the fourteenth century. Nicholas
> of Ostia was in Florence, as pacificator, from early
> March to early June in 1304.
> Lionardo Bruni, in his *Life of D..nte*, declares that
> the exiled Whites 'considered many schemes and
> finally fixed their seat at Arezzo, where they gathered
> a great force and appointed Count Alessandro da
> Romena their captain, with twelve councillors, amongst
> whom was Dante.' From this it has been conjectured
> that the 'A. ca.' of this letter stands for 'Alexander

Capitaneus,' and that as Dante was one of his council it is likely that it was he who drew up this memorial. But it is nowhere expressly assigned to Dante, and it is doubtful whether he was associated with the Whites at the time when it was written. It cannot, therefore, be assigned to him with any confidence.

It is clear that the letter is a genuine document, though it is impossible to determine the precise point of the negotiations into which it fits.

The question of Dante's authorship of this letter is treated at great length by Zenatti (who supports it) in his *Dante e Firenze*, 2nd Appendix. It had previously been examined by Del Lungo (who regards it as a genuine document, but written after Dante had broken with the Whites) in his *Dino Compagni*, vol. II., Appendix XIII. (1879).

1. The opening words of the letter, *Præceptis salutaribus moniti*, are taken from the Mass.
48. There is no clue to the identity of brother L.

EPISTOLA II

Death of Alexander da Romena

1. The illustrious Count Alexander, your uncle, who within these last days has returned to the celestial fatherland, whence, after the spirit, he came, was my lord, and his memory will lord it over me so long as I live; since his munificence, which is now abundantly remunerated with fit rewards above the stars, made me, by his own will, his subject from olden [10] time, which munificence, accompanied in him by every other virtue, made his name illustrious beyond the claims of the heroes of Italy. And what else did his heroic blazon declare save ' we display the scourge that puts vices to flight'? For outwardly he bore silver scourges

on a purple field, and inwardly a mind which drove off vices in love of virtue. Let grief, then, grief come upon that mightiest of Tuscan families to which belonged the glory [20] of so great a man; and let grief come upon all his friends and subjects whose hope death hath cruelly scourged. And amongst these last must I too grieve in my misery; for, banished as I am from my fatherland, and undeservedly exiled, I was wont, when I pondered on my misfortunes, straightway to find the consolation of a precious hope in him.

His blazon and his character

2. But although, when we have lost the things perceived by sense, the bitterness of grief presses upon us, yet if we ponder the things perceived by intellect which survive, verily [30] the sweet light of consolation rises upon the eyes of the mind. For he who paid honour to the virtues upon earth, now hath honour paid to him by the virtues in heaven; and he who was a Paladin of the Roman court in Tuscany, is now in glory a chosen courtier of the eternal palace, in the Jerusalem above, with the chiefs of the blessed. Wherefore, my dearest lords, I implore you with suppliant exhortation that ye be minded to grieve in moderation, and to turn your backs upon things of sense [40], save in so far as they may be examples to you; and like as he most rightly made you the heirs of his goods, so do you yourselves, as the nearest to him, clothe yourselves with his excellent character.

3. But, for the rest, I, your vassal, pray pardon of your discretion for my absence from the tearful obsequies; for it was neither negli-

The writer's absence gence nor ingratitude that restrained me, but the unlooked-for poverty which my exile has brought about; for she [50], fierce persecutress as she is, has already thrust me, horseless and unarmed, into the dungeon of her captivity, and, though I strive with all my power to escape, she, holding the mastery on every side, relentlessly compasses my detention.

This letter (preserved in the same Vatican MS. that contains *Epistola* I.) bears the description:—
'This epistle was written by Dante Alighieri to Oberto and Guido, Counts of Romena, after the death of the Count Alexander of Romena, their uncle, condoling with them on his demise.'

It will be observed that this superscription is not an integral part of the letter, but is merely the account given of it by the copyist or by the authority he followed.

On the supposition that the letter is really Dante's we should have to note the contradiction between its affectionate and respectful tone and the terrible reference to the same Alexander in *Inferno*, XXX. 77. Many writers have been scandalised by what they call the 'ingratitude' of the reference in the *Inferno*, and some have attempted (in vain) to establish a distinction between the two Alexanders. But if there were any scandal at all, it would be in the insincerity of this epistle (if Dante had the same knowledge of Alexander at the time of his death that he had when he wrote the *Comedy*), rather than in the severity of the passage in the *Inferno*.

The general opinion of scholars, however, is that the letter is not Dante's, but is either a deliberate forgery (which seems extremely improbable), or a genuine letter of condolence written by one of the numerous exiles, and falsely attributed to Dante.

Alexander was the chief of the Romena branch of the Conti Guidi, and the date of his death is, so far as I know, still doubtful. The date of 1305, given in some books, is based on a quite arbitrary conjecture.

It must, therefore, remain uncertain for the present whether or not Dante had already broken with the exiles at the time of Alexander's death.

Oberto and Guido were the sons of Alexander's younger brother Aghinolfo (Latham).

EPISTOLA III

Dante writes to lord Moruello, marquis Malaspina.

1. For fear that the master should have no knowledge of the captivity of the servant, and of the graciousness of the affection that commands him, and for fear that confused narrations, which are often wont to become seedbeds of false opinion, should declare the captive to be neglectful of his duty, it has pleased me to address to the sight of your magnificence the concatenation of this present rescript. *The writer taken captive*

2. It chanced, then, that when I had parted from the threshold [10] of that court (for which I was afterwards to sigh) wherein, as you have often marked with wonder, I had leave to follow the offices of liberty, no sooner had I set my feet by the streams of the Arno, in security and carelessness, than straightway behold a woman appeared to me, descending like a lightning flash, strangely harmonious with my condition both in character and in person. Oh, how was I struck dumb at her apparition! But my stupor yielded to the terror of the thunder that followed. For like as thunders [20] straightway follow flashes from heaven, so when the flame of this beauty had appeared,

by love terrible and imperious Love laid hold of me, terrible and imperious; raging, moreover, like a lord banished from his fatherland returning after long exile to what is all his own! For he slew or banished or enchained all opposition in me. He slew that praiseworthy determination in the strength of which I held aloof from women, those instruments of his enchantment; and the unbroken meditations [30] wherein I was pondering on things both of heaven and of earth, he relentlessly banished as things suspected; and finally, that my soul might never again rebel against him, he chained my free will; so that I needs must turn not whither I would, but whither he wills. Love, therefore, reigns within me, and there is no power to oppose him. And how he rules me you must inquire below, outside the boundary of these presents.

This letter appears in the same Vatican MS. that contains the last. Internal evidence inclines most scholars to accept it as genuine. The concluding lines evidently refer to a poem that was enclosed in the letter, and the inevitable inference is that it was the 'Mountain Ode' which is translated in the T. C., *Convivio*, pp. 417 ff. This has suggested to more than one Dante scholar the idea that the 'assiduous meditations' mentioned in line 29 refer to Dante's elaboration of the *Convivio*.

We know that Dante was in relations with the Malaspina in 1306; and the following conjectural piece of biography seems to reach a high probability: During the years 1306-8, or thereabout, Dante was much at the court of the Malaspina, working hard at the *Convivio*, dissociating himself from the amorous tradition of his early years, and regarded as a miracle of continence. An incidental encounter with a lady in the Apennines shattered his resolves and broke off his enterprise, which was then further impeded by the events that followed Henry's election, and was finally abandoned. Compare T. C., *Convivio*, Appendix, especially page 422.

The opinion that the letter was written during Henry's presence in Italy, and that the 'court' referred to in line 10 is his, I regard as highly improbable.

Several members of the Malaspina family were called Moroello (see T. C., *Purgatorio*, p. 89). The recipient of this letter would doubtless be the Count of Giovagallo, who married Alagia dei Fieschi (*Purgatorio*, XIX. 142 and T. C., *Purgatorio*, p. 91), and who is referred to in *Inferno*, XXIV. 145. In this case he would be the same man to whom (according to a tradition preserved by Boccaccio) Dante intended to dedicate the *Purgatorio* (cf. *Purgatorio*, VIII. 109 ff.). His death is placed at about 1315 (Toynbee), which is earlier than the probable date of the completion of the *Purgatorio*; but it is touching to think of the great confession of *Purgatorio*, XXX. and XXXI., Dante's final pronouncement on his own aberrations, as associated in his original intention with the friend who had been intimate with the evasions of the *Convivio* and with the relapse which broke them short.

The text of this letter was dealt with very freely by Witte, whom the Oxford Dante still follows. It was published after the manuscript, by Zenatti (in his recent *Dante e Firenze*, Appendix III.), and I have preferred to face the difficulties of the text as it stands, rather than follow Witte's somewhat arbitrary reconstruction.[1]

Zenatti has made it pretty clear that Moroello, Cino, and Dante, about the years 1306 and 1307, were exchanging letters and poems in a correspondence of which this and the following *Epistle* are portions.

Under such conditions something like a jargon or private language is likely to establish itself, and one

---

[1] An equally arbitrary, though more seductive, reconstruction has been made by Torraca (*Bullettino della Società Dantesca Italiana*, 1903, p. 143).

can hardly tell whether the difficulties of the opening portion of this letter and the occurrence (in line 2) of such a (non-existent) word as *gratuitatio*[1] are due to this cause or merely to the negligence of the scribe, who is certainly not above suspicion. (Cf. note on line 19.).

1-3. I read '*vincula servi, suique affectus gratuitatis dominantis.*'

5. l. *negligentem.*

16 l. *forma* (in place of *fortunæ*).

17. l. *apparitione.*

19. l. *divinis,* with Witte and Moore. The MS. has *diurnis;* but Boccaccio (who borrowed a great part of this letter for one of his own) appears to have read *divinis.* See Zenatti, p. 434.

21. l. *hujus.*

25. l. *enim* (in place of *ei*).

28. The Oxford text is 'mulieribus suisque cantibus,' which might be translated either 'women and songs about them' or 'women and their enchantments.' But the MS. reading is 'mulieribus suis cantibus,' which I can only understand as 'women, who are his [Love's] instruments of enchantment.' In any case those who believe that Dante had been recently occupied with the *Convivio* can hardly suppose he was under a vow to abstain from 'songs about women.'

---

[1] *Gratuitas* is a recognised word, but the genitive, *gratuitatis,* which would be very close to the reading of the MS., gives no sense.

EPISTOLA IV

To the exile of Pistoja he who is undeservedly exiled from Florence sends wishes for long health, and declares the ardour of perpetual affection.

1. The flame of thy love hath uttered forth the word of eager confidence to me, wherein, dear friend, thou dost ask me whether the mind can be transformed from passion to passion; from passion to passion, that is, according to the same capacity, but objects numerically, not specifically, differing. And though the answer would more rightly issue from thy mouth, thou hast none the less chosen to make [10] me the authority concerning it; that by my exposition of a matter so hotly questioned, thou mayest enlarge the prestige of my name. How pleasing, how acceptable, and how grateful this is to me, words cannot express without vexatious derogation; wherefore, considering the cause of this silence, thou art thyself to take the measure of what is unexpressed.

A love problem answered in verse

2. Lo, I offer thee below, in phrase of Calliope, that wherein is sung the opinion (though [20] indicated after the figurative fashion of poets) that the intense love of one specific object may be dulled and may finally perish; and also that the destruction of one may be the begetting of another, which is formed anew in the mind.

3. And confidence in this, though it be a thing brought home by experience, can be fortified by reason and authority; for every

and in prose faculty which perishes not after the decay of a single act, is reserved by nature for another; wherefore [30] the faculties of sense, if the organ abides, are not destroyed by the perishing of one of its acts, but are naturally reserved for another.

Since, then, the concupiscible faculty which is the seat of love is a power of sense, it is manifest that after the death of one passion, wherein it was reduced to act, it is reserved for another. The major and minor propositions of the syllogism, the entry to which lies easily open, may be left to your diligence to prove.

4. [40] The authority of Naso, in the fourth *De Rerum Transformatione*, which directly and literally concerns the matter in hand, thou shouldest carefully inspect; to wit, where the author says (in the story of the three sisters, who despised the deity in the Seed of Semele), speaking to the Sun, who, deserting and neglecting other nymphs of whom he had previously been enamoured, had recently fallen in love with Leucothoe: 'What now, son of Hyperion,' and what follows.

5. [50] For the rest, dearest brother, I exhort thee, to the best of thy power, to be patient against the darts of Rhamnusia. Read, I pray thee, the *Fortuitorum Remedia*, which are ministered to us by Seneca, most illustrious of philosophers, as by a father to his sons, and never let that saying flow out of thy memory: 'If ye had been of the world, the world would have loved its own.'

This strange composition, treating a sufficiently obvious love problem with all the pomp and solemnity of a philosophical or theological discussion, is preserved in a manuscript of Boccaccio's (*Medicæo-Laurentian*, XXIX. 8), in which it appears between two letters of Dante's (*Epistolæ* VII. and IX.).

The identification of the two exiles as Dante and Cino is conjectural; but it is generally accepted, and may be regarded as at least suggested by the position in which Boccaccio placed the letter.

The letter evidently belongs to the same group as *Epistola* IV., and its tone is doubtless dictated by the esoteric traditions and conventions observed by the intimates, Dante, Cino, and Moroello, in their correspondence. A strong presumption in favour of its authenticity is raised by the reference in line 20 to a composition 'in phrase of Calliope' (that is to say 'in verse'), which we cannot help identifying as the sonnet (XXXVI. in Moore's edition) '*Io sono stato con Amore insieme.*'

A translation is subjoined :—

I have been acquaint with Love since my ninth circling sun, and I know how he draws the rein and strikes the spur, and how folk laugh and groan beneath him.

Whoso urges reason or virtue against him is as one who sounds his trumpet in the storm, thinking where the thunder rolls to quench the fury of the blasts.

Wherefore within the circle of his wrestling ground,[1] free will was ne'er emancipated yet, and counsel is launched in vain against him.

Aye, truly with new spurs he may ply the flank, and whatsoever be the pleasure that presently doth tame us needs must we follow it, if worn out be the other.

If this epistle is really from Dante to Cino, as seems probable, it may well date from 1306 or 1307, not later. Compare *De Vul. El.*, I. 11 : 30, *note* (p. 34).

40-49. Alcithoe, daughter of Minyas, in contempt

---

[1] l. *palestra*.

of Bacchus ('the Seed of Semele'), persuaded her sisters and domestics to keep to their spinning and weaving in honour of Minerva while the Bacchic orgies were going on. The three sisters beguiled the time by telling stories, amongst them that of the love of Apollo (son of Hyperion) for Leucothoe.

50. *To the best of your* (or possibly *my*) *power*. So it seems simplest to take *ad potentiam;* but other translators find in it some such meaning as 'a propos of faculties or powers of the mind, let me exhort you, etc.

51. *Rhamnusia*, that is Nemesis. So called from her temple at Rhamnus, near Athens; here apparently the name is to be taken in the wider sense of 'hostile fortune.'

53. *Fortuitorum Remedia*. A work attributed to Seneca in the Middle Ages, the real author of which was Martin of Dumio in Portugal, a sixth-century saint and bishop (Toynbee).

EPISTOLA V

On the kings of Italy all and several, on the senators of her fostering city, on her dukes, marquises, counts, and peoples, the humble Italian Dante Alighieri, the Florentine, exiled counter to his deserts, imploreth peace.

A new dawn 1. Lo now is the acceptable time wherein arise the signs of consolation and peace. For a new day beginneth to glow, showing forth the dawn which is even now dissipating the darkness of our long calamity; and already the breezes of the east begin to blow, the lips of heaven glow red, and confirm the auspices of the nations with a caressing calm. And we, too, shall see the looked-for joy, we who have kept vigil through the long night in the [10] rises upon desert. For peace-bringing Titan shall arise, Italy and Justice, which, without the sun hath languished like the heliotrope, will revive again so soon as he shall brandish his first ray. All they who hunger and thirst shall be satisfied in the light of his rays, and they who love iniquity shall be confounded before his shining face. For the strong lion of the tribe of Judah hath lifted up his merciful ears, and, taking pity on the wail of universal captivity, hath raised up a second [20] Moses to snatch his people from the burdens of the Egyptians, leading them to the land that floweth with milk and honey.

2. O Italy! henceforth rejoice; though now to be pitied by the very Saracens, yet soon to be envied throughout the world! because thy bridegroom, the solace of the world and the glory of thy people, the most clement Henry, Divus and Augustus and Cæsar, is hastening to the bridal. Dry thy tears and remove the marks of grief [30], O thou fairest one; for nigh at hand is he who shall release thee from the prison of the impious, and, smiting the malicious, shall destroy them with the edge of the sword, and shall give out his vineyard to other husbandmen such as shall render the fruit of justice at time of harvest.

3. But will he not have compassion on any? Yea! he will pardon all who implore his mercy, since he is Cæsar and his majesty floweth from the fount of compassion. His [40] judgment abhorreth all severity, and, smiting ever on this side of the mean, planteth itself beyond the mean in rewarding. Will he then applaud the

Fitting dispositions towards audacities of worthless men, and drink to the undertakings of presumption? Far be it! For he is Augustus. And, if Augustus, will he not avenge the deeds of backsliders and pursue them even unto Thessaly—the Thessaly, I mean, of final extinction?

[50] 4. O blood of the Lombards, put off thy contracted barbarism, and if aught of the seed of the Trojans and the Latins remain, give place thereto, lest when the eagle from above shall come swooping down like a thunderbolt he find his own nestlings cast out and the place of his proper offspring seized by crows. Ah, see to it, ye tribe of Scandinavia, that so far as lieth in you, ye learn to long for his presence at whose coming ye now rightly tremble! Nor let illusive greed [60] seduce you, siren-like, doing to death, by some charm, the vigil of reason. 'Come before his face with confession of submission, and rejoice in penitential psalmody,' remembering that 'whoso resisteth the power resisteth the ordinance of God,' and whoso fighteth against the divine ordinance kicketh against a will co-equal with omnipotence; and 'it is hard to kick against the prick.'

5. But ye who grieve under oppression [70], uplift your heart; for your salvation is nigh at hand. Take the harrow of fair humility, and breaking up the clods caked by the heat of your wrath, make level the acre of your minds, lest haply the celestial shower, anticipating the seed ere ye have sown it, fall from on high in vain; that the grace of God leap not back from you like the daily dew from a rock; but rather, that ye conceive like a fertile valley, and thrust forth

the green [80], the green, that is, that bears the fruit of true peace; that when your land is keeping spring in this verdure, the new ploughman of the Romans may, with the more love and confidence, yoke the oxen of his counsel to the plough. Be merciful, be merciful even henceforth, O dearest ones who have suffered wrong with me, that the Hectorean pastor may recognise you as sheep of his fold. For though temporal punishment be divinely committed to him, yet (that he may savour of the goodness [90] of him from whom, as from a single point, the power of Peter and of Cæsar brancheth) he delicately correcteth his household, and yet more gladly doth take compassion on it.

the representative of justice and mercy

6. And therefore, unless hindered by the inveterate offence which oft in serpent fashion doth twist round and turn upon itself, ye may perceive on either side that peace is prepared for all and every, and may taste already the first fruits of the hoped-for joy. Awake then all ye dwellers in Italy and [100] arise before your king since ye are destined not only to obey his command, but, as free-born children, to follow his guidance.

7. Nor do I exhort you only to arise, but to stand dumb before his presence. Ye who drink his streams and sail upon his seas; who tread upon the sands of the shores and the summits of the alps which are his; who possess whatsoever public rights ye enjoy, and all things ye hold in private, by the chain of his law [110], not else; deceive not yourselves in ignorance, nor dream in your hearts and say: 'We have no lord': for all that heaven circles

The authority of the Roman empire is his orchard and his lake. For 'the sea is God's and he made it, and his hands established the dry land'; and that being so, it is clear, from miraculous events, that God chose the Roman prince before, and the church declareth that by word of the Word that he confirmed him after.

[120] 8. For if 'from the creation of the world the invisible things of God are perceived by the mind through those things which are made,' and if the less known things are perceived through the better known to us; it is likewise the business of the human apprehension to understand the mover of heaven and his will, through the motion of heaven; and this predestination will grow clear to him who considereth even a little. For if we traverse past times from the first spark of this flame when hospitality was denied to the Argives by the [130] Phrygians, and if we review the doings of the world even to the triumphs of Octavian, we shall see that some of them utterly transcend the summits of human virtue, and that God therein wrought in a measure through men as though through new heavens. For it is not always we who act. Nay, sometimes we are God's instruments, and human wills, which are by nature free, are sometimes driven without touch of lower [140] affection, submissive to the eternal will, serving it often though they know it not.

9. And if these things, which are as it were the premises for the proof of the thing we seek, suffice not, who that taketh his start from the conclusion reached by them shall escape the compulsion to think with us, when he sees the

twelve years' peace, embracing all the world, sanc-
and revealing the face of the syllogiser, that tioned by
is, revealing the Son of God, as with accom- Christ
plished deed ? And he himself, when [150]
he had become man for the revealing of the
Spirit, and was preaching the gospel upon earth,
as though partitioning the two kingdoms, and
distributing the universe between himself and
Cæsar, ' Render,' he said, ' to either the things
that are his own.'

10. But if a stubborn mind demandeth
further proof, not yet assenting to the truth,
let it examine the words of Christ, even when
already bound; for when Pilate urged on him
his power, our Light declared that office to come
from above of which [160] he who then bore it
in the vicarious authority of Cæsar made his boast.
Walk not, therefore, as the Gentiles walk in
the vanity of their thought, clouded in dark-
ness, but open the eyes of your mind and see
that the Lord of heaven and earth hath
ordained to us a king. He it is whom Peter,
the vicar of God, exhorteth us to honour,
whom Clement, the present successor of Peter,
doth illuminate with the light of the apostolic
benediction; that where the spiritual ray suffic-
eth not there [170] the splendour of the lesser
luminary may give light.

> This letter is preserved in the Vatican MS. above
> referred to; and also in another Roman manuscript
> (in the *Biblioteca Nazionale*). There can be no doubt
> as to its authenticity. On the contrast offered by the
> high-wrought expectancy and passion of this and the
> following letters to the self-restraint of the *De Mon-
> archia*, consult pp. 287-289 of this volume. The only

discrepancy of doctrine between the letter and the *De Monarchia* that a microscopic examination could reveal is to be found in the fact that Dante here implicitly makes his peace with the symbolism by which the sun is taken to represent the papacy and the moon the empire (lines 165-170), though he rejects it in the third book of the *De Monarchia*. The same remark applies to the next epistle (lines 54, 55), and *Epist.* IX. 8: 159.

The exact date of this letter cannot be determined, but we may suppose that it was written in September 1310 or thereabouts.

The following dates may be of use to the student in reading this and the two next letters:—

Henry's election	Nov. 1308.
His coronation at Aix-la-Chapelle	June 1309.
He crosses the Alps and enters Turin	Sept. and Oct. 1310.
Dante's letter (v) to the princes of Italy	(?) Sept. 1310.
Robert of Naples in Florence .	Sept. 1310.
Florentines refuse to receive Henry's ambassadors	Oct. 1310.
Henry crowned at Milan . .	Jan. 1311.
The Florentines resolve to renew their fortifications . . .	Feb. 4, 1311.
Dante's letter (vi) to the Florentines	Feb. 28, 1311.
Henry lays siege to Cremona .	Feb. 12, 1311.
Florentines refuse to send an ambassador to Henry at Pisa .	(?) March 1311.
Dante's letter (vii) to Henry .	April 16, 1311.
Henry takes Cremona . .	April 20, 1311.
Many Florentine exiles recalled .	April 26, 1311.
Henry takes Brescia by siege .	May & June 1311.
The emperor's headquarters at Genoa and then at Pisa .	Winter of 1311-1312.
Death of the empress at Genoa .	Nov. 1311.
Rebellion of Brescia and Cremona	Winter of 1311-1312.
Henry leaves Pisa for Rome .	April 1312.
Is crowned at St John Lateran (St Peter's being in possession of King Robert's faction) .	May 1312.

Moves north and lays siege to Florence	Sept. 19 to end of Oct. 1312.
Withdraws to Casciano and Poggibonsi, and then to Pisa	Winter & spring, 1312-1313.
Moves south from Pisa with reinforcements	Aug. 5, 1313.
Dies of fever at Buonconvento, near Siena	Aug. 24, 1313.

48. *Thessaly.* Julius Cæsar defeated Pompey at Pharsalia, in Thessaly.

69-93 It is well to note the generous and forgiving temper which, in the hour of his anticipated triumph, inspired Dante towards his political opponents.

86. *Hectorean* = Trojan = Roman = Imperial.

114. Because, to begin with, it is all God's; and, in the next place, his miraculous preparation for the Roman empire constituted a gift of it all to the Roman emperor in advance, and the testimony of Christ constitutes a confirmation of the gift *post factum*.

120. Created things are the divinely appointed means of indicating the invisible things of God to the human intellect (Romans I. 20); and the right order of philosophical inquiry is to proceed from what is more known to us to what is less known to us (Aristotle's *Physics*, I. 1). Therefore, the proper concern of the human mind is to examine the movements of the heavens (*i.e.* the course of human history as dominated by the heavens), and so discover the will of God.

129. Dares Phrygius (cap. II.) tells how the Argonauts, on their way to Colchis, touched at the port of the Simois. Laomedon drove them off. Hence the first sacking of Troy under Hercules, and the rape of Hesione, followed in due course by the rape of Helen in reprisal.

160. 'Pilate said unto him, Speakest thou not unto me? Knowest thou not that I have power to release thee? Jesus answered, Thou couldest have no power at all against me, except it were given thee from above' (John XIX. 10, 11).

EPISTOLA VI

Dante Alighieri, the Florentine, exiled counter to his deserts, to the most infamous Florentines within.

The miseries of an imperial interregnum

1. The tender providence of the eternal King,—who, though he perpetually sustains celestial things by his goodness, yet looks down on our affairs below and deserts them not,—hath committed human things, for governance, to the holy Roman empire, that the mortal race might be at peace under the serenity of so great a guardianship, and, as nature demandeth, might in all places live the civil life. And though this be proved by the sacred utterances, and though antiquity [10], leaning only on the support of reason, beareth witness thereto, yet it is no small confirmation of the truth that when the throne of Augustus is vacant all the world turneth out of its course, the helmsman and rowers in the ship of Peter slumber, and wretched Italy, deserted, and abandoned to private caprices, destitute of all public guidance, is tossed with such battling of winds and waves as words may not express, nay, the wretched Italians themselves can scarce measure with their tears. Wherefore, let all who [20] in rash presumption do magnify themselves against this most manifest will of God, be now smitten with pallor, as the judgment of the stern Judge draweth nigh—unless the sword of him who said, 'Vengeance is mine,' have fallen out of heaven.

2. But you, who transgress divine and human law, whom a dire rapaciousness hath found ready to be drawn into every crime, —doth not the dread of the second death pursue you [30]? For ye first and alone, shunning the yoke of liberty, have murmured against the glory of the Roman prince, the king of the world and the minister of God, and on the plea of prescriptive right have refused the duty of the submission which ye owed, and have rather risen up in the insanity of rebellion! Or are ye ignorant in your madness and your spleen that public rights have limitation only with the limitation of time, and can be called to no reckoning by prescription? For the sanctions of the laws [40] proclaim aloud, and human reason perceiveth by searching out, that the supremacy over public things, howsoever long neglected, can never lose its force, nor, however emaciated, be overcome. For that which maketh for the advantage of all cannot perish, nor even be weakened, without detriment to all. The which God and nature wills not, and the consensus of mortals would utterly abhor. Wherefore, then, stirring up so vain a [50] thought as this, do ye, a second race of Babylonians, desert the compassionate empire and seek to establish new kingdoms, making the civic life of Florence one, and that of Rome another? Wherefore should not the like envy attack the apostolic monarchy, that if Delia be reduplicated in the heavens Delius should be reduplicated in like fashion? But if the requital of your evil enterprises is not a terror to you, let this then terrify your stubborn minds, that not only wisdom

Enormity of the opposition of Florence to the empire

Its futility but the beginning thereof hath been taken from you as a penalty [60] for your sin. For no condition of the delinquent is more terrible than when he doeth after his will shamelessly and without fear of God. Full often, in truth, is the impious man smitten with this punishment, that he should be forgetful of himself in death, since he hath been forgetful of God in life.

3. But if your insolent arrogance hath so bereft you of the dew of the Most High (even as the mountains of Gilboa), that it was no terror [70] to resist the decree of the eternal senate, nor a terror that ye are not terrified, surely that base terror, human to wit and mundane, cannot be lacking when the inevitable shipwreck of your proudly exalted blood, and your right lamentable rapine hastens on! Or do ye, girt by your contemptible vallum, trust in defence? Oh, harmonious in ill, oh, blinded by wondrous greed, what shall it avail to have girt you with a vallum and to have [80] fortified you with outworks and battlements, when, terrible in gold, that eagle shall swoop down on you who soaring, now over the Pyrenees, now over Caucasus, now over Atlas, ever strengthened by the breath of the soldiery of heaven, looked down of old upon vast oceans o'er which lay his flight! Oh, most wretched of men! How shall it be with you, when ye stand dumb in the presence of him who shall tame the insane Hesperia? The hope which ye cherish in vain, and against all virtuous use, shall not be furthered by this your resistance; but rather [90] shall such an obstacle make the advent of the just king flame up the more, and mercy, who

doth ever accompany his army, shall fly away **Woes to**
indignant; and where ye think to defend the **come**
corridor of false liberty, there shall ye fall into
the dungeons of true slavery. For we are to
believe that by a wondrous judgment of God it
doth sometimes come to pass that by the very
path whereby the impious man thinketh to
escape the punishment he doth deserve, he is
hurled therein the more grievously; and he who,
knowing and willing, hath wrestled against [100]
the divine will, must needs take service under it
when he knoweth not nor willeth.

4. The fortifications which ye have not reared
in prudence against necessity, but changed at ran-
dom and for wantonness, which gird no Pergama
risen once again,—these ye shall mournfully gaze
upon as they fall in ruins before the battering-
ram, and are burnt with fire. Ye shall see
that populace which now doth rage hither and
thither, for and against, then of one mind clamour-
ing dire threats against you, for [110] they may
not be hungry and timid at one same time. Ye
shall look upon the grievous sight of your
temples, thronged with the daily concourse of
matrons, given up to the spoiler; and of your
wondering and unknowing little ones, destined
to expiate the sins of their sires. And—if my
presaging mind be not deceived, as it announceth
that which it hath learned from truth-telling
signs, and arguments that may not be gainsaid,
—your city, worn out with long-drawn suffer-
ings, shall be given at last into the hands of the
aliens, the greatest part [120] of you scattered
in death and captivity, while the few that are
left to endure their exile shall look on and weep.

Vain hopes and empty precedents And, briefly to sum up all, what sufferings that glorious city of Saguntum bore in faithfulness for liberty, those same must ye of force endure shamefully, in perfidy, for slavery.

5. And draw not courage from the unlooked-for fortune of the men of Parma, who (when hunger, counsellor of ill, urged them), murmured one to another [130], 'Let us die, and rush into the midst of arms,' and broke into the camp of Cæsar in Cæsar's absence. For even they, though they had their victory over Victoria, nevertheless came by disaster over that disaster in memorable guise. But think rather of the thunders of the former Frederick. Think of Milan and Spoleto. For, by the consideration of their perversion and likewise eversion, your over-swelling flesh will have a chill [140] and your too glowing hearts will shrink. Oh, vainest of the Tuscans, insensate alike by nature and ill custom, little do you think or understand, in your ignorance, how the feet of your diseased mind go astray, in the darkness of the night, before the very eyes of the full-fledged! For the full-fledged and uncontaminated in the way look upon you as ye stand on the threshold of the prison, repelling whosoever hath pity upon you, lest haply he should deliver you from your captivity and from the [150] fetters that bind your hands and feet. Nor in your blindness do ye perceive the lust that hath sway over you, lulling you with poisonous whisper, holding you back with scourging threats, making you captive to the law of sin and forbidding you to obey the sacred laws that copy the image of natural justice; the observance whereof, if it be joyous,

if it be free, is not only proved to be no slavery, **Freedom**
but to him who looketh in clearness [160] is **of service**
seen itself to be supreme liberty. For what else **of mad**
is liberty save the free course from will to act **recalci-**
which the laws make easy for those who submit **trance**
to them? Since then they alone are free who
of their own will obey the law, what are ye to
think of yourselves who whilst ye make parade
of the love of liberty conspire against the uni-
versal laws, and against the prince of the laws?

6. Oh, most wretched offspring of Fiesole!
Oh, Punic barbarism once again! Do the things
that I have [170] touched on strike too little
terror into you? Nay, I believe that, for all the
hope ye simulate in countenance and lying word,
ye tremble in your waking hours and ever start
from your slumbers shuddering at the omens
that have crept into your dreams or rehearsing
the counsels of the daytime. But if in your
well-merited trepidation ye regret your madness,
but yet grieve not for it, be it further imprinted
on your minds (that the streamlets of fear and
woe may flow into the bitterness of repentance)
[180] that this baton-bearer of the Roman
estate, this divine and triumphant Henry, thirst-
ing not for his own but for the public ease, hath
shrunk on our behalf from no arduous task,
freely sharing in our sufferings, as though the
prophet Isaiah had pointed the finger of prophecy
upon him, after Christ, when by the revelation
of the Spirit of God he foretold 'truly he hath
borne our weaknesses and hath carried our woes.'
Therefore, if ye cease to dissemble [190], ye
yourselves perceive that the time is at hand for
most bitter remorse for your rash undertakings.

Inevitable chastisement Yet may not late penitence, of such a sort, give birth to pardon. Rather is it itself the beginning of seasonable chastisement. For the saying is: The sinner is smitten that he may come back to the way without backsliding.

Written the day before the Kalends of April, on the confines of Tuscany, under the source of the Arno, in the first year of the most auspicious progress to Italy of Henry the [200] Cæsar.

This Epistle also appears in the Vatican MS. already mentioned. When Dante realised that Florence was heading the resistance to the emperor his grief and indignation knew no bounds. This letter is doubtless what Lionardo Bruni refers to when, after telling how Henry's expedition threw all Italy into a fever of expectation, he goes on to say: 'Whereon Dante could not hold his purpose of awaiting grace, but exalting himself with disdainful mind, began to revile them who were in possession of the city, calling them infamous and evil, and threatening them with the punishment they deserved at the hands of the emperor, from which, he said, it was evident that they could have no escape.' This alone would suffice (could there be any doubt otherwise) to prove the authenticity of the Epistle. We should note that (in spite of the furious denunciations of this and still more of the following letter) Lionardo assures us that Dante 'retained so much reverence for his fatherland, that when the emperor advanced on Florence and encamped hard by the gate, he would not accompany him.' Compare *Epistola* V. 5.

22, 23. *Unless* . . . *have fallen from heaven*, i.e. unless Heaven have lost its power to execute justice.

50. *Babylonians*, i.e., Babel-builders = impious rebels. *Compassionate*. *Cf.* § 3 of the previous letter.

54, 55. A *reductio ad absurdum*. If you attack the unity of the imperial regimen (the lesser light = the moon = Delia), why not attack the unity of the papal regimen (the greater light = the sun = Delius)?

59. *The beginning thereof.* 'The fear of the Lord is the beginning of wisdom.'

79 ff. *I.e.* how do you expect your fortifications to hold out against the Roman power, which of old passed Europe, Asia, and Africa, commanding oceans and mountains in its victorious flight, inspired by heaven?

102-106. The attempt to fortify Florence is no well-conceived design to ward off danger, but a mere whim. And the cause you are defending is not that of Troy = Rome = just administration of human affairs.

110. 'Nescit plebes jejuna timere' (*Lucan*, III. 58). 'A starving population knows not what fear means.' When Florence feels the pinch of hunger the people will no longer be timidly submissive to the leaders.

132. Victoria was the name of Frederick II.'s fortified camp, taken by the men of Parma in the desperate sally that compelled the emperor to raise the siege (*Villani*, VI. 34). Dante says they reaped ultimate disaster themselves from the disaster they inflicted on Frederick.

196. Apparently a proverb. Does Dante mean that the corrective punishment has only a limited application, and that Florence, as a backslider, must now expect conclusive condemnation?

EPISTOLA VII

> *Of the most sacred triumphant one, and sole lord, Lord Henry, by divine providence king of the Romans, ever Augustus, his most devoted servants Dante Alighieri the Florentine, exiled counter to his deserts, and all the Tuscans generally who desire the peace of the land, do kiss the feet.*

1. As testifieth the unmeasurable love of **Peace** God, the inheritance of peace hath been left to

Long wept for and still delayed us, that in its marvellous sweetness the hardships of our warfare might be softened, and by its practice we might earn the joys of the triumphant fatherland. But the envy of the ancient and implacable foe, who plotteth ever and in secret against the prosperity of man, by persuading some to forfeit their heritage of their own will, hath, in the guardian's absence, impiously stripped us others thereof [10] against our will. Hence we have long wept by the streams of Confusion, and without ceasing have implored the protection of the righteous king, that he should scatter the following of the cruel tyrant and re-establish us in our just rights. And when thou, successor of Cæsar and of Augustus, leaping over the ridges of the Apennines, didst bring back the venerated Tarpeian standards, forthwith our long sighing desisted and the floods of our tears were dried. And, even as the rising of the longed-for [20] Titan, the new hope of a better age flashed upon Latium. Then many a one, anticipating in his joy the wishes of his heart, sang with Maro of the kingdom of Saturn and of the returning Virgin.

2. But because our sun (whether the fervour of our longing or the appearance of the truth stirs up the thought) already either seemeth to delay or is thought to be receding, as though Joshua or the Son of Amoz did again command it, we are compelled in our uncertainty [30] to question, and to break into the words of the Precursor, 'Art thou he who should come or do we look for another?' Yet although long thirst, as it is wont, in its frenzy turneth to

doubt (just because they are close at hand) even those things which are certain, nevertheless, we believe and hope in thee, averring that thou art the minister of God and the son of the church and the promoter of Roman glory. And I too, who write for myself and for others, have seen thee, as [40] beseems imperial Majesty, most benignant, and have heard thee most clement, when that my hands handled thy feet and my lips paid their debt. Then did my spirit exult in thee, and I spoke silently with myself, ' Behold the Lamb of God! Behold him who hath taken away the sins of the world.'

The Roman empire over the world

3. But we marvel what may be the cause of this so sluggish delay. Victor long ago in the valley of the Po, thou dost desert, pass [50] over, and neglect Tuscany, no otherwise than as though thou didst suppose the laws of the empire thou hast to guard to be circumscribed by the boundaries of Liguria, not perceiving (as we suspect) that the power of the Romans is neither cramped within the limits of Italy nor the margin of three-cornered Europe. For although under violence it has drawn in its reins on every side into narrower space, yet, by inviolable law, it doth reach the flow of Amphitrite, and scarce deigneth to be bounded [60] by the barren wave of ocean. For it is written for us,

'*Nascetur pulchra Troianus origine Cæsar,
Imperium Oceano, famam qui terminet astris.*'[1]

[1] 'There shall be born a Trojan Cæsar of fair origin, who shall bound his empire by the ocean, his fame by the stars' (*Æneid*, I. 286 *sq.*).

con- And when (as loweth our evangelic ox, kindled
firmed by by the flame of the eternal fire) Augustus had
Christ given out the edict that all the world should be
enrolled, if this edict had not issued from the
council chamber of the most righteous prince-
dom, the only begotten Son of God, made man,
would never, by way of professing himself sub-
ject after his [70] assumed nature to the edict,
have chosen that time to be born of a virgin;
for he whom it behoved to fulfil all righteousness
would not have urged by his example that which
was unjust.

4. Be ashamed, then, to be entangled so long
in a little narrow plot of the world, thou for
whom all the world looketh! And let it not
escape the vision of Augustus that the tyranness
of Tuscany is strengthened in the confidence of
delay, and daily exhorting the pride of the
malignant ones [80], gathereth new strength
and addeth audacity to audacity. Let that word
of Curio to Cæsar ring forth once more—

' *Dum trepidant nullo firmatæ robore partes,*
Tolle moras ; semper nocuit differre paratis ;
Par labor atque metus pretio maiore petuntur.' [1]

Let that voice of the chider ring forth from the
clouds once more against Æneas—

' *Si te nulla movet tantarum gloria rerum,*
Nec super ipse tua moliris laude laborem [90],

---

[1] ' Whilst the factions are trembling, with no con-
firmed strength, banish delay! They who are ready
ever suffer by deferring. Equal toil and fear are
encountered for a greater prize ' (*Lucan*, I. 280-282).

*Ascanium surgentem et spes heredis Iuli
Respice ; cui regnum Italiæ Romanaque tellus
Debentur.*' [1]

must be vindicated by Henry

5. For John, thy royal first-born, the king whom the world's posterity to come anticipates, after the setting of the day that now is rising, is for us a second Ascanius, who, following in the footprints of his great sire, shall rage like a lion all around against every Turnus, and shall be gentle as a lamb towards [100] the Latins. Let the deep counsels of the most sacred king take heed lest the heaven-inspired judgment of Samuel once more whet these words, 'When thou wast little in thine own eyes, wast thou not made the head of the tribes of Israel? And God anointed thee to be king over Israel, and God sent thee on the way and said: *Go, slay the sinners of Amalek.*' For thou too hast been anointed king, that thou mayst slay Amalek and spare not Agag, and mayst avenge him who sent [110] thee against a brutish folk and against their inconsiderate festivities, which in truth Amalek and Agag are said to mean.

6. Dost thou delay at Milan, through spring as well as winter, and think to destroy the poisonous hydra by smiting off her heads? But hadst thou thought upon the mighty deeds of glorious Alcides thou wouldst have recognised that thou, like him, art mocked; for the pestilent

---

[1] 'If the glory of such deeds move thee not at all, and thou wilt not base the toil on thine own praise, think of the rising Ascanius and the hopes of thine heir Iulus, to whom the kingdom of Italy and the Roman land are due' (*Æneid*, IV. 272 *sq.*).

The unclean flux from Florence creature, as her teeming heads multiplied, grew stronger for mischief, until [120] the great-souled one choked at once the source of her life. For it sufficeth not to cut off the branches of trees, wouldst thou extirpate them, for they thrust forth green branches still the more so long as their roots be sound to give them food. What wilt thou boast to have accomplished, thou only ruler of the world, when thou hast twisted the neck of the rebellious Cremona? Will not some sudden madness swell up at Brescia or at Pavia? Yea, and when this [130] shall have sunk down chastised, straightway another at Vercelli or Bergamo or elsewhere will rise again until the root cause of this teeming be removed, and, the root of so great error being uptorn, the thorny branches wither with the trunk.

7. Dost thou not know, most excellent of princes, and from the watch tower of highest exaltation dost thou not perceive where the fox of this stench skulks in safety from the hunters? For the culprit drinketh not of the headlong Po, nor of [140] thy Tiber, but her jaws do ever pollute the streams of the torrent of Arno; and (knowest thou not perchance?) this dire plague is named Florence. She is the viper that turns upon the entrails of her mother. She is the sick sheep that infects the flock of her lord with her contagion. She is the foul and impious Myrrha that burns for the embraces of her father Cinyras. She is that passionate Amata who rejected the wedlock decreed by fate, and feared not to summon to herself the son-in-law that [150] fate denied her; who

called him forth to war, in her madness, and must be
at last, expiating her evil deeds, hanged herself staunched
in the noose. In truth, with the fierceness of
a viper she is striving to rend her mother, for
she hath sharpened the horns of rebellion against
Rome, who created her in her image and after
her likeness. In truth doth she breathe out
poisonous fumes, exhaling infection whence the
neighbouring sheep pine even without knowing
it, whilst [160] she with her false blandish-
ments and fictions draweth her neighbours to
her and bewitcheth them when drawn. In
truth doth she burn for the embraces of her
father, since she striveth, in wicked wantonness,
to violate against thee the assent of the supreme
pontiff, who is the father of fathers. In truth
doth she resist the ordinance of God, worship-
ping the idol of her proper will; and whilst
scorning her rightful king, she blusheth not, in
her madness, to traffic in laws which are not
hers, with a king who is not her own, for power
[170] that she may use amiss. But the in-
furiated woman doth but await the halter where-
with to noose herself. For often is one betrayed
into reprobate conceit, that when betrayed he
may do the things which beseem him not.
Then, though they be unjust deeds, yet are
they recognised as just penalties.

8. Come, then, banish delay! thou lofty
scion of Jesse. Take to thee confidence from
the eyes of the Lord God of Sabaoth, before
whom thou standest, and lay this Golias low
with the sling [180] of thy wisdom and the
stone of thy strength; for when he falleth,
night and the darkness of fear shall overwhelm

and the the camp of the Philistines; the Philistines shall
very flee, and Israel shall be delivered. Then shall
memories our heritage, the taking away of which we weep
of evil
sweet- without ceasing, be restored to us again. And
ened even as we now groan, remembering the holy
Jerusalem, exiles in Babylon, so, then, citizens,
breathing again in peace, we shall look back in
our joy upon the miseries of [190] Confusion.

Written in Tuscany, under the source of the Arno, fourteen days before the Kalends of May, 1311, in the first year of the most auspicious progress to Italy of the divine Henry.

  This letter again is preserved in the Vatican MS., but other copies of it are also extant. It is one of the three expressly referred to by Villani, and is described by him as 'written to the emperor when besieging Brescia [it should rather be Cremona], reproving him for his delay, almost in prophetic strain.'

  1. *John* XIV. 27. Note the contrast between church militant and church triumphant.
  10, 11. *Psalm* CXXXVII. [Vulgate CXXXVI. 1], Babylon = confusion.
  17. *Tarpeian* is apparently used merely as equivalent to *Roman*, so that the whole phrase will mean 'didst restore the imperial eagle to Italy.'
  23. The reference is to Virgil's *Eclogue*, IV. The Virgin is Astræa, or Justice.
  28. The son of Amoz = Isaiah. The reference is to the putting back of the shadow on the dial in sign of the new term of life granted to Hezekiah.
  33, 34. The meaning is somewhat doubtful. I take it to be that when we have long thirsted for a thing we cannot believe that it has really come.
  64-73. Compare *De Monarchia*, II. 12.
  65, 67. *I.e.* as the evangelist Luke, under divine inspiration, declares.
  85. This last line does not really belong to the

VIII.   EPISTOLAE   331

other two; and it is by no means clear what sense Dante attached to it in this connection. For Dante's final judgment on Curio, see *Inferno*, XXVIII. 94-102.

88-92. The words were spoken by Mercury to Æneas, to make him quit his life of ease and security with Dido. Æneas = Henry VII. Ascanius or Iulus = John, Henry's son, who became, by marriage, King of Bohemia in 1310, and (when he had lost the sight of both his eyes) died in the battle of Crecy, in 1346.

111, 112. I take this to refer to some current interpretation of the meaning of these names.

147-150. Cinyras = the pope. Æneas (the fate-appointed spouse) = the emperor. Turnus (the arbitrarily substituted son-in-law) = Robert of Naples. Dante himself explains the cipher in the passage that follows.

155-157. *Horns of rebellion.* A month or so before this letter was written, Henry had required the Florentines to send an ambassador to Pisa, bearing their submission to him. Betto Brunelleschi had replied, on behalf of the Signoria, that 'the Florentines never lower their horns for any lord' (*Dino Campagni*, III. 35). *In her own image,* see *Villani,* I. 38; III. 2.

EPISTOLA VIII

To the Italian cardinals Dante Alighieri of Florence.

1. 'How doth the city sit desolate, who was filled with people! The mistress of the nations hath become as a widow.' The greed of the chief Pharisees which made the ancient priesthood hateful, in former times not only transferred the ministry of the offspring of Levi but begat siege and ruin for David's chosen city. And he who alone is eternal, looking down

Deserted Rome

[10] from the lofty watchtower of eternity, did through the Holy Spirit impress the same by his command upon the mind, worthy of God, of a man who was a prophet; who thereon wept for the holy city Jerusalem, as extinct, in the words set down above, and oh, grief! repeated but too often.

mourned over and scoffed at

2. And we too, who confess the same to be Father and Son, the same to be God and Man, and in like manner the same to be Mother and Virgin, we for whom and for whose [20] salvation the words were uttered to him thrice-questioned concerning love, 'Peter, feed my sacred flock,' grieve to look upon Rome (to whom after so many glorious triumphs Christ confirmed with word and deed the empire of the world, whom that great Peter, and Paul the preacher to the Gentiles, consecrated as the apostolic seat with the sprinkling of their own blood, whom, widowed and deserted [30], we must now needs wail over, with Jeremiah, not after him in mourning, though mourning after him), no less than to look upon the lamentable wound of heresy.

3. The champions of impiety, Jews, Saracens, and Gentiles, scoff at our sabbaths; and, as it is written, cry out 'where is their God?' and perchance ascribe it all to their own plots and power against the protecting angels. And, what is more horrible, certain astronomers, crudely prophesying [40], declare that to be of necessity which in truth ye, making ill use of the liberty of the will, have rather chosen.

4. But ye, as it were the officers of the first rank of church militant, neglecting to guide the

chariot of the spouse along the manifest track of **Perverse**
the Crucified, have gone astray no otherwise **drivers**
than the false driver Phaeton. And ye whose **and**
duty it was to guide the flock that followed you **guides**
through the glades of this pilgrimage, have led
both it and yourselves to the precipice [50].
Nor do I rehearse examples for your imitation,
because you have turned your backs and not your
faces to the chariot of the bride, and ye may in
truth be considered as those who were shown to
the prophet turned the reverse way toward the
temple. Ye have despised the fire sent down
from heaven, where now the altars burn with
strange fire; ye have sold doves in the temple,
where those things which cannot be measured
for price are put up for sale, unto destruction
[60]. But look to the cord, look to the fire,
and despise not his patience who awaits your
penitence. And if ye are in doubt concerning
the precipice of which I have spoken, what more
shall I declare in answer save that like unto
Demetrius ye have consented to Alcimus?

5. Perchance ye will cry in indignant
rebuke, 'And who is this, who, fearing not the
swift punishment of Uzzah, raiseth himself up
to the ark [70], tottering though it be?' In
truth I am one of the least of the sheep on the
pastures of Jesus Christ. I have no pastoral
authority to abuse, for riches are not mine. Not
therefore by grace of wealth, but of God, I am
what I am; and the zeal of his house hath eaten
me up. For even by the mouth of sucklings
and babes hath the truth, well pleasing to God,
ere now been uttered; and the man born blind
confessed the truth which the Pharisees not only

The ark and the oxen [80] suppressed but even strove in their malignity to turn back. It is thus that I am persuaded to my daring deed; and moreover I have with me the Philosopher as my instructor, who, in his teaching on the whole body of morals, declareth that the truth must be preferred to every friend. Nor will the presumption of Uzzah (which some might think could be cast against me as though I were rashly breaking in) infect me with the poison of his crime; for he turned him to the ark, I to the kicking oxen that drag it through devious ways [90]. Let him rescue the Ark who opened his eyes to bring salvation upon the storm-tossed ship.

6. It seems not then that I have provoked any to rail against me; but rather that I have kindled the blush of confusion in you and in others, shepherds only in name, throughout the world (unless shame be altogether rooted out), because that, for all there be so many that exercise the office of pastor, and so many sheep that are neglected and untended on the pastures (even if they be not driven out), yet is there only one voice [100], only one that wails, and that one a private voice, to be heard at the funeral, as it were, of mother church.

7. And what wonder? Each one hath taken to him avarice for wife, even as ye; and never is she the mother of pi[e]ty and of justice, as is charity, but ever of impiety and of iniquity. Ah! pitying mother, bride of Christ, what sons dost thou produce, in water and in the spirit, to thy shame! Not [110] Charity nor Astræa, but the daughters of the horseleech have become thy daughters-in-law. And what offspring they

bring forth for thee, not the pontiff of Luni alone but all the rest also bear witness. Thy Gregory lieth neglected amongst spider webs, Ambrose lieth in the clergy's forgotten lumber rooms, Augustine lieth neglected, Dionysius, Damascenus, and Beda are flung aside, and they all declaim a certain *Speculum*, Innocent, and him of Ostia. Why so? Because those [120] sought God as the goal and the supreme good; and these seek fortune and benefices.

Greed rebuked by a humblest instrument

8. But, O my Fathers, think not that I am a phœnix in the world; for every one is whispering, thinking, or dreaming what I speak out. And who are they that bear not witness to the things they have discovered? Some indeed are dumb with amazement. But will they keep silence for ever, and never bear witness to their maker? The Lord liveth; and he who moved the tongue of Balaam's [130] ass is lord also over the modern brutes.

9. Even now have I grown garrulous, for ye have forced me to it. Shame upon you that ye have received your correction and admonishment from so far below you rather than from the heaven that should absolve you! And in truth shame does its office rightly with us when the knocking is upon that side whereon it plays upon our hearing as well as our other senses, and may beget penitence, its first-born, in us, and she again may give birth [140] to the purpose of amendment.

10. And that a noble patience may foster and defend this purpose, do ye all set before the eyes of men, in the measure of your power to represent it, the present state of the city of Rome,

Rome's appeal to her sons now destitute of either light, an object to wake pity in Hannibal himself, to say naught of others, sitting solitary and widowed, as hath been declared above. And most of all is this addressed to you who have known the sacred Tiber as infants [150]. For although the head of Latium must be reverently loved by all Italians as the common source of their civility, yet it should rightly be deemed your duty to worship it most closely, since to you it is the source of your very being also. And if, in the present time, misery hath crushed the other Italians with grief and confounded them with shame, who shall doubt that you who were the cause of the unwonted eclipse—shall we say of Rome or of the sun—must blush and grieve? And thou above all, Orsini! [160], lest thy disgraced colleagues should still be stripped of their glory, because of thee; and that, with the authority of the apostolic supremacy, they should resume the venerable insignia of the church militant which they were compelled undeservedly, and not because they had served their time, to lay down. And thou, too, follower of the other trans-Tiberine faction, in order that the wrath of the pontiff that was gone might grow green again in thee, like an ingrafted branch in a trunk not its own, hadst the heart, as though thou hadst not yet stripped off that Carthage once [170] subdued, to prefer this passion to the country of the illustrious Scipios, with no rebuke from thy judgment!

11. Wherefore, albeit the note and scar of infamy must burn the apostolic seat like fire, and befoul her for whose keeping heaven and earth

are reserved, yet amends may come if all ye on her own behalf and the world's
who were the authors of this going astray fight
manfully and with one mind for the bride of
Christ, for the seat of the bride, which is Rome
[180], for our Italy, and, to speak more fully,
for the whole estate of those on pilgrimage
on earth; that from the wrestling ground of
the contest already entered on (while even
from the edge of the ocean all eyes are fixed
thereon), ye, making glorious proffer of yourselves, may hear the cry, 'Glory in the
highest'; and the shame of the Gascons,
who burn with so dire lust as to seek to usurp
to themselves the glory of the Latins, may be a
warning to [190] posterity for all ages to come.

This letter is preserved in Boccaccio's manuscript
(*Mediceo-Laurentian*, XXIX. 8). It was written to
the cardinals assembled at Carpentras, near Avignon,
in 1314, to appoint a successor to Clement V. It
is one of the letters mentioned by Villani, and there
can be no reasonable doubt as to its authenticity. It
is interesting as showing Dante's intense reverence
for the papal dignity, and his genuine sense of
desolation at its seat being removed from Italy.

16-32. 'We, who hold the Christian faith, grieve
to look upon Rome, no less than upon heresy.'

53, 54. See Ezek. VIII. 16.

60. *Cord* (*funiculus*). Christ cast out the traffickers
with a 'flagellum de funiculis' (John II. 15).

61. *The fire* wherewith Korah and his followers
(Num. XVI. 35), or Nadab and Abihu (Lev. X. 2),
were consumed.

65, 66. 1 Maccabees VII. Alcimus, an opponent of
Judas Maccabæus, secured the support of Demetrius,
the successor of Antiochus Epiphanes. He aspired
to the high priesthood. Alcimus=Clement V.?
Demetrius=Philip the Fair?

67. *Uzzah.* 2 Sam. VI. 6, 7.

84, 85. 'For I take it that we shall haply think it better, and indeed a duty, to suppress even the promptings of friendship in order to keep the truth intact, especially if we profess ourselves philosophers. And though both be dear, we must pay the greater honour to the sacred truth' (Arist. *Eth. Nic.* I. 4. 1).

90, 91. *I.e.* 'waked from his sleep and saved it.' Matt. VIII. 24 *sqq.* and the parallel passages.

112, 113. *Pontiff of Luni.* Gherardo., a member of the Malaspina family, who distinguished himself by resistance to Henry VII., and was at enmity with the rest of his house (Latham). The Latin is 'præter Lunensem pontificem omnes alii contestantur,' the natural translation of which would be, 'all the rest except the priest of Luni,' which could only be taken sarcastically, like the 'fuor che Bonturo' of *Inferno* XXI. 41. But 'præter' can also mean 'besides,' 'in addition to,' and I have, with some hesitation, taken it in this meaning. Dante frequently uses it so, *e.g.*, *De Monarchia* II., 7 : 49 and 9: 61, and line 82 of this very Epistle.

114-121. Theology is neglected, and the books of ecclesiastical and civil law (the knowledge of which brings money and preferment) are studied instead. Compare *Paradiso*, IX. 133-138; XII. 83. The *Speculum* was a book of both civil and canon law by Durandus, written about 1270 (Toynbee).

135-140. I understand Dante to mean that it is well if shame gives us warning in articulate language, as by some outspoken reproof, instead of being brought home to us too late by the consequences of our neglect. But the passage is obscure.

141-158. 'To bring men to wholesome shame, set the afflictions of Rome vividly before their eyes.' *A noble patience*, 'gloriosa longanimitas,' is a strange expression for the patient efforts at self-reform. In itself the phrase would rather suggest the long-suffering of God; but to render it so would seem to involve considerable violence to the rest of the sentence.

158, 159. *Of Rome or of the sun*, 'Sui vel solis,' *i.e.* it is doubtful whether the removal of the papal seat to Avignon should be regarded as an eclipse of Rome or an eclipse of the papacy.

159-172. The account given by Villani (VIII. 80) of the intrigues that preceded the election of Clement V., makes these references perfectly clear. Matteo Rosso degli Orsini and Francisco Gajetano were the heads of the Orsini faction; but Napoleone degli Orsini dal Monte (the Orsini here addressed by Dante) was not himself of the Orsini faction, but was allied with the Colonna, whom Boniface VIII. had hated and disgraced. It was for the sake of restoring them that he entered upon the intrigues which finally resulted in the election of Clement V. Fraticelli gives an extract from a letter subsequently addressed by him to Philip the Fair, in which he takes upon himself the chief blame for the election of Clement, and expresses deep shame at the spectacle of the latter's deeds.

Gajetano, on the other hand, who shared Boniface's hatred of the Colonna, allowed himself to be overreached, while he thought he was securing the election of one who would share his views. Lines 165-172 are obviously addressed to him. They may be paraphrased 'as though a Carthaginian [*i.e.* enemy of Rome] at heart, you revived in your own person the malignant hostility of the late pope Boniface to the Colonna, and felt no qualms in allowing this vindictive passion to weigh against your duty to the country of the Scipios.'

Both Napoleone and Gajetano, then, the chief instruments of Clement's election, were led by private motives of love or hate into committing a great public wrong; and Dante now calls upon them, above all others, to make restitution.

176. *Her* = Rome.

EPISTOLA IX

To a Florentine friend.

Conditions of recall from exile

1. With grateful mind and close attention did I perceive from your letter, received with due reverence and affection, how deeply you have my recall at heart. And thereby you have bound me under the closer obligation because it so rarely chanceth that exiles find friends. But I go on to answer the contents of it. And if my answer be not such as perchance the pusillanimity of [10] certain might seek, I would beg you, in all affection, to winnow it in your judgment before you pronounce upon it.

2. This, then, is what has been indicated to me by the letters of your nephew and mine, and many other friends, as to the decree recently passed in Florence concerning the pardon of the exiles: That if I will consent to pay a certain sum of money, and be willing to bear the brand of oblation [20], I may be absolved and may return at once. Wherein are two things ridiculous and ill-advised, O father! I say ill-advised by those who have expressed them; for your letter, more discreetly and advisedly drawn up, contained no hint of them.

3. Is this the glorious recall whereby Dante Alighieri is summoned back to his fatherland after suffering well-nigh fifteen years of exile? [30]. Is this the reward of innocence manifest to all the world, of unbroken sweat and toil in study? Far be it from the familiar of philo-

sophy, this abject self-abasement of a soul of clay! To allow himself to be presented at the altar, as a prisoner, after the fashion of some Ciolo or other infamous wretch. Far be it from the preacher of justice, when he hath suffered a wrong, to pay his coin to them that inflicted it as though they had deserved well of him.

indignantly rejected

[40] 4. Not this the way of return to my country, O my father! but if another may hereafter be found by you or any other, which hurts not Dante's fair fame and honour, that will I accept with no lagging feet. If no such path leads back to Florence, then will I never enter Florence more. What then? May I not gaze upon the mirror of the sun and stars wherever I may be? Can I not ponder on the sweetest truths wherever I may be beneath the heaven [50], but I must first make me inglorious, nay infamous, before the people and the state of Florence? Nor shall I lack for bread.

This letter again is preserved by Boccaccio in his precious manuscript. It is clear from the use he makes of it in his 'Life of Dante' that he thoroughly believed in its authenticity, which indeed need not be doubted. There is, however, a genuine difficulty. Line 29 approximately fixes the date of this letter, and identifies the act of grace to which it refers as that of June 2, 1316. Now from this act are excluded all who have borne arms against Florence, all who were exiled under the authority of Cante Gabrielli, from November 1301 to July 1302, and all who were condemned for malversation in office. Thus Dante was excluded under three several heads from all benefit under the provision. How, then, could he thus repudiate the conditions of a recall that was never offered him? It has been suggested that Dante's friends wrote to him, in their haste, before the exact conditions were known; but does it not seem more probable that they had received private assurances that grace would be extended to Dante if he would make express application, and would submit himself to the conditions?

Of the recipient of this letter we know nothing except what we gather from the letter itself, viz., that he was a priest, and that he and Dante had a nephew in common. (See lines 22, 41, and 13, 14.)

19. *Bear the brand of oblation*, *i.e.* allow myself to be presented as an offering to St John at the high altar of his church.

24-26. Are we to gather that the letter which Dante is answering only spoke of the possibility of his being included in the act of grace, without dwelling on the conditions, which were enumerated in the other letters?

34, 35. The text has *victus* = 'vanquished,' but we should certainly read *vinctus* = 'a prisoner.' It was a regular part of the ceremony of 'oblation' that the offender should enter one of the public prisons of Florence, and then ask to be offered, as a redeemed prisoner, to God and to St John.

The Ciolo here referred to is mentioned in a decree of 1311, wherein (in prospect of the conflict with Henry) a number of Florentine exiles are recalled. Others, of whom a list is given, are excluded. Amongst these last are Dante himself, and 'all the Abbati except Ciolo.' Ciolo, therefore, who is not exempted from pardon, must have ingratiated himself in some way with the Florentines. Dante takes him as a type of abject submission.

EPISTOLA X

To the magnificent and victorious lord, Lord Can Grande della Scala, vicar-general of the most sacred imperial princedom in the city of Verona and in the state of Vicenza, his most devoted servant Dante Alighieri, a Florentine by birth, not by character, wishes long protracted life and felicity, and the perpetual growth of the glory of his name.

1. The illustrious praise of your munificence, which wakeful fame scatters abroad as she flies, draws divers in such divers directions as to exalt these in the hope of prosperous success and hurl down those into terror of destruction. Now this report, exceeding all deeds of moderns, I was once wont to think extravagant, as stretching beyond the warrant of truth; but, lest continued doubt should keep me too much in [10] suspense, even as the queen of the south sought Jerusalem or as Pallas sought Helicon, so did I seek Verona, to scrutinise by the faithful testimony of my own eyes the things which I had heard. And there I beheld your splendour, I beheld and at the same time handled your bounty; and even as I had formerly suspected excess on the side of the reports, so did I afterwards recognise that it was the facts themselves that exceeded. Wherefore it came to pass that whereas the mere report had already secured my good will, with a certain submission of mind, at the sight of the source and origin

Can Grande great in fame and fact

Disparity no bar to friendship itself I became your most devoted [20] servant and friend.

2. Nor do I think I am laying myself open to a charge of presumption (as some perhaps might urge) by arrogating to myself the name of friend, since unequals no less than equals are united in the sacrament of friendship. For should one care to examine those friendships from which delight and advantage have sprung, right often will he discover on inspection that such have united pre-eminent persons to their inferiors. And if attention be turned to the true friendship [30] which exists for its own sake, will it not abundantly appear that the friends of illustrious and supreme princes have for the most part been men obscure in fortune but shining in integrity? Why not? Since even the friendship of God and man is in no sort hindered by disparity. But if any one thinks my assertions too bold, let him hearken to the Holy Spirit declaring that certain men share his own friendship, for in *Wisdom* we read, concerning Wisdom [40], ' For she is an infinite treasure to men, and they that use it are made partakers of the friendship of God.' But the artlessness of the vulgar herd judges without discrimination, and even as it supposes the sun to be a foot across, so is it deceived by vain credulity as to character. But it is not fitting for us, to whom it has been granted to know the best that is in us, to follow the footprints of the herd; nay, rather are we bounden to oppose its [50] wanderings; for we who have vigour of intellect and reason, being endowed with a certain divine liberty, are held to no precedents,

And no wonder, for such are not directed by the laws but rather the laws by them. It is clear, then, that what I said above, namely, that I am your most devoted servant and your friend, is in no sort presumptuous.

Dedication of the Paradiso

3. Cherishing your friendship, then, as my dearest treasure, I desire to [60] preserve it with loving forethought and considered care; and therefore, since in the teaching of ethics we are instructed that friendship is equalised and preserved by what is proportionate, it is in my vows to keep the path of proportion in my return for bounty received. Wherefore I have often and eagerly scrutinised such small gifts as I have, and have set them side by side, and then conned them over again, considering which would be the more worthy and the more acceptable to you. And I have found [70] nothing more suited to your pre-eminence than the sublime cantica of the *Comedy* which is adorned with the title of *Paradise*; which cantica, under cover of the present epistle, as though dedicated under its own special heading, I inscribe, I offer, and conclusively commend to you.

4. Neither will my glowing affection permit me to pass over in absolute silence the thought that in this dedication there may seem to be greater [80] measure of honour and fame conferred on the patron than on the gift. And what wonder? since in its very inscription I appeared to those who looked closely, to have already uttered a presage of the destined increase of the glory to your name, and this of set purpose. But now, zeal for your glory, for which I thirst, making little of my own, urges me

The part and the whole forward to the goal set before me from the beginning.

And so, having brought to a close what I have written in the shape of a letter, I will at once assume the office of lecturer, and sketch in outline something by way of introduction to the work [90] I offer you.

5. As the Philosopher said in the second *Metaphysicorum*, 'as a thing is related to existence, so is it related to truth,' the reason of which is that the truth about a thing (which is established in the truth as in its subject) is a perfect likeness of the thing as it is. Now of things which exist some so exist as to have absolute being in themselves; others so exist as to have a being dependent on [100] something else, by some kind of relation, for example 'being at the same time' or 'being related to something else,' like the correlatives 'father and son,' 'master and servant,' 'double and half,' 'whole and part,' and the like, as such; and because the being of such depends on something else, it follows that the truth of them also depends on something else; for if we have no knowledge of half we can never understand double, and so of the rest.

6. [110] Therefore if we desire to furnish some introduction to a part of any work, it behoves us to furnish some knowledge of the whole of which it is a part. Wherefore I too, desiring to furnish something by way of introduction to the above-named portion of the *Comedy*, have thought that something concerning the whole work should be premised, that the approach to the part should be the easier and

more complete. There are six things then which must be inquired into at the beginning of [120] any work of instruction; to wit, the *subject, agent, form,* and *end,* the *title of the work,* and the *branch of philosophy* it concerns. And there are three of these wherein this part which I purposed to design for you differs from the whole; to wit, *subject, form,* and *title;* whereas in the others it differs not, as is plain on inspection. And so, an inquiry concerning these three must be instituted specially with reference to the work as a whole; and when this has been done the way will be sufficiently clear to the introduction of the part. After that we shall [130] examine the other three, not only with reference to the whole but also with reference to that special part which I am offering to you.

Six points of inquiry, Letter and allegory.

7. To elucidate, then, what we have to say, be it known that the sense of this work is not simple, but on the contrary it may be called polysemous, that is to say, 'of more senses than one'; for it is one sense which we get through the letter, and another which we get through the thing the letter signifies; and the first is called literal, but the second [140] allegorical or mystic. And this mode of treatment, for its better manifestation, may be considered in this verse: 'When Israel came out of Egypt, and the house of Jacob from a people of strange speech, Judæa became his sanctification, Israel his power.' For if we inspect the letter alone the departure of the children of Israel from Egypt in the time of Moses is presented to us; if the allegory, our redemption wrought by

Subject, form Christ; if [150] the moral sense, the conversion of the soul from the grief and misery of sin to the state of grace is presented to us; if the anagogical, the departure of the holy soul from the slavery of this corruption to the liberty of eternal glory is presented to us. And although these mystic senses have each their special denominations, they may all in general be called allegorical, since they differ from the literal and historical; for *allegory* is derived from *alleon*, in Greek [160], which means the same as the Latin *alienum* or *diversum*.

8. When we understand this we see clearly that the *subject* round which the alternative senses play must be twofold. And we must therefore consider the subject of this work as literally understood, and then its subject as allegorically intended. The subject of the whole work, then, taken in the literal sense only, is 'the state of souls after death' [170], without qualification, for the whole progress of the work hinges on it and about it. Whereas if the work be taken allegorically the subject is 'man, as by good or ill deserts, in the exercise of the freedom of his choice, he becomes liable to rewarding or punishing justice.'

9. Now the *form* is twofold, the form of the treatise and the form of the treatment. The form of the treatise is threefold, according to its threefold division. The first division is that by which the whole work [180] is divided into three cantiche; the second that whereby each cantica is divided into cantos; the third, that whereby each canto is divided into lines. The form or method of treatment is poetic,

fictive, descriptive, digressive, transumptive; and **and title of the whole** likewise proceeding by definition, division, proof, refutation, and setting forth of examples.

10. The *title of the work* is, 'Here beginneth the *Comedy* of Dante Aligheri, a Florentine by birth, not by [190] character.' To understand which, be it known that *comedy* is derived from *comus*, 'a village,' and *oda*, which is, 'song'; whence comedy is, as it were, 'rustic song.' So comedy is a certain kind of poetic narration differing from all others. It differs, then, from tragedy in its content, in that tragedy begins admirably and tranquilly, whereas its end or exit is foul and terrible; and it derives its name from *tragus* [200], which is a 'goat' and *oda*, as though to say 'goat-song,' that is fetid like a goat, as appears from Seneca in his tragedies; whereas comedy introduces some harsh complication, but brings its matter to a prosperous end, as appears from Terence, in his comedies. And hence certain writers, on introducing themselves, have made it their practice to give the salutation: 'I wish you a tragic beginning and a comic end.' They likewise differ [210] in their mode of speech, tragedy being exalted and sublime, comedy lax and humble, as Horace has it in his *Poetica*, where he gives comedians leave sometimes to speak like tragedians and conversely :—

' *Interdum tamen et vocem comœdia tollit,*
Iratusque Chremes tumido delitigat ore ;
Et tragicus plerumque dolet sermone pedestri.' [1]

[1] 'Sometimes Comedy herself raises her voice, and

and of the part And hence it is evident that the title of the present work is '*the Comedy*.' For if we have respect [220] to its content, at the beginning it is horrible and fetid, for it is hell; and in the end it is prosperous, desirable, and gracious, for it is *Paradise*. If we have respect to the method of speech the method is lax and humble, for it is the vernacular speech in which very women communicate. There are also other kinds of poetic narration, as the bucolic song, elegy, satire, and the utterance of prayer, as may also be seen from Horace in his *Poetica*. But concerning them [230] nought need at present be said.

11. There can be no difficulty in assigning the *subject* of the part I am offering you; for if the subject of the whole, taken literally, is 'the state of souls after death,' not limited but taken without qualification, it is clear that in this part that same state is the subject, but with a limitation, to wit, 'the state of blessed souls after death'; and if the subject of the whole work [240] taken allegorically is 'man as by good or ill deserts, in the exercise of the freedom of his choice, he becomes liable to rewarding or punishing justice,' it is manifest that the subject in this part is contracted to 'man as by good deserts, he becomes liable to rewarding justice.'

12. And in like manner the *form* of the part is clear from the form assigned to the whole; for if the form of the treatise as a whole is threefold, in this part [250] it is twofold only,

wrathful Chremes denounces with tempestuous lips. And the tragedian often lowers his wail to pedestrian tone.'

namely, division of the cantiche and of the cantos. The first division cannot be a part of its special form, since it is itself a part under that first division.

Agent, end, and branch of philosophy

13. The *title of the work* is also clear, for if the title of the whole work is 'Here beginneth the Comedy,' and so forth as set out above, the title of this part will be 'Here beginneth the third cantica of Dante's Comedy, which is entitled Paradise.'

14. Having investigated the three things in which the [260] part differs from the whole, we must examine the other three, in which there is no variation from the whole. The *agent*, then, of the whole and of the part is the man already named, who is seen throughout to be such.

15. The *end* of the whole and of the part may be manifold, to wit, the proximate and the ultimate, but dropping all subtle investigation, we may say briefly that the end of the whole and of the part is to remove those living in this life from the state of misery and lead them to the state [270] of felicity.

16. But the *branch of philosophy* which regulates the work in its whole and in its parts, is morals or ethics, because the whole was undertaken not for speculation but for practical results. For albeit in some parts or passages it is handled in the way of speculation, this is not for the sake of speculation, but for the sake of practical results; because, as the Philosopher says in the second *Metaphysicorum* [280], 'practical men sometimes speculate on things in their relative and temporal bearings.'

17. These, then, premised, we must approach the exposition of the letter, after the fashion of a kind of prelibation; but we must announce in advance that the exposition of the letter is nought else than the development of the form of the work. This part, then, namely the third cantica, which is called *Paradise*, falls by its main division into two parts, to wit, the [290] *prologue* and the *executive portion*. The second begins here, 'riseth unto mortals through divers straits.'

18. Concerning the first part you are to know that although it might, in the common way, be called an *exordium*, yet in strict propriety it should have no other name than *prologue*, which is what the Philosopher seems to be at in the third *Rhetoricorum*, where he says that 'the proem is the beginning of a rhetorical discourse, as a prologue is of a poetic one [300], and a prelude in flute-playing.' It is further to be noted that the prefatory enunciation, commonly called an exordium, is differently conducted by poets and by orators; for orators are wont to make a prelibation of what they are about to utter, calculated to prepare the mind of the hearer; whereas poets not only do this, but also utter some certain invocation after this. And this is to their purpose, for they have need of ample invocation, since [310] they have to implore something above the common scope of man from the higher beings, as in some sort a divine gift. Therefore the present prologue is divided into two parts; in the first of which is premised what is to be said; in the second Apollo is invoked. And the second

Promise and performance

part begins here, 'O, good Apollo, for the crowning task,' and the rest.

19. With reference to the first part be it noted, that for a good exordium three things are needed [320], as saith Tully in the *Nova Rhetorica*, to wit, that one should render his hearer benevolent and attentive and tractable; and this, especially in a marvellous kind of matter, as Tully himself says. And since the matter with which the present treatise is concerned is marvellous, the intention is, at the beginning of the exordium or prologue, to excite those said dispositions, in connection with the marvellous. For he says that he will tell such part as he could retain of [330] what he saw in the first heaven; in which utterance all those three things are comprehended. For the profit of the things to be said secures benevolence, their wondrous nature attention, their being possible docility. He gives their profitableness to be understood, when he declares that he is going to relate those things which chiefly attract the longing of mankind, to wit, the joys of Paradise; he touches on their wondrous nature when he promises to tell of such lofty and sublime things, to wit, the conditions of the celestial kingdom [340]; he shows that they are possible when he says that he will tell those things which he had power to retain in his mind; and if he had such power, then shall others have it too. All these things are indicated in those words, wherein he says that he was in the first heaven, and that he is purposed to tell concerning the celestial kingdom whatsoever he had power to retain in his mind, as a treasure. Having therefore taken

Functions of a prologue

Creation derived from God note of the excellence and perfection of the first part of the prologue, let us proceed to the letter.

20. He says, then, that the 'glory of the first mover' [350], who is God, 'reglows in all parts of the universe,' yet so as to be in 'some part more' and in 'another less.' Now that it reglows everywhere reason and authority declare. Reason thus: Everything that is has its being either from itself or from another. But it is obvious that to have being from itself is competent only to one, to wit the first or initial being, which is God. And since to have being does not imply [360] self-necessity of being, and self-necessity of being is competent to one only, to wit the first or initial Being, which is the Cause of all; therefore all things that are, save that one itself, have their being from another. If, then, we take any one of the individual phenomena of the universe it must evidently have its existence from something; and that from which it has it has [its existence] either from itself or from something else; if from itself then it is the prime existence; if from something else, then that again must have its existence from itself or from something else. And so we should [370] go on to infinity along a line of effective causes, as is proved in the second *Metaphysicorum;* and since this is impossible we must at last come to the prime existence, which is God, and thus mediately or immediately everything which is has its being from him; for it is by what the second cause received from the first cause that it has influence upon that which it causes, after the fashion of a body that receives and reflects a

ray. Wherefore the first cause is cause in a higher degree; and [380] this is what the book *De Causis* says, to wit, that 'every primary cause is more influential on that which it causes, than a universal secondary cause.' So much as to being. *in its being and in its essence*

21. But as to essence I prove it thus: Every essence, except the primary, is caused; otherwise there would be more than one existence of self-necessity, which is impossible. What is caused is either of nature or of intelligence; and what is of nature is [390] consequentially caused by intellect, since nature is the work of intelligence. Everything, therefore, which is caused, is caused by some intellect, mediately or immediately. Since, then, virtue follows the essence whose virtue it is, if the essence be intellectual the whole virtue is of one [intelligence] which causes it; and thus, like as before we had to come to a first cause of being itself, so now of essence and of virtue [400]. Wherefore it is clear that every essence and virtue proceeds from the primal one, and the lower intelligences receive it as from a radiating source, and throw the rays of their superior upon their inferior, after the fashion of mirrors. Which Dionysius, speaking of the celestial hierarchy, seems to handle clearly enough, and therefore it is said in the book *De Causis* that 'every intelligence is full of forms.' It is clear, then, how reason declares the divine [410] light, that is, the divine excellence, wisdom, and virtue, to reglow everywhere.

22. And authority does the same as science; for the Holy Spirit says by Jeremiah, 'Do I

Omni-presence of God does not preclude degrees not fill heaven and earth?' and in the psalm, 'Whither shall I go from thy spirit, and whither shall I flee from thy presence? If I ascend into heaven thou art there; if I descend into hell thou art present. If I take my wings,' and the rest [420]. And *Wisdom* says that 'the spirit of the Lord filled the whole world,' and *Ecclesiasticus*, in the forty-second, 'His work is full of the glory of the Lord.' Whereto the scripture of the pagans bears co-witness, for Lucan in the ninth,

> '*Juppiter est quodcumque vides quocumque moveris.*'[1]

23. It is therefore well said when it says that the divine ray, or divine glory *pierces and reglows* through the universe [430]. It pierces as to essence; it reglows as to being. And what he adds as to *more and less* is manifest truth; since we see that one thing has its being in a more exalted grade, and another in a lower, as is evident with respect to the heaven and the elements, whereof that is incorruptible and these corruptible.

24. And having premised this truth, he goes on from it with a circumlocution [440] for Paradise, and says that he 'was in that heaven which receives most abundantly of the glory or the light of God'; wherefore you are to know that that heaven is the supreme heaven, containing all the bodies of the universe and contained by love, within which all bodies move (itself

---

[1] 'Whatsoever thou seest, wheresoever thou goest, is Jupiter.'

abiding in eternal rest), receiving its virtue from no corporeal substance. And it is called the *Empyrean*, which is the same as the heaven [450] flaming with fire or heat, not because there is any material fire or heat in it, but spiritual, to wit holy love or charity.

The heaven of supreme light

25. Now that it receives more of the divine light can be proved by two things. First, by its containing all things and being contained by none; secondly, by its eternal rest or peace. As to the first the proof is this: That which contains is related by natural position to that which is contained, as the [460] formative to the formable, as is stated in the Fourth *Physicorum*. But in the natural position of the whole universe the first heaven contains all things; therefore it is related to all things as the formative to the formable, which is the same as being related by way of cause. And since every causative power is a certain ray emanating from the first cause, which is God, it is manifest that that heaven which is most of the nature of cause receives [470] most of the divine light.

26. As to the second point it is proved thus: Everything that moves, moves for the sake of something which it has not, and which is the goal of its motion; as the heaven of the moon moves because of some part of itself which has not the position towards which it is moving; and inasmuch as every part of it, not having attained every position (which is impossible), moves to some other, it follows that it always moves and [480] never rests, in accordance with its appetite. And what I say of the heaven of the moon must be understood of all the rest

The empyrean heaven tranquil and perfect except the first. Everything that moves, then, has some defect, and does not grasp its whole being at once. That heaven, therefore, which is not moved by anything has in itself and in its every part, in perfect fashion, everything which it is capable of having; so that it needs no motion for its perfecting. And since all perfection is a ray of the primal perfection [490], which realises the highest degree of perfection, it is manifest that the first heaven receives most of the light of the primal being, which is God. It is true that this argument appears to proceed from the negation of the antecedent, which is not in itself conclusive, as a form of argument; but, if we consider its content, it is conclusive, because it refers to an eternal being, the defect in which would be susceptible of being eternalised. Wherefore if God gave it no movement [500] it is clear that he did not give it material that was defective in anything; and on this supposition the argument holds, by reason of its content. It is the same way of arguing as if I were to say: 'If he is a man he is able to laugh'; for in all convertibles the like reasoning holds, in virtue of the content. So it is evident that when he says, 'in that heaven which receives most of the light of God,' he means to describe Paradise, or the empyrean heaven, by circumlocution.

[510] 27. And concordantly with all this the Philosopher declares in the first *De Cælo* that heaven has matter more honourable than the things below it in proportion as it is more remote from the things here; and we might further adduce what the apostle says *Ad Ephesios*

concerning Christ, 'who ascended above all the heavens, that he might fill all things.' This is that heaven of the 'delights of the Lord,' concerning which delights [520] it is said against Lucifer through Ezekiel, 'Thou, the seal of similitude, full of wisdom and perfect in beauty, wast in the delights of the Paradise of God.'

Understanding and memory

28. And when he has said that he was in that place of Paradise, described by circumlocution, he goes on to say 'that he saw certain things which he who thence descends cannot relate'; and he tells the reason, saying that 'the intellect is so engulfed' in the very thing for which it longs [530], which is God, 'that memory cannot follow.' To understand which things be it known that the human intellect, when it is exalted in this life, because of its being co-natural and having affinity with a sejunct intellectual substance, it is so far exalted that after its return memory fails it, because it has transcended the measure of humanity. And this we are given to understand by the apostle, speaking *ad Corinthios*, where [540] he says, 'I know such a man (whether in the body or out of the body I know not, God knoweth), who was rapt into Paradise and heard hidden words, which it is not lawful for a man to utter.' Behold, when the intellect had transcended human measure in its ascent, it remembered not the things that took place beyond its own range. And this we are also given to understand in Matthew, where the three disciples fell upon their faces, and record [550] nothing thereafter, as though they had forgotten. And in Ezekiel it is written, 'I saw and fell upon my

Revelations vouchsafed to sinners

face.' And if all this suffices not the carpers, let them read Richard of St Victor in his book *De Contemplatione*, let them read Bernard *De Consideratione*, let them read Augustine *De Quantitate Animæ*, and they will cease to carp. But if they yelp against the assignment of so great exaltation, because of the sin of the speaker, let them read [560] Daniel, where they will find that Nabuchodonosor, too, was divinely enabled to see certain things against sinners, and then dropped them into oblivion; for he 'who makes his sun to rise upon the good and the evil, and sends his rain upon the just and the unjust,' sometimes in compassion, for their conversion, sometimes in wrath, for their punishment, reveals his glory, in greater or less measure, as he wills, to those who live never so evilly.

[570] 29. He saw, then, as he says, certain things 'which he who returns has not knowledge, nor power to relate'; and it must be noted carefully that he says, has 'not knowledge, nor power.' He has not knowledge, because he has forgotten; and he has not power, because if he remembered and retained the matter, nevertheless language fails: for we see many things by the intellect for which there are no vocal signs, of which Plato gives sufficient hint in his books by having recourse to metaphors; for he saw many things by intellectual [580] light which he could not express in direct speech.

30. Then he says that 'he will tell those things which he was able to retain concerning the celestial kingdom'; and this, he says, is 'the matter of his work'; and of what nature

and extent these things are will be revealed in the executive part. *Invocation and narrative*

31. Then when he says, 'O good Apollo,' and the rest, he makes his invocation. And that part is divided into two parts: in the first he makes petition in his invocation; in the second he suasively urges upon [590] Apollo the petition he has made, announcing a kind of remuneration. And the second part begins here, 'O divine power.' The first part is divided into two parts, in the first of which he seeks the divine aid, and in the second touches upon the necessity of his petition, which is its justification. And it begins here: 'up to this point one peak of Parnassus,' and the rest.

32. This is the general purport of the second part of the Prologue; but I will not [600] at present expound it in detail, for I am pressed by my narrow domestic circumstances, so that I must needs relinquish this and other matters profitable to the common good. But I hope from your munificence that I may have opportunity, at some other time, to proceed to a profitable exposition.

33. Now concerning the executive part, which was co-ordinate in the division of the whole with the Prologue, nought shall be said at present either concerning its divisions or its purport, save this, that there will [610] be a process of ascending from heaven to heaven; and the narrative will tell of blessed souls discovered in each orb, and how true blessedness consists in the sense of the prime source of truth, as is evident by John in the passage: 'This is true blessedness, to know thee, the true God,' and

God the conclusive goal — the rest; and by Boethius in the third *De Consolatione*, in the passage: 'To behold thee is the end.' Whence it comes about that to make manifest the glory of blessedness in those souls, many things will be asked of [620] them (as of those who look upon all truth) which have much profit and delight. And inasmuch as, when the source or origin has been found, to wit, God, there is nought to seek beyond, since he is A and O, that is, the beginning and the end, as the vision of John calls him, the treatise ends in God himself, who is blessed *in sæcula sæculorum.*

The authenticity of this important work has been hotly challenged, but evidence in support of it has been gradually accumulating, and it may now be accepted without misgiving. The subject is fully treated by Dr Moore in the third volume of his *Studies in Dante*, pp. 284-374.

The reader who desires to know something of Can Grande in detail is referred to Wicksteed and Gardner's *Dante and del Virgilio*, Prolegomena, Albertino Mussato.

In lines 1-90 I have followed the text published by Witte (*Dante Forschungen*, I. 504 ff.); in the rest of the letter the text of Moore's Oxford Dante.

11. Ovid, in the fifth book of the *Metamorphoses*, tells how Pallas visited Thebes and Helicon in order to test the truth of the stories about Hippocrene. Note Dante's characteristic habit of taking parallel illustrations from sacred and profane stories.

25-30. There is an express reference here to Aristotle's classification of friendships (*Eth. Nic.* VIII. 3), into those inspired by interest, by pleasure, and by virtue.

46 ff. Those who have come to the conscious exercise of reason, have 'recognised the best element in human nature.'

50-54. Compare *De Monarchia*, I. 3: 90-92 (Aristotle, *Pol.* i. 2, 2).

62, 63. *In dogmatibus moralis negotii,* i.e. Aristotle's *Eth. Nic.* (IX. 1. 1).

73, 74. '*Sub præsenti epistola, tanquam sub epigrammate proprio dedicatum.*' The present epistle is the 'epigamma' or superscription which dedicates the work.

77-90. This difficult passage seems to mean that the epistle, when carefully examined, will exhibit the author as less intent on glorifying his poem than on glorifying his patron; and that the superscription, with its prayer for his growing fame, sufficiently indicates this. The 'titulus' of line 81 would then be not the title of the cantica 'Paradise,' but the superscription of the letter itself. There would be nothing out of place in the past, '*viaebar*,' which would be more or less in proper epistolary style, which, in Latin, always regards the letter from the point of view of the reader, as a thing already completed and done.

91-109. The *Paradiso* is part of the *Comedy*. A part, as such, only exists in relation to the whole of which it is a part. The truth about things is an image or reflection of the things themselves; therefore the truth about the *Paradiso* only exists in relation to the truth about the *Comedy*. So if I am to tell the truth about the *Paradiso*, I must tell it in relation to the truth about the *Comedy*.

The passage of the *Metaphysics* referred to occurs at the end of the first chapter of the book, known as ' Little Alpha,' which is numbered in the Latin translations as Book II. The form in which Dante cites it is, ' *Sicut res se habet ad esse, sic se habet ad veritatem,*' which does not correspond with either of the versions current in his time. Albertus Magnus, however, says in his paraphrase, (II. 4), '*unumquodque sicut se habet ad esse, ita se habet ad veritatem,*' and no doubt this is the source of Dante's phrase. Albert has explained that in the same way as many things may be hot, but fire is the principle and cause of heat in all the rest, so many things may be true, but certain things must be the principles and causes of truth in all the rest. These principles are to be investigated in the study of 'first philosophy' or 'metaphysics,' and since nothing causes them to be true, ' but they are the cause of truth to all other things, and since the principles of being, and of truth, and of knowing are identical, it necessarily follows that everything is related to being as it is related to truth.' This may explain Dante's phrase in line 95, that a thing ' is established (*consistit*) in the truth as in its subject'; that is to say, that the ultimate truth is the 'underlying' reality or 'substrate' that confers truth on things and enables it to be known. But the passage remains difficult, and can only be explained by a *tour de force*. It would be more natural to regard the thing as the subject or 'substrate' of the truth about it, and it is tempting to read '*re*' for '*veritate*' in line 95, and take the '*quæ*' of line 94 as referring to '*veritas*.' ' For the truth about a thing (which is rooted in the thing as in its subject) is, etc.' But I can suggest no handling of the passage that seems satisfactory.

102. *Father and son . . . as such*. A father, as a man, might be known without any knowledge of his son, or any knowledge whether he had one.

120-123. This was the accepted method of commenting in Dante's time, as may be seen from some of the early commentaries on his own works, and also from a contemporary Latin commentary on Albertino Mussato's *Ecerinis*,[1] written during Dante's lifetime. The first four of these six points are equivalent to the four 'causes' (material, efficient, formal, and final) of the existence of the work. Compare T. C., *Convivio*, p. 329.

133-135. Compare this passage with *Convivio*, II. 1, and note the much firmer handling and increased clearness of conception which mark this present passage.

167-175. That is to say, the literal subject is the state of souls after death; and the allegorical subject is Man, as a moral agent, qualifying himself for his future state, and already manifesting its essence.

183-187. The only point of this account of the *Comedy* which presents any difficulty is the term *transumptivus*, which Giuliani, followed by others, declared

[1] Published in Padrin's edition of the *Ecerinide* (Bologna, 1900).

to mean 'concisely.' But there is no manner of doubt, especially from its use in the commentaries on Mussato's *Ecerinis*, that the word means 'figurative' or 'metaphorical,' as has generally been supposed.

188 ff. These ideas as to the nature of comedy and tragedy, and the derivation of the terms, were current in Dante's time, and may be found in Uguccione's *Derivationes*, as to which see T. C., *Convivio*, IV. 6, and *note*.

280, 281. The passage (in the first chapter of 'Little Alpha') explains that practical men also theorise, or speculate, though not on the abiding and essential aspects of things, but rather on their transitory and relative aspects.

286, 287. The *form of the work*, as we have seen, is taken to mean its divisions. All students of the *Vita Nuova* and of the *Convivio* must have noticed the immense importance which Dante attaches to the divisions of his poems, and his conviction that to point them out is to throw essential light on the meaning. He is followed in this by the early commentators.

291. *Riseth unto mortals*, etc. This and all the subsequent quotations from the *Comedy* are given not in Italian, but in Latin.

320. The passage occurs in the *Rhetorica ad Herennium*, I. 4. In Dante's time this treatise was attributed to Cicero, and was known as the *Rhetorica Nova*, the *De Inventione* being the *Rhetorica Vetus* (Rashdall).

366-369. Throughout this passage the text reads *ab aliquo*, but perhaps the true reading is *ab alio*. At any rate that is the sense.

381-383. On the treatise *De Causis*, see T. C., *Convivio*, p. 146.

384. We may learn from lines 429, 430, below, that the difference between the *esse* (being) and the *essentia* (essence) of a thing is that its *esse* is its actual existence, as it stands, and its *essentia* is its ideal existence, as it is in the mind of God.

394-399. This passage is obscure through its brevity, and perhaps the text is corrupt. Probably a careful study of the *Celestial Hierarchy* of Dionysius, and the *De Causis* (referred to below) might throw some light upon the matter. In the *Celestial Hierarchy* (Cap. XI.) the angels are called *essentiæ*, and the divine or celestial intelligences are spoken of as containing in themselves *essentiam*, *virtutem*, and *operationem*. In the *De Causis*, on the other hand (text to Lecture X. in the Commentary of Aquinas), the angels are called *intelligentiæ*, and they are said to be all of them full of forms, but the higher ones of the more universal forms; and further on (Lecture XVII.) we are told that the more unified a virtue is the greater is its range, in proportion as it draws nearer to pure unity. I suspect some cross argument depending on the equivocal use of *essentiæ* and *intelligentiæ*, but the main idea, I think, is clear enough, namely, that as you can argue physically from a series of efficient causes to a prime cause, so you can argue intelligentially from the essential significance of every being, derived from some higher intelligence, to a single supreme intelligence which is the source of all.

460. What Aristotle really says (*Physics*, IV. 4, 10 f.) hardly justifies the wide inference here drawn. He is speaking of such things as liquids, contained in vessels, in which the containing vessel determines the shape of the contained liquid. Compare the *Quæstio*, etc., § 11 and *note*. Dante apparently understands him to say that anything which 'contains' another holds to it (as Latham expresses it) the relationship of a mould to the plastic substance it shapes.

466. Since all causal power is an emanation or ray from God, it may be treated as light; and, therefore, that heaven which is most causal has most light.

493-498. The reading of 493, 494, in the editions is *ad destructionem antecedentis*. But this must be wrong, first, because that is not the form of the argument, and secondly, because it is a generally sound form, and would need no apology if it were employed. (See p. 220 of this volume.) I have no hesitation in substituting *a destructione*. The argument is: A thing that moves is not satisfied; the empyrean heaven does not move, therefore it is satisfied. Now this is proceeding from the denial of the antecedent to the denial of the consequent, as though you were to say, 'If A is B, then C is D; but A is not B, therefore C is not D,' which is not legitimate as a general form. But there are many legitimate arguments the general form of which, apart from its special content, is not conclusive. Thus you cannot argue from the fact that all A's are B's to the fact that all B's are A's; but if you happen to know that B is the definition of A, or otherwise that the B's do not extend beyond the A's, then in virtue of the content (that is to say, the specific things for which A and B stand in this instance) you can convert the proposition that all A's are B's into the proposition that all B's are A's. Thus, for instance, 'man is a laughing animal,' holds, when converted, as 'a laughing animal is a man.' In the case under discussion a thing that moves is not satisfied, but a thing may be dissatisfied and yet not move, simply because it cannot. Therefore, in a general way, you cannot say that because a thing does not move it is satisfied. But in the case of a direct creation by God, which is to endure for ever, you cannot admit the hypothesis of a suppressed dissatisfaction that cannot utter itself. Therefore the fact that the empyrean heaven does not move proves that it is satisfied.

512. Aristotle (*De Cælo*, I. 2, 9 ff.) argues that the matter of the heavens must differ from the elements of which the earth and its immediate envelopes, air and fire, are composed. 'Propter quod ex omnibus utique his aliquis syllogyzans credet quod est aliquod (præter corpora quæ hic et circa nos) alterum segregatum, tanto honorabiliorem habens naturam, quanto quidem plus elongatum est ab his quæ hic.' Dante apparently took this as one of the premonitions in Aristotle of the empyrean heaven. Compare *Convivio*, II. 4: 33, 34. But this particular passage does not justify his interpretation.

533-538. Since each man has a certain relation, or natural affinity, with some angelic being or power (compare *Paradiso*, XXII. 112-117), he is capable of being rapt into the intellectual vision of an angel ('sejunct intellectual substance'). But if this takes place while he is still 'living in this life,' when he returns to human consciousness he will again be subject to human limitations, and will therefore be unable to retain his vision.

552-569. The point on which Dante insists with such earnestness and anxiety is, that he did actually experience things which he cannot relate. If he is met with carping incredulity he will appeal to scriptural authority for the reality of such visions, beyond the range of human intellect; and if these examples seem too remote and inaccessible, he will add the experiences of the great mystics (three of whom he specifies, with appropriateness sufficiently vindicated by the admirably illustrative quotations given by Witte, *apud* Latham); and if they still object that such saintly men may not be cited as precedents by a sinner like Dante, he will answer that the sinner Nebuchadnezzar had such things revealed to him by God that he could not retain them, but plunged them into forgetfulness.

605. This startling passage calls to mind Boccaccio's statement that in his declining years Dante was engaged in private tuition. It would seem that the pressure of the work he had to do for his living cramped him in his wider schemes. This most marvellous of all begging letters cannot have been written before 1319 (see p. 377 of this volume), at which time Dante was the honoured guest of Guido da Polenta at Ravenna. His appeal for pecuniary assistance to Can Grande, therefore, if seriously meant, is somewhat perplexing.

Note to the *Letters*.

I am under considerable obligations to Latham's *Dante's Eleven Letters* (Houghton, Mifflin & Co., 1902) throughout this portion of the work.—P. H. W.

ECLOGUES

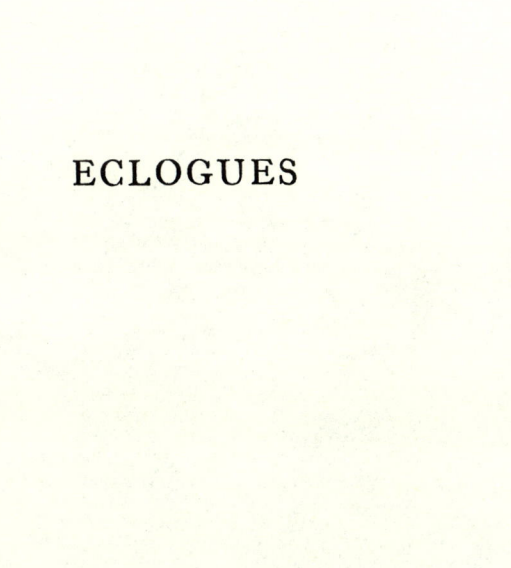

DANTE AND DEL VIRGILIO

In the year 1319 Giovanni del Virgilio, professor of Latin in the university of Bologna, wrote an epistle in Latin hexameters to Dante, then residing in Ravenna, couched in terms of affectionate respect and admiration, but reproaching him for writing in Italian instead of Latin, and urging him to compose 'something for students.' He suggested a variety of contemporary political themes as subjects for a Latin poem. It was grievous, he thought, that so great a poet as Dante should desert the practice of all his precursors, and should insult the Muses by clothing them in the unworthy garb of the vernacular. If he would adopt his suggestion of a Latin poem, or (apparently) even if he would promise to do so, Del Virgilio himself would be proud to place the laurel crown upon his head, before the applauding students of Bologna, if Dante would deem him worthy of such an office.

To these proposals Dante answered, in the poem that follows (*Eclogue* I.), with patient sweetness of temper (enhanced rather than otherwise by a touch of gentle and pathetic sarcasm) in the form of a pastoral eclogue. Fortunately the whole correspondence was preserved by Boccaccio, and so annotated (either by himself or by one writing very shortly after him) as to enable us to interpret the cipher with considerable security.

Perhaps a paraphrase will be the best form in which to present a general commentary.

Dante and his friend or assistant, Ser Dino Perini of Florence, were engaged in some humble sort of academic pursuit (perhaps connected with the teaching of the art of Italian poetry, which Boccaccio informs us Dante practised at Ravenna), when Del Virgilio's letter arrived. Perini was full of curiosity as to its contents, and Dante, after attempting to put him off, explained to him that it dealt with matters far above the range of his (Perini's) literary flights, which only extended to the study and teaching of the vernacular, whereas Del Virgilio's missive was full of the ripest and loftiest university culture; but Perini (as though another Syrophœnician woman) pleaded that if Dante would expound these high matters to him, not only might he comprehend something of their merit himself, but might even convey some portion of it to the humble students of Italian literature, to whom, as Dante's subordinate, he ministered. Then Dante replied that Del Virgilio, most disinterested of students, by his single efforts kept the service of the Muses alive in the university of Bologna, else wholly given up to the lucrative study of law; and that he now invited him (Dante) to receive the laurel crown at his hands.

Perini. Surely you will accept?
Dante. Such a function would doubtless make

stir enough.[1] For it would be a startling innovation on the neglect into which poets and poetry have fallen. But how should I venture into the turbulent and hostile Bologna? Would it not be better to await my recall to my native city and there assume the crown?

Perini. Better indeed! But time flies. A second academic generation of friends and students already finds you lingering in Ravenna.

Dante. Ah, but when the *Paradiso* becomes known, surely I shall be recalled and crowned (compare *Paradiso*, XXV. 1-9). If indeed, Del Virgilio will sanction my receiving such an honour in virtue of my poor Italian verse!

Perini. What are we to do to convince him?

Dante. My mind is teeming with the matter of the *Paradiso*, which is already taking shape; and I will presently send ten cantos to Del Virgilio, in which, mayhap, he will find after all 'something for students,' clad in vesture not wholly 'unworthy of the Muses.'

Meanwhile Perini had better attend to his humble duties, and learn to be content with his meagre fare.

*** The numbering of the lines follows the original.

ECLOGUE I

In letters black, upon receptive white,   The
I saw the modulations milked for me   letter re-
From the Pierian bosom. As it chanced,   ceived
Telling, as is our wont, our pastured goats,

[1] I abandon with some hesitation the suggestion put forward on p. 225 of *Dante and Giovanni del Virgilio* (see note on p. 385 of this volume).

Mopsus from the heights of Mænalus

Under an oak, I and my Melibœus
Had taken stand; when he (by longing urged
To learn the song) cried, 'Tell me, Tityrus,
'What Mopsus wills.' I laughed, Mopsus; but he
Urged me until for very love at last
I yielded; and, scarce covering my mirth—
'Ah, fool!' I said, 'What madness this? Thy care
'The goats bespeak, though by lean fare dis-
tressed!   [10]
'Where Mænalus' high peak the sinking sun
'Conceals, lie shady pastures all to thee
'Unknown; with many a varying hue inlaid
'Of flowers and grasses; round them gently flows,
'Under the osiers, with perpetual wave
'His banks bedewing from his brimming verge,
'A streamlet; offering a ready way
'Wherein may gently flow the watery store
'Furnished by mountain heights. There, even there,
'Whilst in lush grass his oxen sport, the toils
'Of men and gods doth Mopsus contemplate,
'Exultant! Then through breath-receiving reeds   [20]
'His inward joy reveals; until the herds
'Follow the dulcet strain, and from the mount
'Lions, no longer fierce, haste to the fields.
'The waves are stayed, and Mænalus himself
'Inclines his foliage.'
                    'Tityrus! what though
'Mopsus in unknown pastures sings; yet I
'Those unknown songs might practise for my goats,
'Poor wanderers, if thou wouldst show the way.'
So he, and what could I, when thus he pressed

Breathless? 'O Melibœus, others vie
' To master lore litigious. Mopsus still
' Year in year out himself hath dedicate   [30]
' To the Aonian mountains; hath grown pale
' Beneath the shadows of the sacred grove,
' Drenched by prophetic waters, inly filled,
' Aye to the palate, with the milk of song!
' He to the leaves sprung from the Peneid's change
' Invites me.'
    ' And thine answer? Thinkest thou
' Thus still to wear thy temples unadorned,
' A shepherd ever on the rustic plains?'
Said Melibæus.
     ' Scattered to the winds
' The glory, aye, the very name of bards!
' O Melibœus,' I had said, ' And scarce
' One vigil-keeping Mopsus hath the muse
' Known to maintain!' Then indignation gave
A voice to utter these: ' What bleating sounds
' Would gather from the flocks o'er hill and plain
' If to a pæan I should smite the strings   [40]
' With leaf-entwined hair! But let me shun
' The glades and pastures that know not the gods!
' Were it not better my triumphant locks
' Should hide beneath the green their hoariness,
' Erst auburn-glowing, by the ancestral stream,
' Should ever I return to deck them there,
' Of Arno.'
    ' Nay, who doubts it?' he replied,
' But mark time's flight, O Tityrus, how swift!
' And goats whose dams we mated waxing old!'

' Ah! when the gliding universal orbs
' And the star-woning spirits, in my song,
' E'en as the nether realms, shall stand revealed,

Offers the laurel crown to Tityrus, who could only accept it from Florence

*in
guerdon
for the
Paradiso*

'Then,' I replied, 'my joy shall be to bind
'My brow with laurel and with ivy;—leave [50]
'Of Mopsus asked.'
     'Of Mopsus? Why of him?'
The other said.
    And I myself replied:
'Hast thou not marked the scorn wherewith he greets
'The speech of Comedy which women's chat
'Stales on the lip, which the Castalian sisters
Blush to receive?' And, Mopsus, here I read
Thy verses once again.
     He shrugged, and said,
'How to our side shall Mopsus, then, be won?'

'A ewe is mine!' I said, 'to thee well known,
'Choicest of all the rest, who scarce supports,
'So doth she teem with milk, her udders' weight
'(Herbage fresh cropt she chews beneath a rock [60]
'Immense) associate with no flock, nor known
'To any fold. Of her own will she comes,
'And never driven, to the milking-pail.
'Her do I purpose with deft hand to milk.
'From her ten measures will I fill to send
'To Mopsus. And do those give heed, the while,
'To the wanton goats; and learn thy teeth to fix
'In stubborn crusts.'
    Such words beneath the oak
Did I and Melibœus sing; what time
Our humble cot prepared our oaten meal.

  10. The Latin (like the translation) is ambiguous.

But it seems to be the young shepherd, not the goats, who has to face the hardships of meagre fare. Compare the closing lines of the poem.

33. Daphne, daughter of Peneus, changed to a laurel.

37. Del Virgilio was the only professor of literature in Bologna, and even he had a hard fight with poverty, while the professors of law grew rich.

49. *Nether realms*, *i.e.* purgatory as well as hell. Del Virgilio's political allusions date his letter early in 1319, and from this phrase of Dante's we learn that the two earlier cantiche, but not the third, were known at that date.

57-64. Some have supposed these lines to refer to ten Eclogues (the Virgilian number) contemplated by Dante; and others have made other suggestions. But surely the most obvious interpretation is the best. The allusion can only be to ten cantos of the *Paradiso*.

Del Virgilio was delighted with Dante's reply, and more especially with the pastoral humour he had adopted. He flung himself into it with all his heart, hailing his friend as a second Virgil, and was apparently quite satisfied with this response to his suggestion of Latin poetry; at least he lays no further stress on that matter; and he also accepts Dante's decision as to receiving the laurel crown nowhere but in Florence. He speaks with generous indignation of Dante's exile, and devoutly hopes that he may indeed revisit his native stream of Arno, and have his locks decked (in anticipation, apparently, of the ceremony of coronation) by 'Phyllis' self' (that is, as I take it, by Gemma, though others insist that 'Phyllis' must be a pastoral impersonation of Florence). Meanwhile he implores him at least to come and visit him, and assures him that there is no cause for the apprehension he has expressed, and that he may safely visit Bologna.

Apparently Dino Perini had the honour of taking Dante's letter to Del Virgilio, and it was he who brought back the reply. Dante and his friend Fiducio dei Milotti were discussing Del Virgilio's strange affection for Bologna, at the very moment when Dino Perini came hastening back with his answer. He recited the ninety-seven lines (three short of a hundred) of the epistle, and Fiducio, full of apprehension, implored Dante not to desert the place to which his fame was already so closely linked, nor to risk approaching the terrible cave of 'Polyphemus' (it is uncertain who is referred to under this name); for should any evil befall him his friends at Ravenna would be inconsolable. Dante replies that for all the inferiority of Bologna, he would undertake the journey for Del Virgilio's dear sake, were it not that he does indeed dread the terrible Polyphemus; Fiducio presses this point still further, and Dante assents. Guido da Polenta, Dante's protector at Ravenna, overheard the whole conversation and reported it to the writer.

It will be noted that this second eclogue does not in any express way claim to be the work of Dante. The pastoral cipher on its geographical side is tangled. The way in which Dante himself is spoken of is more in the tone of an ardent disciple than of a man writing of himself, and the poem (*Eclogue* II.) adds no trait to our knowledge of Dante. The commentator above referred to has preserved a tradition that Del Virgilio received no answer to his second letter till Dante's son, after his father's death and a year after Del Virgilio had sent his letter, conveyed this answer to him.

All this justifies some doubt as to Dante's full authorship of the poem and his responsibility for its present form. It is, however, generally accepted as Dante's authentic work, and in any case it is a genuine contemporary document and in no sense a forgery. It may, and probably does, stand closer to Dante than it claims to do; but at any rate no claim that it does make can for a moment be disputed.

ECLOGUE II

The shepherds' talk interrupted

THEIR Colchian fleeces doffed, Eöus swift
And th' other steeds the beauteous Titan bore.
And, momently, the track in equal poise
Held either chariot-bearing orb, what point
It felt the first down-swerving from the height.
Sun-smitten things, but now by self-cast shade
Out-lengthed, their shadows overpassed; the fields
All unprotected, burned. And woodward now
Had Tityrus and Alphesibœus fled
(Themselves compassionating and their herds)
Seeking the copse where, 'twixt the ash's growth,
Linden and plane find frequent space. And there,—
The while reposing on the woodland grass [10]
Cattle, with goats between, sniff the cool air—
Tityrus, drowsed by odours somnolent,
With maple leaves, reclining, shields his age;
And, to discourse, Alphesibœus stands,
Leaning upon a gnarlèd pear-wood staff
Wrenched from its stock.
            'That souls,' quoth he, 'of men
'Make for the stars, whence they were newly come
'When first our frames they entered; that white swans
'Love to make ring Cäyster with their joy
'In temperate heavens and in plashy vale;
'That fishes of the sea gather, and quit [20]
'That sea, just where the streams first touch the realm

'Of Nereus; that the Caucasus is dabbed
'With blood Hyrcanian-tiger-spilt, the sands
'Of Lybia swept by serpent-scales, I not
'Admire; for, Tityrus, each thing delights
'In what to its own life conforms; but I
'Marvel, and marvel all my fellow-swains
'Holding Sicilia's pastures, that the rocks
'That parch 'neath Etna's summit should delight
'Mopsus.'

by the missive of Mopsus

So he. When, lo! (his panting breath
Checking his speed) toil-heated Melibœus
Approaches and scarce gasps 'Look Tityrus!'
His throbbing throat the seniors laugh to see [30]
No less than the Sicanians laughed of old
Seeing Sergestus wrenched from off the rock.
From the green sod raising his hoary locks,
The aged swain thus to the panting boy,
With nostrils still distent: 'What novel cause
'Has urged thee, in the wantonness of youth,
'The bellows of thy bosom thus to strain
'With rapid course?'
Here naught in answer he;
But rather placed against his quivering lips
The pipe he held; whence to our greedy ears
Issued no simple breath; but as he toils
To give the reed a voice (strange things but true
Am I to tell) the reed's self uttered forth, [40]
*It chanced on the well-watered slopes where Rhine
And Sarpina* and had but three more breaths
Been urged beyond those breathed, a hundred strains

Tityrus must not desert Pelorus

Had the mute rustics charmed.
             Tityrus felt
The purport; felt it too Alphesibœus,
And gave it words. To Tityrus he turned:
' Old venerated Sire! and wilt thou
' Dare to desert Pelorus' dewy fields
' And brave the Cyclops' den?'
             ' What is thy fear?
' What dost thou probe!' he cried.
             ' My fear? What probe?'
Returned Alphesibœus, 'Can'st not feel
' The power divine, vocal within the flute? [50]
' (Such power was in the reeds by whispers bred,
' Whispers that told what shame his temples bore,
' The monarch's, who, at Bromius' mandate, tinged
' Pactolus' sands.) It summons thee to shores
' Strewed with Ætnean pumice. Trust not thou
' Delusive favours! Pity, loved old Sire,
' The Dryads of the place. Thine own flocks pity.
' Thee absent will the mountains weep, and thee
' Our glades and streams; and, sharing in our fears
' Of worse to come, the nymphs. Envy no more
' Will vex Pachynus; and we swains shall grieve
' E'er to have known thee. Think not then to leave, [60]
' O loved old Sire, the springs and pastures, famed
' For thy name's living sake.'
             ' O more than half,—
' And rightly—of this breast,' touching his own,
The aged Tityrus cried, ' Mopsus, with me
' In love united (for their sakes who fled
' In terror from Pyreneus' evil will),
' Deeming I dwell on shores to Padua's right

ECLOGUES

'And left of Rubicon, where Adria   Nor will
'Bounds the Emilian land, of Ætna's shore   he
'Commends the pastures, ignorant that we [70]
'Dwell on a mount Trinacrian, than which
'No other hill of Sicily more rich
'Doth pasture flocks and herds. But though
    the rocks
'Of Ætna vie not with Pelorus' sward,
'Yet, to see Mopsus, I would take my way,
'My flocks abandoned, but for dread of thee,
'O Polyphemus!'
               'Polyphemus,' cried
Alphesibœus, 'who dreads not? His jaws
'Familiar with the drip of human gore,
'Since when, scarce 'scaping, Galatea saw
'Forsaken Acis mangled; while herself
'Love's power had barely shielded from the
    rage   [80]
'That boiled so fiercely. Achimenides
'Near breathed his last barely at sight of him,
'Drenched with his comrades' blood. My life!
    I pray
'Never may such dread purpose master thee
'As that Rhine with his neighbour nymph enclose
'That head illustrious, which the pruner speeds
'To grace with leaves undying, from the boughs
'Culled of the exalted virgin.'
                          Not unpleased,
In silence, Tityrus with full assent
Received the words of th' flock's great fosterling.
But since, by now, so prone the yoke-mates
    cleft   [90]
The ether that the shadow each thing cast
Stretched far beyond its height, the crook-
    bearers,

Iolas Quitting the woods and the cool vale, returned
reports After their flocks; the shaggy goats before
To pastures soft, like home-comers, led on.

Wily Iolas, lurking close at hand,
The whilst, heard all, and all he heard rehearsed.
He unto us, and, Mopsus, we to thee.

1-6. The golden hues of the dawn have long ago been flung off by the horses of the sun, whose chariot was in mid-heaven. Shadows were shorter than the things that cast them; shade was scanty, and all the fields were baking under the mid-day sun.

31. In the funeral games described in *Æneid*, V. Sergestus in the boat race strikes a rock, and his damaged vessel when finally pushed off makes a sorry show to the Sicilian spectators.

36. Del Virgilio had represented the words of Dante's first *Eclogue* as borne to him supernaturally upon the breeze. Dante transforms the letter brought back by Dino Perini into a magic flute, which, when breathed upon it by the messenger's lips, sings the poem committed to it by the distant bard.

41. *It chanced*, etc. These are the opening words of Del Virgilio's poem of 97 lines.

Rhine, here and in line 85, stands for the Reno that flows by Bologna.

51 ff. Midas, at whose touch all things turned to gold, was ordered by Bacchus (Bromius) to bathe in Pactolus in order to get rid of this inconvenient virtue. When he did so the sands of Pactolus turned to gold. The rest of the story is well known. Midas judged Pan superior to Apollo as a musician, and had asses' ears given him in consequence. He concealed his deformity from all except his barber, who, bursting with his secret, confided it to the reeds, which thenceforth proclaimed it in their rustlings.

78, 79. The story of Acis and Galatæa, and the love of Polyphemus for the latter, is told by Ovid, *Met.* XIII. 750 ff.

82. For Achimenides, the companion of the ad-

ventures of Ulysses in the cave of the Cyclops, see *Æneid*, III. 588 ff.

86, 87. The 'exalted virgin' seems merely to mean the laurel.

NOTE TO THE *Eclogues*.

Dante's correspondence with Del Virgilio (together with the latter's other poems) is edited, with a prose translation, introductions, and commentary, in *Dante and Giovanni del Virgilio*, by Wicksteed and Gardner (A. Constable, 1902).

It had previously been translated into English blank verse by Plumptre in the second volume of his *Commedia and Canzoniere*, 1887, and is contained in vol. iv. of the cheap edition (Isbister, 1899).   P. H. W.

THE QUAESTIO DE AQUA ET TERRA

QUAESTIO DE AQUA ET TERRA

A golden and right profitable discussion, made public by Dante Alagherii, the most illustrious Florentine poet, in shape of a discourse on the nature of the two elements, water and earth.

To all and singular who shall inspect these presents, Dante Aligheri of Florence, least amongst true students of philosophy, giveth greeting, in him who is the beginning of truth and the light. **Inscription**

On the general scope of this treatise see note on pp. 424, 425.
God is not only the source of objective truth, but is also the light by means of which we see it.

§ 1.

Be it known to you all that when I was in Mantua a certain discussion arose, which, following the appearance rather than truth, received manifold expansion, but remained undecided. Wherefore since I have been nurtured from my boyhood in the love of truth, I could not endure to abstain from discussing the aforesaid question, but determined to demonstrate the truth about it, and further [10] to refute the arguments urged on the other side, in equal love **Origin of this treatise** of truth and hatred of falsehood. And lest the spleen of the many who are wont to foist lies, in their absence, upon those they hate, should pervert, behind my back, what I had rightly uttered, it was my further pleasure, in this attestation prepared by my own fingers, to leave a record of my conclusion, and to design with my pen the form of this whole disputation.

14, 15. *Should pervert.* The text reads *transmutent*, a plural verb to the singular subject *livor*, a mistake which suggests careless transcription.

§ 2.

The question The question, then, turned on the position and shape, or form, of two elements, *water*, to wit, and *earth ;* and what I here mean by form is what the Philosopher puts down as the fourth kind of 'quality' in the *Predicaments.* And the discussion was limited to this inquiry (as the principle of the truth to be investigated) 'Whether water, in its own sphere, that is in its natural [10] circumference, was in any part higher than the earth which emerges from the waters, and which we commonly call the habitable quarter.' And it was argued on the affirmative, for many reasons; some of which reasons were so insignificant that I passed them by, but five I retained as having some apparent validity.

3-6. The first of Aristotle's predicaments is, in Latin phrase, the *quiddity* or 'whatness' of a thing; the fourth is its *quality* or 'what-likeness.' Of this Aristotle makes several divisions, enumerating for example inherent capacities (*e.g.*, for laughter), and acquired accomplishments (*e.g.*, skill in music). The fourth of these kinds of quality, or 'what-likeness,' is 'form' in the sense of 'shape'; and the author explains that he does not use 'form' in the scholastic sense of 'constituent principle,' but merely as the equivalent to 'shape.'

7, 8. At the beginning of each book of the *De Monarchia*, Dante lays down the fundamental principle, conformity to which is to be the test of the arguments and conclusions of the book. Such a fundamental principle will be established for the present inquiry if we can answer, with regard to the relations of earth and water, the question here proposed.

§ 3.

The first argument ran thus: Two circumferences, which are not uniformly distant from each other, cannot have a common centre. The circumference of water and the circumference of earth are not uniformly distant. Therefore, etc. Then it went on: Since the centre of earth, as all admit, is the centre of the universe; and anything that has a position in the world other than it, is higher than it; we must conclude that [10] the circumference of water is higher than the circumference of earth, since the circumference corresponds to the centre all round. The major premise of the chief syllogism appeared to be manifest from the theories demonstrated in geometry, the minor by the evidence of the senses, because we see that in some places the circumference of earth is included in the circumference of water and in some places excluded.

Geometrical argument

12. It is assumed throughout that the radius of the sphere of water will at anyrate not be smaller than the radius of the sphere of earth.

§ 4.

Argument from relative nobility

Second argument: To the nobler body the nobler place is due. Water is a nobler body than earth, therefore the nobler place is due to water. And since place is nobler in proportion as it is higher, because it is nearer to the most noble envelope, which is the first heaven; therefore, etc. It remains that the place of water is loftier than the place of earth, and secondly that water is loftier than earth, since [10] the position of the place and of the thing placed is identical. The major and minor of the chief syllogism of this argument were taken as obvious.

7. *It remains.* The text has *relinquo*, which White translates 'I admit.' But in stating these five arguments the author never seems to speak in his own person. Nor can I find authority for such a use of *relinquo*. I am inclined to suppose there has been a false expansion of a contraction in the manuscript, and that we should read *relinquitur*.

§ 5.

Argument from the senses

The third argument was this: Every belief that contradicts the senses is a false belief. The belief that water is not loftier than earth contradicts the senses. Therefore it is a false belief. The first premise was said to appear from the Commentator on the third *De Anima*; the second or minor from the experience of sailors, who, when at sea, observe the mountains beneath them; which they prove by saying that [10] when they climb the mast they see them, but not when on the deck; and this they think is due to the land being far beneath them and depressed below the ridge of the sea.

6. The *Commentator* is of course Averroes. No passage in his commentary on the third book of the *De Anima* has been found to justify this appeal. It should be noted, however, that Dante (or whoever the author may be) does not make himself directly responsible for the reference.

7-14. If you climb a cairn on the top of a mountain you may be able (on looking back in the direction in which you have ascended) to see a cottage, for example, near the foot of the mountain, which you could not see from the base of the cairn, since it was then hidden by a shoulder of the mountain over which you now see it. Thus the sailors imagined that the fact of their seeing the land they had recently left from the top of the mast when they could no longer see it from the deck, showed that they had been ascending, and now saw the land below them over the shoulder of a sea-mountain. In the same way, on *approaching* the land, they would think they were *descending*. Dante gives the true interpretation of this phenomenon in § 23.

§ 6.

Fourthly, it was argued thus: If earth were not lower than water, the earth would be entirely waterless, at any rate in the exposed portion about which we are inquiring; and so there would be no springs, nor rivers, nor lakes; the opposite of which we see. Wherefore the opposite of that from which this follows is true, namely, that water is higher than earth. The sequence is proved by the fact that water is naturally [10] borne downwards; and since the sea is the prime source of all waters (as is shown by the Philosopher in his *Meteorics*), if

Argument from springs

the sea were not loftier than the land no water would move to the land, since in every natural movement of water the source must needs be the loftier.

8. The *sequence*, 'consequentia.' That is to say, 'that the absence of water from the earth would really follow upon the land being higher than the sea.' Compare *De Monarchia*, II. 12: 24-29*n*.

12. What Aristotle actually says (*Meteorica*, II. 2, 27) is exactly the opposite, namely, that the sea is to be regarded rather as the goal than the source of the flowing waters; but note, here again, that the author is not responsible for this perversion, and when he comes in § 23 to refute this fourth argument, he makes a perfectly correct use of the *Meteorics* himself, and passes over the perversion of his opponent in apparent contempt.

§ 7.

Argument from moon's excentricity

It was also argued fifthly: Water seems mainly to follow the motion of the moon, as appears by the flow and ebb of the sea. Since then, the orbit of the moon is excentric, it seems reasonable that water in its sphere should imitate the excentricity of the orbit of the moon, and so be itself excentric; and since this could not be without its being higher than the land, as was shown in the first argument, the same [10] conclusion follows as before.

§ 8.

False conclusion

By these arguments, therefore, and others to which we need pay no heed, they who hold that water is loftier than the exposed or habitable earth endeavour to show that their opinion is true, though sense and reason contradict it. For by sense we perceive that throughout the whole earth rivers flow down to the sea, whether northern or southern, eastern or western; which [10] would not be unless the sources of the rivers and the course of their channels were higher than the surface of the sea. Reason will be shown below to be on the same side, as will be demonstrated by many arguments in expounding or determining the position and form of the two elements, as was hinted above.

§ 9.

This will be the order. First, the impossibility of the water at any part of its circumference being loftier than this emergent or uncovered land will be demonstrated. Secondly, it will be shown that the emergent land is everywhere loftier than the whole surface of the sea. Thirdly, a rejoinder will be urged against the conclusions established, and this rejoinder will be refuted. Fourthly, the final and efficient causes of this elevation or emergence [10] of land will be shown. Fifthly, the arguments above noted will be answered.

Order of demonstration

7, 8. On the term *rejoinder*, see § 18 : 1*n*.

§ 10.

As to the first point, then, I say that if water, considered at the circumference, were at any point higher than the land, it would necessarily be in one of these two ways: either by water being excentric, as the first and fifth arguments

Alternatives

maintained, or by its not being excentric indeed, but having a hump in some place, wherein it should rise above the earth. No otherwise [10] could it be, as is sufficiently manifest on close consideration. But neither of these cases is possible; therefore neither is that [possible] from which one or the other of the two necessarily followed. The sequence, as laid down, is manifest from the *locus* on the adequate division of cause. The impossibility of the consequent will appear by what we are about to prove.

7. *Not being excentric.* The text reads *excentrica*, which is a palpable mistake. We must either insert 'non' or read 'concentrica.'

12, 13. The Fraticellian reading, 'vel per quod, alterum,' is unauthorised and futile. The *editio princeps* has 'alterum vel alterum.' The reading is perfectly satisfactory and the sense clear. 'One or other of two consequences must necessarily follow from the supposition; and since both these consequences are impossible, the supposition from which one or the other necessarily follows is also impossible.'

15. See *De Monarchia*, II. 12: 61 and *note:* 'Locus a divisione est habitudo unius condividentium ad relinquum, ut *Si Socrates est animal, aut est animal rationale aut irrationale*' (Petrus Hispanus: Tractatus Quintus). Compare the form of Beatrice's argument in *Paradiso*, II. 73-84.

§ 11.

Axioms   To prove what we have to say, two points must be conceded: the first is that water naturally moves downward, and the second that water is naturally a fluid body and incapable of being bounded by a boundary intrinsic to itself. And if any one were to deny these two principles, or either of them, our proof would not appeal to him, since, if any one denies the principles of any science, there can [10] be no discussion with him in that science, as is shown in the first *Physicorum*. For these principles are discovered by the senses and by induction, whose province it is to discover such, as is clear from the first *ad Nichomachum*.

5, 6. '*Et non terminabile termino proprio*,' that is to say, a liquid has no fixed boundaries of its own like a solid, but must be bounded by something else.

§ 12.

For the refutation of the first member of the consequent, I say that it is impossible for water to be excentric; which I demonstrate thus: Were water excentric, three impossibilities would follow, the first of which is, that water would naturally move both up and down; the second is, that water would not drop along the same line as earth; the third [10] is, that gravity would be predicated in a different sense of each of them. All which seem to be not only false but impossible. The sequence is thus established. Let the circumference marked with three crosses be heaven, that marked with two crosses water, and that marked with one, earth. And let the centre of heaven and earth be the point marked A, and the centre of water, which is excentric, the point marked B, as shown in the marked figure. I say, then, that if there should be water at [20] A having a free course, it would naturally move to B, since everything that has

A reductio

ad weight naturally moves to the centre of its proper circumference; and since moving from A to B is moving up (since A is absolutely down, with reference to everything), water will naturally move up, which was the first impossibility mentioned above. Again, let there be a clod of earth at Z, and let there be a quantity of water at the same place, and let there be no obstacle [30]. Then, since everything that has weight moves, as already declared, to the centre of its proper circumference, the earth will move along

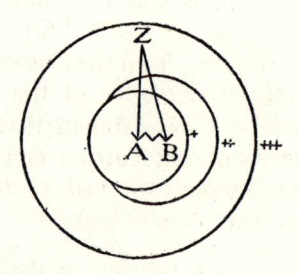

the straight line to A, and the water along the straight line to B; but this will of necessity be along different lines, as is clear from the marked figure; and not only is this impossible, but Aristotle would laugh to hear it; and this is the second point which had to be shown. The third I thus set forth: Heavy and light [40] are affections of elementary bodies, which move in straight lines; and the light ones move up, but the heavy down. For what I mean by heavy and light is mobile, as the Philosopher *in Cælo et Mundo* has it. If, then, the water move to B and the earth to A, then, since they are

both heavy bodies, they will move to different absurdum
'downs,' the meanings of which cannot be the
same, since one is 'down' absolutely and the
other [50] relatively. And since difference of
meaning in the ends argues difference in the
things which conduce to them, it is manifest
that the meaning of fluidity will be different in
the case of water and of earth; and since differ-
ence of meaning with identity of name consti-
tutes equivocality, as is clear from the Philosopher
in *Antepraedicamentis*, it follows that gravity
would be predicated in different senses of water
and of earth, which was the third member of
the sequence that we were [60] to develop.
Wherefore it follows, from the true demonstration
(derived from the character of the bodies con-
cerned) whereby I have shown that this is not
so, that water is not excentric; and this was the
first [member] which we had to refute of the
consequent of the main sequence.

13, 14. *Sequence*, *i.e.* that one of these two results really would follow, as above.

44. Aristotle, *De Cælo*, IV. 1, 7. 'For we call things heavy and light in virtue of their natural capacity to move.'

45-50. This argument, though based entirely on *a priori* assumptions, is penetrating and original. Moreover, it appears to be the only argument in the treatise for which no contemporary or accessible parallel can be found. It is odd that the believers in the late date of the treatise have not, so far as I know, fastened upon this passage as containing ideas beyond the scope of Dante's science.

50-54. Note again in line 53, *fluitatis* for *fluiditatis*. The word is used not as equivalent to our 'fluidity,' but in a broader sense as 'capable of flowing or moving,' as earth will drop through the air or flow down the sides of a steep embankment. The argument is that this capacity for moving towards its centre is the means given by nature to earth or water for reaching its natural place of rest, in reference to its proper centre. If, then, the proper centres were different in each case, the 'fluidity' given as a means of reaching that centre would be a different thing in each case, though bearing the same name. I can by no means accept the suggestion of Böhmer and others to substitute *gravitatis* for *fluitatis*.

In line 52 I take *illa* to be loosely used for *illos*, sc. *fines*.

56, 57. Aristotle's *Categories* (or *Predicaments*), besides treating of things that can be predicated, has an introductory paragraph on homonyms, paronyms, etc. This is referred to as the '*Ante-predicaments*,' just as a series of paragraphs concerning 'opposition,' the different meanings of 'priority,' etc., which follow the treatment of things that can be predicated are quoted as the '*Post-predicaments*.'

59. *The third member of the sequence*. The 'sequence' is 'were water excentric three impossibilities would follow,' in lines 4 f. of this section.

62. *I have shown that this is not so*, i.e. that it is not true that the water is excentric. But I doubt whether the reading of this passage is sound.

63-65. The first member of the consequent of the 'main sequence' (set out in the opening of § 10) was that water is excentric. This has been shown to be false. The antecedent of that 'main sequence' was that 'water is somewhere higher than earth.' The consequent had two alternative members, one of which has been shown to be false. When we have shown that the other is false we shall have proved that the antecedent is false. The 'sequence' of § 10 is called 'the main sequence,' in contradistinction to the 'sequence' of § 12: 4, 5.

§ 13.

The second alternative To refute the second member of the consequent of the main sequence, I say that it is also impossible for water to have a hump, which

I thus demonstrate: Let heaven be the circumference marked with four crosses, water that marked with three, and earth that marked with two; and let the centre of earth, of water (supposed concentric), and of heaven be D. And let us suppose it to be known that water cannot be concentric with earth unless [10] earth have a hump somewhere, above its central circumference (as is clear to those who have studied mathematics), if indeed it emerges anywhere at all from the circumference of the water.

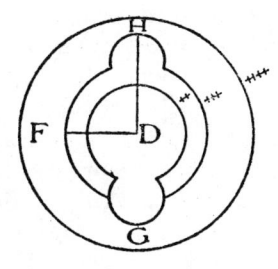

also leads to an absurdity

So let the hump of water be at the place marked H, and the hump of the earth at the place marked G; then let a line be drawn from D to H, and another from D to F. It is clear that the line from D to H is longer than the line from D to F; and therefore its extremity is higher up [20] than the extremity of the other; and since each touches the surface of the water at its extremity, but does not pass it, it is clear that the water of the hump will be 'up' with respect to the surface at which F is. Since, then, there is no obstacle, it follows from our axioms that the water of the hump will flow down until it is equidistant from D with the regular or central circumference;

and thus it will be impossible for the hump to remain, or indeed to exist [30]; which is what we were to show. And besides this most cogent demonstration, it can also be shown by way of probability that water would not have a hump protruding from its regular circumference; for what can be done by one, is better done by one than by several; and the whole matter before us may be effected by a hump of earth alone, as will be seen below. Therefore there is no hump in the water, since God and nature ever [40] doeth and willeth what is better, as is clear from the Philosopher, *De Cœlo et Mundo*, and in the second *De Generatione Animalium*. Thus we have sufficiently established the first point, namely, that it is impossible for water in any portion of its circumference to be loftier, that is remoter from the centre of the universe, than is the surface of this habitable earth, which was the first in order of the things we had to say.

13. The *Ed. Prin.* has *a* before *circumferentia*, which makes both grammar and sense satisfactory. I have altered the punctuation of the Fraticellian text.

34, 35 Compare *De Monarchia*, I. 14: 1-28.

36. *The whole matter before us*, so I understand *totum oppositum;* but the reading seems suspicious.

48, 49. *First in order*, etc., *i.e.* was the point laid down in § 9 as the first to be dealt with.

§ 14.

Concentricity established If, then, it is impossible for water to be excentric, as was shown by the first figure, and also that it should have a hump, as is shown by the second, it must necessarily be concentric [with earth], and also symmetrical, that is equally distant from the centre of the universe at every point of its circumference, as is obvious.

§ 15.

I now proceed to argue thus: Anything that is higher than any part of a circumference equidistant from its centre is remoter from that centre than any part of that circumference. But all the shores, both of Amphitrite herself and of the inland seas, are higher than the surface of the contiguous sea, as is plain to the eye; therefore all the shores are remoter from the [10] centre of the universe, since the centre of the universe is also the centre of the sea, as we have seen; and the surfaces at the shores are parts of the total surface of the sea. And since everything remoter from the universe is loftier, it follows that all the shores are higher than all the sea; and if the shores, then much more the other regions of earth, since the shores are the lower portions of the land, as the rivers show by descending to them. Now the [20] major premise of this demonstration is demonstrated in geometrical theorems; and the demonstration is conclusive, although it derives its force (as in the case of our own proofs above) from a *reductio ad impossibile*. And so we have established the second point.

Exposed land higher than water

25. *The second point*, laid down in § 9.

§ 16.

A difficulty derived But against the things now established it is argued thus: The heaviest body seeks the centre equally from every direction and with the greatest force. Earth is the heaviest body. Therefore it seeks the centre equally from every direction and with the greatest force. And from this conclusion follows, as I shall show, that the earth is equally distant from the centre at every point of its circumference (as is involved [10] in the meaning of the word 'equally'), and that it is lower down than any other body (as is involved in the meaning of 'with the greatest force'); whence it would follow (if water were concentric, as declared) that the land would be submerged on every side, and would not appear; the contrary of which we see. That these results follow from the conclusion I thus explain: Let us make an assumption contrary, or opposite, to this consequence (namely, that it is equidistant at every part), and let us say it is [20] not equidistant. And let us suppose that at one point the surface of the earth is distant twenty stadia, and at another point ten, so that one of its hemispheres will exceed the other in quantity. Nor does it matter whether the difference in distance be little or much, so long as there is a difference. Since, then, there is more virtue of gravity in the greater quantity of earth, the greater hemisphere, by the superior virtue of its [30] weight, will shove the lesser hemisphere until the quantity of each is equalised, by which equalising their weight will be equalised also; and thus the distance on either side will be reduced to fifteen stadia, as we see when we add **from the** weights to the balances to bring them to equality. **nature of** Whereby it is plainly impossible for earth, which **earth** equally seeks the centre, to be diversely or unequally distant from it in its [40] circumference. Therefore the opposite of being unequally distant, namely, being equally distant, is necessary where there is any distance at all; and thus the sequence has been defended so far as refers to equi-distance. That it also follows that it must be below all other bodies (which was likewise declared to follow from our conclusion), I thus maintain: The most potent virtue most potently attains the goal; for what makes it most potent is, that it [50] can most swiftly and easily reach the goal. The most potent virtue of gravity is in the body which most potently seeks the centre; and that body is earth. Therefore earth most potently approaches the goal of gravity, which is the centre of the world. Therefore it will be below all the other bodies, seeing that it seeks the centre most potently; which was the second point to be elaborated. Thus it appears that it is impossible for water to be concentric with earth, which is contrary to the conclusion we had reached.

The author has now provisionally established his point; but he proceeds to challenge his own conclusions.

16. *From the conclusion.* That is the conclusion of the initial syllogism of this counter argument.

40-42. The text is apparently corrupt, '*Ergo necessarium est oppositum suum inæqualiter distare,*' but the meaning is clear. 'If there is any distance at all,' I suppose means, 'in all cases when it cannot actually reach the centre.'

49. The words '*citissima est quod*' of Fraticelli's text do not appear in the *Ed. Prin.*, and I have omitted them.

§ 17.

An attempted rejoinder But this argument does not appear to be conclusive, because the major of the main syllogism does not itself appear to be necessarily true. For it was urged, 'that the heaviest body seeks the centre equally from every direction, and most potently,' which does not seem to be necessary; for though earth is the heaviest body compared to other bodies, yet compared to itself, to wit [10] in its several parts, it may be both the heaviest and not the heaviest; for there may be heavier earth on the one side than on the other. For, since the equalising of a heavy body is not effected by its quantity, as quantity, but by its weight, there might be an equalising of weight where there was no equalising of quantity; and so the demonstration is apparent and not real.

15-17. The text is '*poterit ibi esse adæquatio ponderis, quod non sit ibi adæquatio quantitatis.*'

§ 18.

The rejoinder rejected But this rejoinder is futile, since it proceeds from ignorance of the nature of homogeneous and elementary bodies; for elementary bodies, too, are homogeneous. Homogeneous ones, such as refined gold, and elementary bodies, such as fire and earth, are uniformly qualified in all their parts, by any affection natural to them. Wherefore, since earth is an elementary body, it is uniformly qualified [10] in its parts by nature **Universal** and, so to speak, of itself. Wherefore, since **nature** gravity is naturally inherent in earth, and earth is an elementary body, it must of necessity possess gravity uniformly, in all its parts, in proportion to its quantity; and thus the validity of the initial rejoinder fails. Whence we must answer that the nature of the rejoinder is sophistical, for it fails to distinguish rightly between 'relative' and 'absolute.' And therefore be it known [20] that universal nature is not baulked of her goal. And so, though particular nature may be baulked of her intended goal by the recalcitrance of matter, yet universal nature can in no sort fail of her intention, since both the actuality and the potentiality of things which may be or not be, are equally subject to universal nature. But it is the intention of universal nature that all the forms which are within [30] the potentiality of first matter should be reduced to actuality, and should be actualised in specific fashion, in order that first matter, in its totality, should be submitted to every material form, although in each of its parts it should be submitted to every opposite privation save one. For since all forms which are ideally within the potentiality of matter, are actualised in the mover of heaven, as the Commentator says in the *De Substantia Orbis*, if all these forms [40] were not continuously actualised, the mover of heaven would fail of the complete diffusion of his excellence, which may not be uttered. And since all material forms of things that can come into and pass out of existence, except the forms of the elements, require a mingled and compound controls
particular
nature material and substrate, whereto, as to their end, the elements, as elements, are ordained, and there can be no mixture except where the things to be mixed can [50] come together, as is obvious, it is necessary that there should be some place in the universe where all the things capable of being mixed, to wit, elements, may have leave to come together. But this might not be unless earth at some point emerged, as is plain on reflection. Whence, since every [special] nature obeys the intention of universal nature, it was necessary that over and above the simple nature of earth, which is to be below, it should have another nature whereby to obey the intention of universal [60] nature; namely, that it should be susceptible of being elevated in part by the virtue of heaven, as the obeying by the commanding; just as we see in the case of the appetitive and resenting nature in man, which, although their proper impulse urges them to obey the affections of sense, yet in so far as they are susceptible of obedience to reason, are sometimes restrained from their proper impulse, as appears from the first of the *Ethics*.

> The 'rejoinder' (see the next note for an explanation of this term) in § 17 is perfectly sound, and it is very curious that the author should retreat from it and should substitute the strange argument that follows. The parallel with *Paradiso*, Canto II., is extremely close. There too Dante retreats from a quite sensible explanation of the spots on the moon, and substitutes for it a mystical account on the same plane of ideas as the account given here of the elevation of the earth.
>
> 1. A rejoinder or 'instantia' is an argument urged against a refuting argument. The opponent, in § 16, has attempted to refute the author, who now brings a 'rejoinder' against him. From another point of view

the argument of § 16 might itself be regarded as a 'rejoinder' of the adversary, following on Dante's refutation of his position; and it is so regarded in § 9.

2-6. I have not interfered with the text, which (if suitably punctuated) runs: 'ex ignorantia naturæ homogeneorum et simplicium; corpora enim homogenea et simplicia sunt. Homogenea, ut aurum depuratum, et corpora simplicia, ut ignis et terra,' etc. But I suspect corruption in the reading. The simplest emendation would be to omit 'homogenea et simplicia sunt,' as a gloss that had been incorporated in the text, and to translate 'ignorance of the nature of homogeneous and elementary bodies. For homogeneous bodies, such as refined gold, and elementary bodies, such as,' etc. See *Postscript* on p. 426.

16. *Of the initial rejoinder*, namely that of § 17, to be followed by another rejoinder, in the author's opinion more valid. So at least I understand '*instantia principalis.*'

18, 19. I have altered the punctuation of the editions; and I suppose a second 'secundum' to have fallen out. The rejoinder fails 'secundum *secundum quid et simpliciter*' (compare *secundum non causam ut causa*, *De Mon.*, III. 5: 37 f., and *secundum accidens.*, III. 12: 29 f.), for it treats equal masses of earth as only equal in weight, 'secundum quid,' or on condition, whereas (according to the author's argument) they are really so 'simpliciter.' or absolutely and without qualification.

30-35. Compare *De Monarchia*, I. 3: 72-78, and the reference to Averroes in the note. On 'privation' see T.C., *Convivio*, p. 123. There is no form which matter is capable of receiving which some matter does not receive. But the first matter which has received the form, say, of air, undergoes privation of all the ('opposed' or incompatible) forms of the other elements (water, fire, etc.). So that if we go through the whole schedule of things we shall find that taken *anywhere* (*secundum partem*) first matter is under privation of every form but one, but taken everywhere at once (*secundum suam totalitatem*) it is under all forms always.

38, 39. No such passage has been found in the *De Substantia Orbis*, and indeed it is not couched in the phraseology of that treatise. There has evidently been a lapse of memory on the author's part, but the idea is quite in accordance with the system of Averroes.

§ 19.

Why and how   Therefore though earth according to its simple nature seeks the centre equally, as was said in discussing the rejoinder, yet according to a certain nature it is susceptible of being partially elevated, in obedience to universal nature, that the mingling may be possible. And thus the concentricity of earth and water is preserved, and no impossible consequence follows, if we philosophise rightly [10], as is clear from this figure. Let the circle marked A be heaven; the circle marked B, water; the circle marked C, earth; nor does it matter to the truth propounded whether water appears to outdistance earth little or much. And you are to know that this figure is the true one, for it is such as the form and position of the two elements really are. The other two figures above are false, and were inserted not because it is so, but to make the learner perceive, as saith he in the first [20] *Priorum*. And that the earth emerges in a hump and not by its central circumference is clear when we consider the shape of the emerging land; for the figure of the emergent land is the figure of a half-moon, which could not possibly be the case if it emerged in accordance with its regular or central circumference; for as is demonstrated in mathematical theorems, the regular [30]

surface of a sphere must always necessarily the habit-
emerge from a plane or spherical surface (as able land
the surface of water must be) with a circular
horizon. And that the emergent land has a
shape like that of a half-moon is clear, both
from the natural philosophers who treat of it,
and astronomers who describe the zones, and
cosmographers who set forth the regions of the
earth in all quarters. For, as is held by all these
in common, this habitable part stretches [40]
longitudinally from Gades, established by

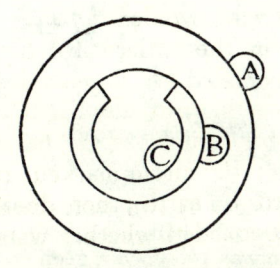

Hercules on the western boundary, to the
mouths of the river Ganges, as Orosius writes.
And this longitude is so great that when, at
equinox, the sun is setting to those who are at
one extremity, he is rising to those who are
at the other, as astronomers have discovered by
eclipse of the moon; so the extremities of the
said longitude [50] must be a hundred and
eighty degrees distant, which is half the distance
of the whole circumference. Latitudinally, as
we commonly receive from the same authorities,
it stretches from those whose zenith is the
equinoctial circle to those whose zenith is the
circle described by the pole of the zodiac round

emerges the pole of the universe, which is distant from
from the the pole of the universe about twenty-three
water degrees. And thus the extension in latitude is
[60] about sixty-seven degrees and no more,
as is evident on reflection; and thus it is clear
that the emergent land must have the figure of a
half-moon, or something like it; for that is the
figure which results from such latitude and
longitude, as is evident. But if it had a circular
horizon it would have a convex circular figure,
and so the longitude and latitude would not
differ in the distance of their extremities, as may
be seen by very women [70]. And so the
third point in the order of what we had to
discuss is elucidated.

21 f. The *Editio Princeps* reads *per centralem circumferentiam patet*.

61-63. *The figure of a half-moon.* As the figure Dante describes is bounded by two great circles, it would not be of the shape of a half-moon, and one would have thought Dante was too good a geometer not to realise this. Fazio Degli Uberti knew better, and described the habitable world as 'almond-shaped.'

'In trovi lungo e stretto l'abitato,
Ritratto quasi qual mandorla vassi.'
Dittamondo, I. vi.

70. See § 9 : 7, 8.

§ 20.

The It now remains to consider the final and the
efficient efficient cause of this elevation of the land,
cause which has been sufficiently demonstrated. And
this is the proper order of art, for the question
whether a thing is, should precede the question
why it is. As to the final cause, what has been

said under the last heading but one may suffice. But for the investigation of the efficient cause of this emergence we must note in advance that [10] the present treatise does not go beyond the scope of nature, for it is confined to mobile existence, to wit water and earth, which are natural bodies; and therefore we are to look for such certainty as is consonant with natural order, which is here our subject-matter; for concerning every kind of thing we are to seek the degree of certainty of which the nature of the thing is capable, as is clear from the first *Ethicorum*. Since, then, it is our inborn method [20] of investigating the truth as to nature to proceed from what is better known to us but less known to nature, to what is more certain and better known to nature, as is clear from the first *Physicorum*, and in such matters effects are better known to us than causes, for it is by them that we are led to the knowledge of causes, as is manifest (for it was the eclipse of the sun that led to the recognition of the interposition of the moon; so that men began to philosophise because of their wonder), the path of investigation in the [30] things of nature must needs be from effects to causes; and this method, though it may yield adequate certainty, yet cannot yield such certainty as the way of investigation in mathematics, which is from causes, or the higher, to effects, or the lower. And so we are to look for such certainty as may be had in this style of demonstration. I say, then, that the efficient cause of this elevation cannot be [40] earth herself; for, since being elevated is a kind of impulse upward, and an impulse upward is contrary to the nature

not in the nature of earth, water, or the moon of earth, and nothing can, in itself, be the cause of what is contrary to its own nature, it remains that earth cannot be the efficient cause of this elevation. And likewise neither can it be water; for since water is a homogeneous body, its virtue must, in itself, be uniformly distributed in [50] all its parts; and so there would be no reason why it should raise it here any more than elsewhere. This same argument rules out air and fire from this causation. And since there is nothing left save heaven, this effect must be referred to it, as to its proper cause. But since there are sundry heavens it remains to inquire to which of them it must be referred as to its proper cause. Not to the heaven of the moon; for, since the organ [60] of its power or influence is the moon herself, and since she departs as far from the equinoctial towards the antarctic pole as towards the arctic, she would elevate it as much on the other side as on this side of the equinoctial, which does not take place. Nor will it do to say that this declination could not take place because of her greater approximation to the earth, due to excentricity; because if the moon had this power of elevation at all (since agents [70] operate with greater power the nearer they are), she would have raised it more there than here.

6. *The final cause* (*i.e.* that for the sake of which the thing happens) has already been shown to be the provision of a place where all the elements may mingle.

11. *Mobile existence*, 'ens mobile.' Aristotle defines 'nature' as including everything that moves.

20-23. Aristotle, at the beginning of the *Physics*, draws a celebrated distinction between the things that come first to us and the things that come first by nature. When we are explaining some familiar fact by giving the reasons for it, we are explaining that which is best known to us and is nearest to us by that which naturally precedes it, and is more obvious or better known as a natural truth on its own merits. When on the other hand we work back from the familiar and intellectually confused to the unfamiliar but (when we reach it) intellectually clear, we have reasoned from what is better known to us to what is better known in nature. Effects, then, are first to us, but causes are first in nature. A favourite example is found in the increased luminosity of a planet when it is nearer to us. If we argue 'Venus is very bright, therefore she is near us,' we are arguing from effect to cause, from what is first to us to what is first in nature. If we argue 'Venus is very near us, therefore she is so bright,' we are arguing from what is first in nature to what is first to us.

54. The *alterius* of the text is apparently a mistake for *ulterius*.

65-71. I can make nothing of this passage as it stands. The context seems to demand *elevatio* for *declinatio* in line 66, for the point is that if the elevation of the earth were due to the moon, there ought to be such an elevation below the equator as well as above it. If we read *elevatio*, the passage would appear to mean that it is no use trying to explain the emergence of the earth above but not below the equator by the different distances of the moon from the earth in her perigee and apogee, for this would tell the wrong way. So Dr Moore also understands it (*Studies*, II. 339).

If this is the meaning of the passage, it rests on an extraordinary blunder, namely, the belief that when the moon is in perigee she is always south of the equator (on the analogy of the sun, who, as a matter of fact, is always below the equator when the earth is in perihelion). But the moon's apsides make a complete revolution from west to east in about nine years, so that within that period the moon has been in perigee at every part of the zodiac. Dante's authorities, Alfraganus for example, were perfectly aware of this motion of the moon's nodes.

The passage needs further investigation, but if this

is the right interpretation of it, it constitutes a real difficulty in accepting Dante's authorship of the treatise, substantially as we have it. The profundity of Dante's astronomical knowledge, however, has perhaps been somewhat exaggerated. The strength and precision of his physical imagination, and his unapproached power of keeping constantly in his mind the most intricate physical conditions of his *mise en scène*, are indeed a source of perpetual wonder. The *Comedy* abounds in subtle and unobtrusive touches, which show that the phenomena of the heavens (in the simplified form under which he had conceived them for his poetical purposes) were as inevitably present to his mind as were the heat of the sun or the light of the moon to his bodily senses, wherever he happened to be. He could no more *accidentally forget* on the mount of purgatory than in the streets of Verona or Ravenna whether he was in sunshine or shade. But there is nothing to show that he was a profound astronomer, in the sense of having pushed his studies beyond the elements of the science. Could it then be shown (though I am not aware that it can) that there was in Dante's time a semi-popular idea that the moon was always south of the equator in perigee, I do not think we could be quite confident that Dante's scientific knowledge would enable him to reject it. Nevertheless such a blunder, if not inconceivable, would remain very strange and unexpected.

§ 21.

nor in any other heaven

This same line of reasoning rules out all the planetary orbs from such causation, and since the *primum mobile*, or ninth sphere, is uniform throughout, and therefore uniformly endowed with virtue throughout, there is no reason why it should lift the earth more from this side than from that. Since, then, there are no other moving bodies except the starry heaven, which is the eighth [10] sphere, this effect must necessarily be referred to it. And to make this evident, be it known that although the starry heaven has unity in substance, yet it has multiplicity in virtue; and that is why it needed the diversity in its parts which we observe, in order, by diverse organs, to pour down its diverse virtues; and let him who perceives not these things know that he is outside the threshold of philosophy. We observe in this heaven [20] difference in the magnitude and luminosity of the stars and in the figures and forms of the constellations, which differences cannot be for nought, as must be perfectly clear to all who have been nurtured in philosophy. Wherefore the virtues of this star and that differ, and likewise of this constellation and of that. And the virtue of the stars this side of the equinoctial differs from that of those beyond it. Wherefore, since the aspects [30] of things below are like to the aspects of things above, as Ptolemy asserts, it follows that (since that effect can only be referred to the starry heaven, as we have seen) the similitude of the virtual agent abides in that region of heaven which covers this exposed land. And since the exposed land stretches from the equinoctial line to the line which the pole of the zodiac describes round the pole of the universe, as was said [40] above, it is manifest that the lifting virtue is in those stars which are in the region of heaven contained between those two circles, whether it elevates it by way of attraction, as the magnet attracts iron, or by way of impulsion, by generating vapours that force it up, as in the case of special mountain ranges. But now the question arises: Since that region of heaven is borne round us in a circle, why was

save that of the stars

Why not the corresponding elevation circular? I
here and answer that it was not [50] circular, because
not there there was not sufficient matter for so great an
elevation. Then the argument is pushed further,
and it is asked: why was the hemispherical
elevation rather on this side than the other?
To this we must answer according to what the
Philosopher says in the Second *De Cælo*, when he
asks why the heavens move from east to west,
and not the other way. For there he says that
such questions arise from great folly or [60]
from great presumption, because they transcend
our intellect. And therefore we must reply to
this question that the great disposer, the glorious
God, who made his dispositions concerning the
position of the poles, the position of the centre of
the universe, the distance of the extreme circum-
ference of the universe from its centre, and other
like things, ordained these, even as those, as was
best. Wherefore when he said, 'Let the waters
be gathered together into [70] one place and let
the dry land appear,' the heaven was at the
same time endowed with virtue to act and the
earth with potentiality to be acted on.

11-29. Compare *Paradiso*, II. 64-72.

29 *sqq*. I take this passage to mean that it is only
by attributing the phenomenon in question to the
starry heaven that we can find a virtual agent (*i.e.*
an agent acting by its virtue, not by physical impact)
in which there is a permanent similitude of the thing
effected.

In lines 31 ff. the reading of the *Editio Princeps* is
'consequens est quod, cum iste effectus non possit
reduci nisi in cœlum stellatum, ut visum est, quod
similitudo virtualis agentis,' etc. The first or second
quod is superfluous. In line 35, *operit* = 'covers,' must
be taken to mean 'is above.'

53, 54. *Rather on this side than the other,* i.e., in the eastern rather than in the western hemisphere. The elevation is called 'hemispherical' because it is confined to one (the northern) hemisphere.

§ 22.

Let men desist therefore, let them desist, from searching out things that are above them, and let them seek up to such point as they may, that they may draw themselves to immortal and divine things to their utmost power, and may abandon things too great for them. Let them listen to the friend of Job, when he says: 'Wilt thou understand the footprints of God, and search out the Almighty to perfection?' Let them listen to the Psalmist, when he says: 'Thy knowledge is wonderful [10], and has comforted me, and I may not attain to it.' Let them listen to Isaiah, when he says: 'As far as the heavens are above the earth, so far are my ways above your ways'; for he was speaking in the person of God to man. Let them hearken to the voice of the apostle *Ad Romanos:* 'Oh the height of the wealth, of the knowledge, and wisdom of God! how incomprehensible are his judgments and his ways are past finding out.' And finally let them hearken to the proper voice of the Creator [20], when he says: 'Whither I go, ye cannot come.' And let this suffice for the inquiry into the truth we set before us.

Limits of knowledge

1-5. There is a direct reference here to a much discussed passage in the *Eth. Nic.* X. 7, 8. See T. C., *Convivio,* IV. 13 : 72, and *note.*

§ 23.

Refutation   And when we have seen this it is easy to refute the arguments which were urged above on the other side, which was the fifth thing set before us to do. When it was said therefore, 'Two circumferences unequally distant from each other, cannot have a common centre,' I say that this is true, if the circumferences are regular, and without a hump or humps. And when it is said, in the minor, that the [10] circumferences of water and of earth are such, I say that it is not true unless we allow for the hump on the earth; and so the argument does not run. As to the second, when it is said: 'The nobler place is due to the nobler body,' I say that it is true as far as concerns their proper nature; and I grant the minor; but when the conclusion is drawn, that water should therefore be in a more exalted position, I say that it is true so far as the proper nature [20] of each body is concerned, but by reason of a more eminent cause, as said above, it happens that in this part the earth is higher; and thus the argument was defective in the first proposition. As to the third, when it said: 'Any idea which contradicts the senses is a false idea,' I say that the argument proceeds upon a fallacious imagination. For the sailors suppose that the reason why they cannot see the land when they are on deck is that the sea is [30] higher than the land; but it is not so; nay, the contrary result would follow, for they would see more. But it happens because the direct ray from the visible thing is intercepted, between the thing and the eye, by the convexity of the water.

For since the water must needs have a spherical form in every direction around its centre, it must necessarily, at any considerable distance, interpose the obstacle of a certain convexity. As to the fourth, when it was argued: 'If the earth were not lower' [40], and the rest, I say that the argument is founded upon falsity, and is therefore nought. For the vulgar, and such as have no knowledge of physical arguments, believe that water rises to the summits of the mountains and also to the place of springs, in the form of water; but that is quite puerile, for waters are generated there (as the Philosopher shows in his *Meteorics*) by matter which ascends in the form of vapour. As to the fifth, when it is said that water is [50] a body that imitates the orbit of the moon, and therefrom the conclusion is drawn that it must needs be excentric, since the orbit of the moon is excentric, I say that that argument carries no necessity; for though one thing should imitate another in one respect, it is not therefore necessary that it should imitate it in every respect. We see that fire imitates the circulation of the heavens, and yet it does not imitate it in not moving in a straight line, or in not having any contrary to its quality; and so [60] the argument does not run. So much, then, for the arguments.

Thus, then, the determination and treatment is brought to a conclusion concerning the form and position of the two elements, as above proposed.

3. *Fourth.* See § 9.
31, 32. If the sea rose above the earth so as to command it, then the farther the sailors got out to sea, the wider stretch of land would they see.

56-59. According to the Aristotelian physics, the material of the heavens naturally moves with a circular motion. Now 'up' is opposed to 'down,' and 'forward' to 'backward,' etc., but there is no opposite to 'round and round'; therefore the 'up' motion of fire in a straight line is opposed to the 'down' motion of earth in a straight line, but nothing has a motion opposite to the 'round and round' motion of the heavens. Now fire shows its affinity to the heavens, or 'imitation' of them, by getting as near to them as it can and by displaying a certain quality analogous to the ardour of love (*Epist. ad Can Grande*, 448-452); but that does not involve its deserting its own natural motion in a straight line or its having no opposite in its motion. It imitates heaven in some things, but not in all.

§ 24.

Colophon This philosophic question was determined under the rule of the unconquered lord, Lord Can Grande della Scala, representing the sacred Roman empire, by me, Dante Aligheri, least of philosophers, in the illustrious city of Verona, in the sanctuary of the glorious Helen, in the presence of all the clergy of Verona, except certain who, burning with excess of charity, will not accept the invitations of others [10]; and who, in the virtue of humility, poor pensioners of the Holy Spirit, lest they should seem to endorse the excellence of others, refuse to be present at their discourses. And this was accomplished in the one thousand three hundred and twentieth year, from the nativity of our Lord Jesus Christ, on Sunday, which our aforesaid Saviour made venerable to us by his glorious nativity and by his wondrous resurrection, which [20] day was the seventh from the Ides of

January, and the fourteenth before the Kalends of February.

19-21. *I.e.* 20th January, which was, in fact, a Sunday in the year 1320.

NOTE TO THE *Quæstio*.

The *Quæstio de Aqua et Terra* was printed by a certain Padre Moncetti in 1508, professedly from Dante's autograph. No one had ever heard of it before, and neither Moncetti's manuscript nor any other is known to exist. This has naturally caused the authenticity of the work to be disputed; but it has been ably defended by Dr Moore in the second series of his *Studies in Dante*, pp. 303-374. The general position may be summed up thus: The positive external evidence for the authenticity of the work is reduced to the bare assertion of Moncetti, nearly two hundred years after Dante's death; but it should be noted that the text itself bears evidence of having been actually edited from a manuscript, the contractions of which were not always rightly understood by the editor.

An inspection of the *Editio Princeps*, of which there is a copy in the British Museum, makes this very clear. The editor, for instance, habitually expands the sigil for *secundum* into *sed*; in § 16 : 52, 53 he reads the sigil for *quod quidem* as *quicquid*; in § 17 : 9 that for *scilicet* as *sed*; and in § 21 : 6 that for *quare* as *quam*. The hypothesis that Moncetti himself forged this treatise may therefore be dismissed without further discussion. Against Dante's authorship the argument *a silentio* is strong, but naturally such evidence can seldom amount to proof, and it certainly cannot be accepted as deciding the question in this instance.

As to external evidence, it has been conclusively shown that interest in the question itself, and the method in which it is here handled, are characteristic of Dante's time; and the attempts to show that the work displays knowledge which it was impossible for Dante to possess may be regarded as having absolutely failed. Indeed, the real difficulties are of a contrary kind. For §§ 19 and 20, as is pointed out in the notes, seem to contain mistakes which we should hardly have expected Dante to make, to say nothing of the extreme weakness of § 21 : 49-51. Under these circumstances it would evidently be unwise to be dogmatic, but for my own part I have very little hesitation in accepting the treatise as belonging to Dante's age or near it; and the number of minute indications that appear to identify it as Dante's own work is so great that in spite of considerable difficulties I think we are justified in provisionally regarding it, with some confidence, as authentic.

As to the question itself, it rises out of the *a priori* conception that each of the four elements, earth, water, air, and fire, has a sphere to itself: earth as the heaviest at the centre, fire as the lightest at the circumference, water enveloping earth, and air enveloping water. The scheme naturally presented many difficulties. For instance, there was no visible atmosphere of fire enveloping the air, and earth is not enveloped by water. The present treatise was concerned with this second point; and the question was how, with the least violence to the general conceptions on which the scheme of the universe was built, to explain the fact that some portions of the earth rise above some portions of the sea, that is to say, are remoter than they are from the centre of the universe.

The sole authority for the text is the *Editio Princeps* of 1508, which contains, as we have seen, many mistakes. In 1576 the work was reprinted, together with other philosophical treatises, by Franciscus Storella at Naples. This edition inserts as *marginalia* the notes which in subsequent editions have appeared as headings of numbered paragraphs (the original edition having no divisions), and also corrects the most obvious mistakes of expansion, thus disguising to a great extent the evidence of direct dependence upon a misread manuscript. Subsequent editions (so far as a hasty inspection reveals) brought no improvements, and Fraticelli's in 1857 was the worst of them all; not so bad, however, as the same editor's later issue of 1873, which was reproduced in the first edition of Dr Moore's *Oxford Dante*. It is much to be regretted that discussions as to the authenticity of the work should have been conducted upon the basis of this critically worthless text. I have followed the *Editio Princeps* when it is not obviously wrong, and have noted the variants in the Fraticellian text when it seemed important to do so, as well as any emendations of my own. The numerous emendations already embodied in the Fraticellian text I have not noted.

Though the division into paragraphs has no authority, I have retained it for convenience of reference.

The *Quæstio* has been twice before translated into English; first by Charles Hamilton Bromby (Nutt, 1897), and then by Alain Campbell White (Boston, 1903). P. H. W.

P.S.—As the revised proofs of this book were being passed, the third edition of Dr Moore's Oxford Dante appeared. It contains a text of the *Quæstio* thoroughly revised by Dr Shadwell, and it is gratifying to find that the greater part of the readings I have suggested in the notes have been anticipated by him and will henceforth be found in the standard text. The many other emendations proposed by Dr Shadwell I have not, as a rule, been able to use or even adequately to consider, but I have been able to incorporate his substitution of *polorum* for *populorum* in § 21 : 64 f., and his obvious correction of *quinto* for *quarto* in § 23 : 3. And I would further call attention to his proposal in § 18 : 4-6 to include all the words 'sunt homogenea . . . ignis et terra' between brackets, as an alternative to my own suggestions.

My notes contained several references to the *textus receptus* (Fraticelli and Moore), which I have now replaced by 'the Fraticellian text,' but in other respects I have left the textual notes as they were written, to save delay and rearrangement of the type, and also in order that the coincidences between Dr Shadwell's emendations and restorations and my own may have whatever weight may be thought due to them.

When 'the text' is referred to, without qualification, the text of the *Ed. Prin.* is meant.

Postscript to Translator's Note on the De Vulgari Eloquentia, *p.* 124.

The text of the *De Vulgari Eloquentia* printed in the 3rd Edition of the Oxford Dante (October 1904), approximates much more closely to that of Rajna (which I have followed in the translation) than the text of the earlier editions did. Those divergencies between the two texts, however, to which I have thought it necessary to refer in the notes, still exist; except that in II. 7 : 45, the 3rd edition of the Oxford Dante has *dolata* (with Rajna) instead of *locatam*. It seems desirable to take this opportunity of mentioning that blanks are left in the 3rd edition of the Oxford Dante in the following passages, viz.: II. 1 : 28; II. 11 : 30-32, and II. 12 : 80, where the Editor has abandoned the readings of the earlier editions but has not seen his way to adopt the emendations of Rajna.

A. G. F. H.

This volume contains all the extant Latin works of Dante. The translation of the De Vulgari Eloquentia *has been revised for this edition by A. G. Ferrers Howell, who first published it in* 1890. *The translations of the* De Monarchia *and of* Epistolæ *V.-IX. have been revised by Philip H. Wicksteed from provisional translations issued by him to students in* 1896 *and* 1898; *while the translations of the rest of the* Epistolæ (*including that to Can Grande*), *of the* Eclogues, *and of the* De Aqua et Terra, *have been made by him expressly for this edition.*

Each translator takes the full responsibility for his own part of the work, including both text and notes, but each has to acknowledge corrections, suggestions, and contributions from the other, not specified in detail.

BEDFORD STREET, W.C.
November 1904.